COLLINS POCKET REFERENCE

What Happened
WHEN ?

HarperCo

HarperCollins Publishers
P.O. Box, Glasgow G4 0NB

First published 1994

Reprint 10 9 8 7 6 5 4 3 2 1 0

ISBN 0 00 470725 7

A catalogue record for this book is available
from the British Library

Printed in Hong Kong

Contents

CONTENTS

DAY BY DAY

1 JANUARY

New Year's Day, and National Day of Cuba, Sudan, and Haiti.

1785   London's oldest daily paper *The Daily Universal Register* (renamed *The Times* in 1788) was first published.

1801   Italian astronomer Giuseppe Piazzi became the first person to discover an asteroid; he named it Ceres.

1901   The Commonwealth of Australia was formed.

1909   The first payments of old-age pensions were made in Britain, with persons over 70 receiving five shillings (25p) a week.

1958   The European Community was established under the Treaty of Rome.

1959   Fidel Castro overthrew the government of Fulgencio Batista, and seized power in Cuba.

2 JANUARY

1492   Granada, the last Moorish stronghold in Spain, surrendered to the Spaniards.

1635   Cardinal Richelieu established the Académie Française in Paris.

1839   French photographer Louis Daguerre took the first photograph of the Moon.

1959   Russia's *Luna I* was launched on its way to become the first spacecraft to pass close to the Moon.

1971   A barrier collapsed at the Ibrox Park football stadium in Glasgow, crushing 66 fans to death.

1979   Sid Vicious, the Sex Pistols' singer, went on trial in New York for the murder of his girlfriend Nancy Spungen.

3 JANUARY

1521   Pope Leo X excommunicated Martin Luther.

1777   George Washington's forces defeated the British at the Battle of Princeton in the War of Independence.

1924   British archeologists Lord Carnarvon and Howard Carter discovered the sarcophagus of Tutankhamen.

1959   Alaska became the 49th state of the USA.

1962   Pope John XXIII excommunicated Cuban prime minister Fidel Castro.

1993   The USA and Russia signed the second Strategic Arms Reduction Treaty (START) in Moscow.

4 JANUARY

National Day of Myanmar.

1884 The socialist Fabian Society was founded in London.

1885 The first successful surgical removal of an appendix was performed, in Iowa, USA.

1936 The first pop-music chart was compiled.

1944 The British Fifth Army launched an attack on Monte Cassino in Italy.

1972 Rose Heilbron became the first woman judge in Britain at the Old Bailey, London.

1991 The UN Security Council voted unanimously to condemn Israel's treatment of the Palestinians in the occupied territories.

5 JANUARY

1066 Edward the Confessor, king of England, died.

1477 Charles the Bold, king of France, was killed at the Battle of Nancy.

1896 German physicist Röntgen gave the first demonstration of X-rays.

1938 Juan Carlos I, king of Spain, was born.

1964 Pope Paul VI met Patriarch Athenagoras I, the first meeting between the heads of the Roman Catholic and Orthodox Churches in over 500 years.

1976 A law was proclaimed in France making French the only language permitted in advertising.

6 JANUARY

Epiphany.

1540 King Henry VIII married Anne of Cleves, his fourth wife.

1720 The Inquiry into the South Sea Bubble financial crisis published its findings.

1838 The first public demonstration of the electric telegraph was given by its inventor, Samuel Morse.

1928 The River Thames flooded, drowning four people, and severely damaging paintings stored in the Tate Gallery's basement.

1945 The Battle of the Bulge, or Ardennes offensive, ended, with 130,000 German and 77,000 Allied casualties.

1988 La Coupole, the Parisian brasserie made famous by generations of notable artists and writers who frequented it, was sold for £6 million to be converted into an office block.

7 JANUARY

Christmas Day in the Orthodox Church.

1558 Calais, the last English possession on mainland France, was recaptured by the French.

1610 Italian astronomer Galileo discovered Jupiter's four satellites, naming them Io, Europa, Ganymede, and Callisto.

1785 The first aerial crossing of the English Channel was made by Jean Pierre Blanchard and Dr John Jeffries, in a hot-air balloon.

1927 The London–New York telephone service began operating, a three-minute call costing £15.

1975 OPEC agreed to raise crude oil prices by 10%, which began a tidal wave of world economic inflation.

1990 Because of its accelerated rate of 'leaning',The Leaning Tower of Pisa was closed to the public.

8 JANUARY

1815 The Americans, led by Andrew Jackson, defeated the British at the Battle of New Orleans.

1886 The Severn Railway Tunnel – Britain's longest – was opened.

1889 US inventor Herman Hollerith patented his tabulator, the first device for data processing; his firm would later become one of IBM's founding companies.

1916 Allied troops made their final withdrawal from Gallipoli.

1921 David Lloyd George became the first occupant of Chequers, the official country residence of British prime ministers.

1959 French general Charles de Gaulle became the first president of the Fifth Republic.

9 JANUARY

1799 British prime minister William Pitt the Younger introduced income tax, at two shillings (10p) in the pound, to raise funds for the Napoleonic Wars.

1902 New York State introduced a bill to outlaw flirting in public.

1913 Richard Milhouse Nixon, 37th US president, was born.

1969 The supersonic aeroplane *Concorde* made its first trial flight, at Bristol.

1972 The ocean liner *Queen Elizabeth* was destroyed by fire in Hong Kong harbour.

1991 US secretary of state Baker and Iraqi foreign minister Aziz met for 6½ hours in Geneva, but failed to reach any agreement that would forestall war in the Persian Gulf.

10 JANUARY

1840   The penny post began in Britain.
1863   Prime minister Gladstone opened the first section of the London Underground Railway system, from Paddington to Farringdon Street.
1920   The Treaty of Versailles was ratified, officially ending World War I.
1920   The League of Nations held its first meeting in Geneva.
1926   Fritz Lang's film *Metropolis* was first shown, in Berlin.
1946   The first meeting of the United Nations General Assembly took place in London.

11 JANUARY

1569   England's first state lottery was held; tickets were obtainable from the West Door of St Paul's Cathedral, London.
1922   Leonard Thompson became the first person to be successfully treated with insulin, at Toronto General Hospital.
1963   The first disco, called the 'Whisky-a-go-go', opened in Los Angeles, USA.
1973   The Open University awarded its first degrees.
1977   Rolling Stone Keith Richards was tried in London for possession of cocaine, found in his car after an accident, and fined £750.
1991   An auction of silver and paintings that had been acquired by the late Ferdinand Marcos and his wife, Imelda, brought in a total of $20.29 million at Christie's in New York.

12 JANUARY

1866   The Royal Aeronautical Society was founded in London.
1875   Kwang-su was made emperor of China.
1964   The sultan of Zanzibar was overthrown, following an uprising, and a republic proclaimed.
1970   The Boeing 747 aircraft touched down at Heathrow Airport at the end of its first transatlantic flight.
1991   US Congress passed a resolution authorizing President Bush to use military power to force Iraq out of Kuwait.
1993   Sectarian violence continued for the eighth consecutive day in Bombay, India; 200 people died in nationwide clashes.

13 JANUARY

1893 The British Independent Labour Party was formed by Keir Hardie.

1910 Opera was broadcast on the radio for the first time – Enrico Caruso singing from the stage of New York's Metropolitan Opera House.

1964 Capitol records released the Beatles' first single in the USA; 'I Wanna Hold Your Hand' sold one million copies in the first three weeks.

1978 NASA selected its first women astronauts, 15 years after the USSR had a female astronaut orbit the Earth.

1991 Soviet troops killed 15 protesters in Vilnius, capital of Lithuania, in a crackdown on pro-independence forces.

1993 Former East German leader Erich Honecker, who had been awaiting trial on charges of manslaughter, was released from a Berlin prison because of ill health.

14 JANUARY

1858 Attempt on the life of Napoleon III, in Paris.

1875 Albert Schweitzer, French missionary surgeon, was born.

1900 Puccini's opera *Tosca* was first performed, in Rome.

1907 An earthquake killed over 1,000 people in Kingston, Jamaica, virtually destroying the capital.

1943 US President Roosevelt and British prime minister Churchill met at Casablanca.

1954 Baseball hero Joe DiMaggio married film star Marilyn Monroe.

15 JANUARY

1559 The coronation of Queen Elizabeth I took place.

1759 The British Museum opened, at Montague House, Bloomsbury, London.

1797 London haberdasher James Hetherington was fined £50 for wearing his new creation, the top hat.

1927 Captain Teddy Wakelam gave the first live rugby commentary on BBC radio of the match between Wales and England at Twickenham.

1973 President Nixon called a halt to the USA's Vietnam offensive.

1992 The EC granted diplomatic recognition to Slovenia and Croatia, essentially recognizing the dismemberment of Yugoslavia.

16 JANUARY

1547 Ivan the Terrible was crowned first tsar of Russia.
1920 The 18th Amendment to the US Constitution was ratified, prohibiting the sale of alcoholic beverages.
1925 Leon Trotsky was dismissed as Chairman of the Revolutionary Council of the USSR.
1932 Duke Ellington and his Orchestra recorded 'It Don't Mean a Thing' in New York.
1970 Colonel Khaddhafi became virtual president of Libya.
1991 A US-led international force launched Operation Desert Storm on Iraq and Iraqi-occupied Kuwait less than 17 hours after the expiration of the UN deadline for Iraqi withdrawal.

17 JANUARY

1377 The Papal See was transferred from Avignon back to Rome.
1706 Benjamin Franklin, US statesman, philosopher, and scientist, inventor of the lightning conductor, was born.
1773 Captain Cook's *Resolution* became the first ship to cross the Antarctic Circle.
1852 The independence of the Transvaal Boers was recognized by Britain.
1912 English explorer Robert Falcon Scott reached the South Pole; Norwegian Roald Amundsen had beaten him there by one month.
1992 An IRA bomb, placed next to a remote country road in County Tyrone, Northern Ireland, killed seven building workers and injured seven others.

18 JANUARY

1778 Captain Cook discovered the Sandwich Islands, now known as Hawaii.
1871 Wilhelm, king of Prussia from 1861, was proclaimed the first German emperor.
1882 A A Milne, English author, creator of Pooh bear, was born.
1911 The first landing of an aircraft on a ship's deck was made by US pilot Eugene Ely, in San Francisco Bay.
1919 The Versailles Peace Conference opened.
1944 The German siege of Leningrad, which began Sept 1941, was relieved.

19 JANUARY

1764 John Wilkes was expelled from the British House of Commons for seditious libel.

1793 King Louis XVI was tried by the French Convention, found guilty of treason and sentenced to the guillotine.

1942 The Japanese invaded Burma (now Myanmar).

1966 Indira Gandhi became prime minister of India.

1969 In protest against the Russian invasion of 1968, Czech student Jan Palach set himself alight in Prague's Wenceslas Square.

1993 IBM announced a loss of $4.97 billion for 1992, the largest single-year loss in US corporate history.

20 JANUARY

1265 The first English parliament met in Westminster Hall, convened by the Earl of Leicester, Simon de Montfort.

1892 The game of basketball was first played at the YMCA in Springfield, Massachusetts.

1944 The RAF dropped 2,300 tons of bombs on Berlin.

1961 John F Kennedy was inaugurated as the 35th US president, and the first Roman Catholic to hold this office.

1981 Fifty-two Americans, held hostage in the US embassy in Tehran for 444 days by followers of Ayatollah Khomeini, were released.

1987 Terry Waite, the Archbishop of Canterbury's special envoy in the Middle East, disappeared on a peace mission in Beirut, Lebanon.

21 JANUARY

1793 Louis XVI, king of France, was guillotined in Place de la Révolution.

1846 The first issue of the *Daily News*, edited by Charles Dickens, was published.

1911 The first Monte Carlo car rally was held; it was won seven days later by French racer Henri Rougier.

1941 Placido Domingo, Spanish operatic tenor, was born.

1954 The world's first nuclear submarine, the USS *Nautilus*, was launched.

1976 *Concorde* inaugurated its commercial service with simultaneous take-offs, from Paris to Rio de Janeiro and from London to Bahrain.

22 JANUARY

1771 The Falkland Islands were ceded to Britain by Spain.

1905 Insurgent workers were fired on in St Petersburg, resulting in 'Bloody Sunday'.

1924 Ramsay MacDonald took office as Britain's first Labour prime minister.

1972 The United Kingdom, the Irish Republic, and Denmark joined the Common Market.

1973 US boxer George Foreman knocked out Joe Frazier in Kingston, Jamaica, becoming the world heavyweight boxing champion.

1992 Rebel soldiers seized the national radio station in Kinshasa, Zaire's capital, and broadcast a demand for the government's resignation.

23 JANUARY

1556 An earthquake in Shanxi Province, China, is thought to have killed some 830,000 people.

1571 The Royal Exchange in London, founded by financier Thomas Gresham, was opened by Queen Elizabeth I.

1849 English-born Elizabeth Blackwell graduated from a New York medical school to become the first woman doctor.

1943 The British captured Tripoli from the Germans.

1960 The US Navy bathyscaphe *Trieste*, designed by Dr Piccard, descended to a record depth of 10,750 m/35,820 ft in the Pacific Ocean.

1985 The proceedings of the House of Lords were televised for the first time.

24 JANUARY

1916 The US Supreme Court ruled that income tax is unconstitutional.

1916 Conscription was introduced in Britain.

1935 Beer in cans was first sold, in Virginia, USA, by the Kreuger Brewing Company.

1962 French film director François Truffaut's *Jules et Jim* premiered in Paris.

1965 Winston Churchill, British prime minister, died, on the same date as his father Randolphe in 1895.

1978 A Russian satellite crashed near Yellow Knife in Canada's Northwest Territory.

25 JANUARY

1533 King Henry VIII and Anne Boleyn were secretly married.
1917 The USA purchased the Danish West Indies (now the Virgin Islands) for $25 million.
1924 The first Winter Olympic Games were inaugurated in Chamonix in the French Alps.
1938 Due to intense sunspot activity, the aurora borealis, or 'northern lights', were seen as far south as western Europe.
1971 Idi Amin led a coup that deposed Milton Obote and became president of Uganda.
1981 Jiang Qing, Mao's widow, was tried for treason and received a death sentence, which was subsequently commuted to life imprisonment.

26 JANUARY

National Day of Australia and of India.
1841 Hong Kong was proclaimed a British sovereign territory.
1871 England's Rugby Football Union was founded in London, by 20 clubs.
1905 The Cullinan diamond, weighing 1¼ lbs, was found by Captain Wells at the Premier Mine, near Pretoria, South Africa.
1939 In the Spanish Civil War, Franco's forces, with Italian aid, took Barcelona.
1950 India became a republic within the Commonwealth.
1992 Russian President Yeltsin announced that his country would stop targeting US cities with nuclear weapons.

27 JANUARY

1765 Wolfgang Amadeus Mozart, Austrian composer, was born.
1879 Thomas Edison patented the electric lamp.
1926 The first public demonstration of television was given by John Logie Baird, at his workshop in London.
1967 Three US astronauts died in a fire which broke out aboard the spacecraft *Apollo* during tests at Cape Kennedy.
1973 The Vietnam cease-fire agreement was signed by North Vietnam and the USA.
1992 Former world boxing champion Mike Tyson went on trial for allegedly raping an 18-year-old contestant in the 1991 Miss Black America Contest.

28 JANUARY

1521   The Diet of Worms began, at which Protestant reformer Luther was declared an outlaw by the Roman Catholic church.

1807   London became the world's first city to be illuminated by gas light, when the lamps on Pall Mall were lit.

1871   In the Franco-Prussian War, Paris fell to the Prussians after a five-month siege.

1935   Iceland became the first country to introduce legalized abortion.

1942   The British Eighth Army retreated to El Alamein.

1986   The US space shuttle *Challenger* exploded shortly after lift-off from Cape Canaveral, killing five men and two women on board.

29 JANUARY

1848   Greenwich Mean Time was adopted by Scotland.

1856   Britain's highest military decoration, the Victoria Cross, was founded by Queen Victoria.

1886   The first successful petrol-driven motorcar, built by Karl Benz, was patented.

1916   Paris was bombed by German zeppelins for the first time.

1942   The BBC Radio 4 programme *Desert Island Discs*, devised and presented by Roy Plomley, was first broadcast.

1978   The use of environmentally damaging aerosol sprays was banned in Sweden.

30 JANUARY

1649   The Commonwealth of England was established upon the execution of Charles I.

1790   The first purpose-built lifeboat was launched on the River Tyne.

1889   Rudolph, crown prince of Austria, and his 17-year-old mistress, Baroness Marie Vetsera, were found shot in his hunting lodge at Mayerling, near Vienna.

1933   Adolf Hitler was appointed chancellor of Germany.

1948   Mohandas Karamchand Gandhi, called 'Mahatma', Indian leader, was assassinated.

1958   Yves Saint Laurent, aged 22, held his first major fashion show in Paris.

31 JANUARY

1606 The executions of Winter, Rockwood, Keys, and Guy Fawkes, the Gunpowder Conspirators, took place in London.

1858 The Great Eastern, the five-funnelled steamship designed by Brunel, was launched at Millwall.

1876 All Native American Indians were ordered to move into reservations.

1929 The USSR exiled Leon Trotsky; he found asylum in Mexico.

1958 *Explorer I*, the first US Earth satellite, was launched from Cape Canaveral.

1983 The wearing of seat belts in cars became compulsory in Britain.

1 FEBRUARY

1884 The first edition of the *Oxford English Dictionary* was published.

1893 Thomas Edison opened the first film studio – to produce films for peepshow machines – in New Jersey, USA.

1896 Puccini's opera *La Bohème* was first staged in Turin.

1930 *The Times* published its first crossword puzzle.

1958 The United Arab Republic was formed by a union of Egypt and Syria (it was broken 1961).

1979 Ayatollah Khomeini returned to Iran after 16 years of exile.

2 FEBRUARY

Candlemas (Wives' Feast Day).

1801 The first parliament of the United Kingdom of Great Britain and Ireland assembled.

1852 Britain's first men's public flushing toilets opened on Fleet Street, London.

1878 Greece declared war on Turkey.

1972 The British Embassy in Dublin was burned down by protesters angered by the 'Bloody Sunday' shootings in Londonderry.

1986 Women in Liechtenstein went to the polls for the first time.

1989 The USSR's military occupation of Afghanistan ended after nine years.

3 FEBRUARY

1488 The Portuguese navigator Bartholomeu Diaz landed at Mossal Bay in the Cape – the first European known to have landed on the southern extremity of Africa.

1913   The 16th Amendment to the US Constitution, authorizing the power to impose and collect income tax, was ratified.
1919   The League of Nations held its first meeting in Paris, with US President Wilson chairing.
1966   The first rocket-assisted controlled landing on the Moon was made by the Soviet space vehicle *Luna IX*.
1969   At the Palestinian National Congress in Cairo, Yasser Arafat was appointed leader of the PLO.
1989   South African politician P W Botha unwillingly resigned both party leadership and the presidency after suffering a stroke.

4 FEBRUARY

National Day of Sri Lanka.
1904   The Russo-Japanese War began after Japan laid seige to Port Arthur.
1928   Black US entertainer Josephine Baker's provocative performance in Munich drew protests from members of the Nazi party.
1945   Allied leaders Roosevelt, Churchill, and Stalin met at Yalta, in the Crimea.
1968   The world's largest hovercraft was launched at Cowes, Isle of Wight.
1987   The US *Stars and Stripes* won the America's Cup back from Australia.
1993   Russian scientists unfurled a giant mirror in orbit and flashed a beam of sunlight across Europe during the night; observers saw it only as an instantaneous flash.

5 FEBRUARY

1924   The BBC time signals, or 'pips', from Greenwich Observatory were heard for the first time; they are broadcast every hour.
1961   The first issue of the *Sunday Telegraph* was published.
1967   Due to a Musicians' Union ban, the Rolling Stones were not allowed to play their hit 'Let's Spend the Night Together' when they appeared on an ITV show.
1974   Patricia Hearst, granddaughter of US newspaper tycoon William R Hearst, was kidnapped by the Symbionese Liberation Army.
1982   Laker Airways collapsed with debts of $270 million.
1983   Expelled from Bolivia, Nazi war criminal Klaus Barbie flew to France to be tried for crimes against humanity.

6 FEBRUARY

National Day of New Zealand.

1508 Maximilian I assumed the title of Holy Roman Emperor.

1778 Britain declared war on France.

1840 The Treaty of Waitangi was signed by Great Britain and the Maori chiefs of New Zealand, granting British sovereignty.

1918 Women over 30 were granted the right to vote in Britain.

1958 An aeroplane carrying the Manchester United football team crashed on take-off at Munich, killing seven players.

1964 Britain and France reached an agreement on the construction of a Channel Tunnel.

7 FEBRUARY

1301 Edward Caernarvon (later King Edward II) became the first Prince of Wales.

1812 Charles Dickens, English novelist, was born.

1845 The Portland Vase, a Roman cameo glass vase dating to the 1st century BC, was smashed by a drunken visitor to the British Museum.

1863 HMS *Orpheus* was wrecked off the New Zealand coast, with the loss of 185 lives.

1947 The main group of the Dead Sea Scrolls, dating to about 150 BC–AD 68, was found in caves on the W side of the Jordan River.

1991 British prime minister Major and his senior cabinet ministers escaped an apparent assassination attempt when the IRA fired three mortar shells at 10 Downing Street from a parked van.

8 FEBRUARY

1587 Mary, Queen of Scots, was beheaded.

1725 Catherine I succeeded her husband, Peter the Great, to become empress of Russia.

1740 The 'Great Frost' of London ended (began 25 Dec 1739).

1969 The Boeing 747, the world's largest commercial plane, made its first flight.

1972 A concert by Frank Zappa and the Mothers of Invention was cancelled at the Albert Hall, London, because some of their lyrics were considered obscene.

1974 After 85 days in space, the US *Skylab* station returned to earth.

9 FEBRUARY

1801 The Holy Roman Empire came to an end with the signing of the Peace of Luneville between Austria and France.

1830 Explorer Charles Sturt discovered the source of the Murray River in Australia.

1872 Lieutenant Dawson's expedition in search of Dr Livingstone began.

1949 US film actor Robert Mitchum was sentenced to two months in prison for smoking marijuana.

1972 The British government declared a state of emergency due to the miners' strike, which was in its third month.

1991 The republic of Lithuania held a plebiscite on independence which showed overwhelming support for secession from the USSR.

10 FEBRUARY

1763 Canada was ceded to Britain by the Peace of Paris.

1774 Andrew Becker demonstrated his practical diving suit in the River Thames.

1840 Queen Victoria and Prince Albert, both aged 20, were married in St James' Palace.

1931 New Delhi became the capital of India.

1942 The first gold disc – sprayed with gold by the record company RCA Victor – was presented to Glenn Miller for 'Chattanooga Choo Choo'.

1989 Jamaican-born Tony Robinson became Nottingham's first black sheriff.

11 FEBRUARY

1818 Independence was proclaimed by Chile.

1858 Bernadette Soubirous, a peasant girl, allegedly had a vision of the Virgin Mary in a grotto in Lourdes.

1878 The first weekly weather report was published by the Meteorological Office.

1945 The Yalta Conference ended, at which the Allied leaders planned the final defeat of Germany and agreed on the establishment of the United Nations.

1975 Margaret Thatcher became the first woman leader of a British political party.

1990   After more than 27 years in prison, ANC president Nelson Mandela walked to freedom from a prison near Cape Town, South Africa.

12 FEBRUARY

1554   Lady Jane Grey, queen of England for nine days, was executed on Tower Green for high treason.

1797   Over 1,000 French troops, led by Irish-American general William Tate, made an unsuccessful attempt to invade Britain, on the Welsh coast.

1831   Rubber galoshes first went on sale, in Boston, Massachusetts, USA.

1851   Prospector Edward Hargreaves made a discovery at Summerhill Creek, New South Wales, which set off a gold rush in Australia.

1912   China became a republic following the overthrow of the Manchu Dynasty.

1973   The first group of US prisoners of war were released from North Vietnam.

13 FEBRUARY

1689   William of Orange and Mary ascended the throne of Great Britain as joint sovereigns.

1692   The massacre of the Macdonalds at Glencoe in Scotland was carried out by their traditional enemies, the Campbells.

1793   Britain, Prussia, Austria, Holland, Spain, and Sardinia formed an alliance against France.

1917   Dutch spy Mata Hari was arrested by the French.

1960   The French tested their first atomic bomb in the Sahara.

1974   Russian novelist Alexander Solzhenitsyn was expelled from the USSR.

14 FEBRUARY

St Valentine's Day.

1779   Captain Cook was stabbed to death by natives in the Sandwich Islands (now Hawaii).

1797   The naval Battle of St Vincent took place off SW Portugal, in which Captain Nelson and Admiral Jervis defeated the Spanish fleet.

1852   Great Ormond Street children's hospital, in London, accepted its first patient.

1895 Oscar Wilde's *The Importance of Being Earnest* was first staged in London.

1946 The Bank of England was nationalized.

1989 The Ayatollah Khomeini issued a *fatwa* edict calling on Muslims to kill Salman Rushdie for his blasphemous novel *The Satanic Verses*.

15 FEBRUARY

1898 The USS *Maine,* sent to Cuba on a goodwill tour, was struck by a mine and sank in Havana harbour, with the loss of 260 lives.

1922 The first session of the Permanent Court of International Justice in The Hague was held.

1971 Britain adopted the decimal currency system.

1974 The battle for the strategic Golan Heights between Israeli and Syrian forces began.

1978 Mohammad Ali lost his world heavyweight boxing title to Leon Spinks in Las Vegas.

1981 For the first time, English Football League matches were played on a Sunday.

16 FEBRUARY

1659 The first British cheque was written.

1887 25,000 prisoners in India were released to celebrate Queen Victoria's jubilee.

1932 Irish general election won by Fianna Fáil party, led by Éamon de Valera.

1940 The British navy rescued about 300 British seamen who were held on board the German ship *Altmark*, in a Norwegian fjord.

1959 Fidel Castro became president of Cuba.

1960 The US nuclear submarine *Triton* set off to circumnavigate the world underwater.

17 FEBRUARY

1864 The first successful submarine torpedo attack took place when the USS *Housatonic* was sunk by the Confederate submarine *Hunley* in Charleston harbour; however, the force of the explosion was so great that the submarine itself was also blown up, killing all on board.

1880 An attempt was made to assassinate the Russian tsar Alexander II with a bomb at the Winter Palace, St Petersburg.

1904 First production of Puccini's *Madame Butterfly*, in Milan.
1958 The Campaign for Nuclear Disarmament (CND) was formed in London.
1968 French skier Jean-Claude Killy won three gold medals at the Winter Olympics in Grenoble.
1972 The House of Commons voted in favour of Britain joining the Common Market.

18 FEBRUARY

National Day of Gambia and Nepal.
1678 Publication of John Bunyan's *Pilgrim's Progress*.
1861 Victor Emmanuel proclaimed king of a united Italy at the first meeting of the Italian parliament.
1876 A direct telegraph link was set up between Britain and New Zealand.
1930 US astronomer Clyde Tombaugh discovered the planet Pluto.
1948 After 16 years in power, the Fianna Fáil party was defeated in the Irish general elections.
1965 The Gambia became an independent state within the Commonwealth.

19 FEBRUARY

1878 US inventor Thomas Edison patented the phonograph.
1897 The Women's Institute was founded in Ontario, Canada, by Mrs Hoodless.
1906 William Kellogg established the Battle Creek Toasted Cornflake Company, selling breakfast cereals originally developed as a health food for psychiatric patients.
1959 Britain, Greece, and Turkey signed an agreement guaranteeing the independence of Cyprus.
1976 Iceland broke off diplomatic relations with Britain after negotiations failed to produce an agreement over fishing limits in the 'cod war'.
1985 The BBC broadcast the first episode of the soap opera *EastEnders*.

20 FEBRUARY

1811 Austria declared itself bankrupt.
1938 Anthony Eden resigned as British foreign secretary after prime

minister Neville Chamberlain decided to negotiate with Italian Fascist leader Benito Mussolini.

1947   Lord Louis Mountbatten was appointed viceroy of India, the last person to hold this office.

1962   US astronaut John Glenn orbited the Earth three times in the space capsule *Friendship 7*.

1985   The sale of contraceptives became legal in the Irish Republic.

1989   An army barracks at Tern Hill, Shropshire, was destroyed by an IRA bomb.

21 FEBRUARY

1804   British engineer Richard Trevithick demonstrated the first steam engine to run on rails.

1931   The *New Statesman* was first published.

1960   All private businesses in Cuba nationalized by Fidel Castro.

1965   Malcolm X, US Black Muslim leader, was shot dead at a meeting.

1972   US President Richard Nixon arrived in Beijing on a visit intended to improve US – Chinese relations.

1989   Czech writer Vaclav Havel jailed for anti-government demonstrations.

22 FEBRUARY

1797   Over 1,000 French troops landed at Fishguard, in South Wales, but were quickly taken prisoner.

1819   Spain ceded Florida to the USA.

1879   US storekeeper F W Woolworth opened his first 'five-and-ten-cent' store in Utica, New York.

1886   *The Times* newspaper published a classified personal column, the first newspaper to do so.

1940   Five-year-old Tenzin Gyatso was enthroned as the 14th Dalai Lama in Lhasa, Tibet.

1946   Dr Selman Abraham Waksman announced that he had discovered streptomycin, an antibiotic.

23 FEBRUARY

1732   First performance of Handel's *Oratorio*, in London.

1820   Discovery of the Cato Street conspiracy; following a tip-off, police arrested revolutionaries who planned to blow up the British Cabinet.

1836 The siege of the Alamo began, under the Mexican general Santa Anna.

1898 Emile Zola was imprisoned for writing his open letter *J'accuse*, accusing the French government of anti-Semitism and of wrongly imprisoning the army officer Captain Alfred Dreyfus.

1919 Benito Mussolini founded the Italian Fascist Party.

1981 Spanish Fascist army officers led by Lt Colonel Antonio Tejero attempted a coup in the *Cortes* (parliament).

24 FEBRUARY

AD 303 Galerius Valerius Maximianus issued an edict demanding the persecution of Christians.

1582 The Gregorian Calendar was introduced by Pope Gregory XIII; it replaced the Julian Calendar, but was not adopted in Britain until 1752.

1920 Nancy Astor became the first woman to address the British parliament.

1932 Malcolm Campbell beat his own land speed record in *Bluebird* at Daytona Beach, USA; he reached a speed of 408.88 kph/ 253.96 mph.

1938 Nylon toothbrush bristles were first produced in the USA – the first commercial use of nylon.

1946 Juan Perón was elected president of Argentina.

25 FEBRUARY

National Day of Kuwait.

1308 Coronation of King Edward II of England.

1570 Pope Pius V excommunicated Queen Elizabeth I.

1841 Pierre-Auguste Renoir, French Impressionist painter, was born.

1913 English suffragette Emmeline Pankhurst went on trial for a bomb attack on the home of David Lloyd George, Chancellor of the Exchequer.

1939 The first Anderson air-raid shelter was built in Islington, N London.

1955 HMS *Ark Royal* was completed, the largest aircraft carrier ever built in Britain.

26 FEBRUARY

1531 An earthquake in Lisbon, Portugal, killed 20,000 people.

1797 The first £1 note was issued by the Bank of England.

1815   Napoleon escaped from exile on the island of Elba.
1839   The first Grand National Steeplechase was run at Aintree.
1935   Robert Watson-Watt gave the first demonstration of radar at Daventry, England.
1936   Adolf Hitler launched the Volkswagen ('people's car'), intended to compete with Ford's Model T and boost the German economy.

27 FEBRUARY

1557   The first Russian Embassy opened in London; exactly one year later, the first trade mission arrived.
1879   US chemists Ira Remsen and Constantine Fahlberg announced their discovery of saccharin.
1881   British troops were defeated by the Boers at Majuba Hill, Transvaal.
1933   The German *Reichstag* (parliament building) in Berlin was destroyed by fire; it is believed that the Nazis were responsible, though they blamed the Communists.
1948   The Communist Party seized power in Czechoslovakia.
1991   The Gulf War came to an end with the liberation of Kuwait and the retreat of Iraqi forces.

28 FEBRUARY

1784   John Wesley, English founder of the Wesleyan faith, signed its deed of declaration.
1900   Relief forces under General Buller reached British troops besieged for four months at Ladysmith, Natal; Boer troops retreated.
1912   The first parachute jump was made, over Missouri, USA.
1948   The last British troops left India.
1975   A London underground train crashed at Moorgate station, killing 42 people.
1986   Swedish prime minister Olof Palme was shot dead as he walked home from a cinema in Stockholm.

29 FEBRUARY

Leap Year Day.
1792   Gioacchino Rossini, Italian composer, was born.
1880   The St Gotthard railway tunnel through the Alps was completed, linking Italy with Switzerland.

1948	The Stern Gang blew up a train carrying British soldiers from Cairo to Haifa; 27 soldiers were killed.
1956	Pakistan became an Islamic republic.
1960	An earthquake killed about 12,000 people in Agadir, Morocco.
1968	English astronomer Jocelyn Burnell announced the discovery of the first pulsar.

1 MARCH

Feast Day of St David and National Day of Wales.

1780	Pennsylvania became the first US state to abolish slavery.
1845	The USA annexed Texas.
1940	English actress Vivien Leigh won an Oscar for her performance as Scarlett O'Hara in the film *Gone with the Wind*.
1949	US heavyweight boxing champion Joe Louis retired after successfully defending his title 25 times.
1954	The USA conducted its first hydrogen-bomb test at Bikini Atoll, in the Marshall Islands.
1966	The uncrewed Soviet spacecraft *Venus 3* landed on Venus.

2 MARCH

1545	Thomas Bodley, founder of the Bodleian Library, Oxford, was born.
1717	The first ballet, *The Loves of Mars and Venus* was performed at the Theatre Royal, Drury Lane, London.
1949	US Airforce captain James Gallagher returned to Fort Worth, Texas, after flying non-stop around the world in 94 hours with a crew of 13 men; tanker aircraft refuelled their plane four times during the flight.
1955	Severe flooding in N and W Australia killed 200 people.
1969	The French-built supersonic aircraft *Concorde* made its first test flight from Toulouse.
1970	Rhodesia proclaimed itself a republic.

3 MARCH

National Day of Morocco.

1802	Beethoven's 'Moonlight Sonata' published.
1831	George Pullman, US designer of luxury railway carriages, was born.
1931	'The Star-Spangled Banner' was adopted as the US national anthem.
1969	US spacecraft *Apollo 9* was launched.

1985 British miners voted to go back to work after a year of striking over pit closures.

1991 Latvia and Estonia voted to secede from the Soviet Union.

4 MARCH

1681 King Charles II granted a Royal Charter to William Penn, entitling Penn to establish a colony in North America.

1861 Abraham Lincoln was sworn in as the 16th president of the USA.

1877 The Russian Imperial Ballet staged the first performance of the ballet *Swan Lake* in Moscow.

1882 Britain's first electric trams came into operation in Leytonstone, East London.

1890 The Forth railway bridge, Scotland, was officially opened.

1968 Tennis authorities voted to admit professional players to Wimbledon, previously open only to amateur players.

5 MARCH

1770 British troops killed five civilians when they fired into a crowd of demonstrators in Boston; the incident became known as the 'Boston Massacre'.

1850 English engineer Robert Stephenson's tubular bridge was opened, linking Anglesey with mainland Wales.

1933 The Nazi Party won almost half the seats in the elections.

1936 The British fighter plane *Spitfire* made its first test flight from Eastleigh, Southampton.

1946 The term 'iron curtain' was first used, by Winston Churchill in a speech in Missouri, USA.

1952 Elaine Page, English musical actress, was born.

6 MARCH

National Day of Ghana.

1836 The 12-day siege of the Alamo ended, with only six survivors out of the original force of 155.

1899 Aspirin was patented by chemist Felix Hoffman.

1930 Clarence Birdseye's first frozen foods went on sale in Springfield, Massachusetts, USA.

1957 Ghana became independent, the first British colony to do so.

1987 A cross-channel ferry left Zeebrugge, Belgium, with its bow doors open; it capsized suddenly outside the harbour, killing over 180 passengers.

1988 British SAS men shot dead three IRA members in a street in Gibraltar, claiming that they had been about to attack a military parade.

7 MARCH

1838 Swedish singer Jenny Lind gave her debut performance in *Der Freischutz*.

1876 Alexander Graham Bell patented the telephone.

1912 French aviator Henri Seimet made the first non-stop flight from Paris to London.

1926 A radio-telephone link was established between London and New York.

1969 The Victoria line was opened as part of London's underground railway.

1971 Women in Switzerland achieved the right to vote and hold federal office.

8 MARCH

1702 Anne became queen of Britain after William III died in a riding accident.

1910 The first pilot's licences were issued, to an Englishman, J T C Moore Brabazon, and a Frenchwoman, Elise Deroche.

1917 The February Revolution began in Petrograd (St (Petersburg), Russia.

1930 In India, a campaign of civil disobedience began, led by Mahatma Gandhi.

1965 3,500 US marines landed in South Vietnam.

1971 US boxer Muhammad Ali was defeated by Joe Frazier.

9 MARCH

1074 Pope Gregory VII excommunicated all married priests.

1796 French army commander Napoleon Bonaparte married Josephine de Beauharnais.

1831 The French Foreign Legion was founded in Algeria; its headquarters moved to France in 1962.

1918 The Russian capital was transferred from Petrograd (St Petersburg) to Moscow.

1923 Lenin retired as Soviet leader after suffering a severe stroke; he died the following year.

1961 Russian dog Laika was launched into space aboard the spacecraft *Sputnik 9*.

10 MARCH

1801 The first census was begun in Britain.

1886 Cruft's Dog Show was held in London for the first time – since 1859 it had been held in Newcastle.

1906 The Bakerloo line was opened on the London underground railway.

1914 English suffragette Mary Richardson slashed Velasquez' *Rokeby Venus* with a meat cleaver.

1969 James Earl Ray was sentenced to 99 years' imprisonment after pleading guilty to the murder of civil-rights leader Martin Luther King.

1974 A Japanese soldier was discovered hiding on Lubang Island in the Philippines. He was unaware that World War II had ended, and was waiting to be picked up by his own forces.

11 MARCH

1682 The Royal Chelsea Hospital for soldiers was founded by Charles II.

1702 The first successful English daily newspaper, the *Daily Courant* was published in London.

1941 US Congress passed the Lend-Lease Bill, authorizing huge loans to Britain to finance World War II.

1985 Mikhail Gorbachev became leader of the USSR.

1988 The Bank of England replaced pound notes with pound coins.

1990 US tennis player Jennifer Capriati, aged 13, became the youngest-ever finalist in a professional contest.

12 MARCH

1609 Bermuda became a British colony.

1904 Britain's first mainline electric train ran from Liverpool to Southport.

1912 The Girl Guides movement (later called Scouts) was founded in the USA.

1930 Indian leader Mahatma Gandhi began his walk to the sea, known as the Salt March, in defiance of the British government's tax on salt and monopoly of the salt trade in India.

1940 The Russo-Finnish war ended with Finland signing over territory to the USSR.

1945 Anne Frank, Dutch Jewish diarist, died in a Nazi concentration camp.

13 MARCH

1781 German-born British astronomer William Herschel discovered the planet Uranus.

1881 Tsar Alexander II of Russia died after a bomb was thrown at him in St Petersburg.

1894 The first public striptease act was performed in Paris.

1928 450 people drowned when a dam burst near Los Angeles, USA.

1930 US astronomer Clyde Tombaugh discovered the planet Pluto; its existence had been predicted 14 years earlier by US astronomer Percy Lowell.

1979 A Marxist coup led by Maurice Bishop took place in Grenada while prime minister Edward Gairy was in New York at a meeting of the United Nations.

14 MARCH

1492 Queen Isabella of Castile ordered the expulsion of 150,000 Jews from Spain, unless they accepted Christian baptism.

1757 British admiral John Byng was executed by firing squad at Plymouth, for having failed to relieve Minorca from the French fleet.

1864 English explorer Samuel Baker was the first European to see the lake he named Lake Albert.

1879 Albert Einstein, German-born Swiss physicist, was born.

1885 Gilbert and Sullivan's *Mikado* was first performed at the Savoy Theatre, London.

1891 The submarine *Monarch* laid the first underwater telephone cable.

15 MARCH

1892 US inventor Jesse Reno patented the first escalator.

1909 US entrepreneur G S Selfridge opened Britain's first department store in Oxford Street, London.

1917 Tsar Nicholas II of Russia abdicated.

1933 Nazi leader Adolf Hitler proclaimed the Third Reich in Germany; he also banned left-wing newspapers and kosher food.

1949 Clothes rationing in Britain ended.

1964 Actors Elizabeth Taylor and Richard Burton were married in Montreal.

16 MARCH

1660   The Long Parliament of England was dissolved, after sitting for 20 years.

1802   The US Military Academy was established at West Point, New York State.

1872   The Wanderers beat the Royal Engineers 1–0 in the first FA Cup Final, at Kennington Oval.

1926   The first rocket fuelled by petrol and liquid oxygen was successfully launched by US physicist Robert Goddard.

1963   William Henry Beveridge, English economist who wrote the report on which the British welfare state was founded, died.

1973   The new London Bridge was opened.

17 MARCH

Feast Day of St Patrick and National Day of Ireland.

1899   The first-ever radio distress call was sent, summoning assistance to a merchant ship aground on the Goodwin Sands, off the Kent coast.

1912   Lawrence Oates died, the English Antarctic explorer and member of Scott's expedition, who walked into a blizzard, saying 'I am just going outside, and may be some time'.

1921   English doctor Marie Stopes opened The Mothers' Clinic in London, to advise women on birth-control.

1939   Robin Knox-Johnston, the first person to sail single-handed, non-stop around the world, was born.

1969   Golda Meir, aged 70, took office as prime minister of Israel, the first woman to do so.

1978   The oil tanker *Amoco Cadiz* ran aground on the coast of Brittany, spilling over 220,000 tons of crude oil and causing extensive pollution.

18 MARCH

1662   The first public bus service began operating, in Paris.

1834   Six farm labourers from Tolpuddle, Dorset, were sentenced to transportation to Australia for forming a trade union.

1891   The London–Paris telephone link came into operation.

1922   Indian leader Mahatma Gandhi was jailed for six years for sedition.

1931   The first electric razors were manufactured in the USA.

1965   Soviet astronaut Alexei Leonov made the first 'walk' in space.

19 MARCH

721 BC The first-ever recorded solar eclipse was seen from Babylon.

1628 The New England Company was formed in Massachusetts Bay.

1813 David Livingstone, Scottish missionary and explorer, was born.

1847 Mary Anning, English paleontologist who discovered the first ichthyosaurus, died.

1932 The Sydney Harbour Bridge, New South Wales, Australia, was opened; it was the world's longest single-span arch bridge, at 503 m/1,650 ft.

1969 British troops landed on the Caribbean island of Anguilla, after the island declared itself a republic; they were well received, and the island remained a UK dependency.

20 MARCH

43 BC Ovid, Roman poet, was born.

1602 The Dutch government founded the Dutch East India Company.

1806 The foundation stone of Dartmoor Prison was laid.

1815 Napoleon returned to Paris from banishment on the island of Elba to begin his last 100 days of power that ended with defeat and exile.

1852 US author Harriet Beecher Stowe's novel *Uncle Tom's Cabin* was published.

1980 Pirate radio ship *Radio Caroline* sank.

21 MARCH

1685 Johann Sebastian Bach, German composer, was born.

1933 Germany's first Nazi parliament was officially opened in a ceremony at the garrison church in Potsdam.

1946 British minister Aneurin Bevan announced the Labour government's plans for the National Health Service.

1960 The Sharpeville Massacre in South Africa; a peaceful demonstration against the pass laws ended with about 70 deaths when police fired on demonstrators.

1963 Alcatraz, the maximum-security prison in San Francisco Bay, USA, was closed.

1990 A demonstration in London against the poll tax became a riot, in which over 400 people were arrested.

22 MARCH

The earliest possible date for Easter.

1824 The British parliament voted to buy 38 pictures at a cost of £57,000, to establish the national collection which is now housed in the National Gallery, Trafalgar Square, London.

1888 The English Football League was formed.

1895 French cinema pioneers Auguste and Louis Lumière gave the first demonstration of celluloid film, in Paris.

1942 The BBC began broadcasting in morse code to the French Resistance.

1945 The Arab League was founded in Cairo.

1948 Andrew Lloyd Webber, English composer of musicals, was born.

23 MARCH

National Day of Pakistan.

1765 The British parliament passed the Stamp Act, imposing a tax on all publications and official documents in America.

1861 London's first trams began operating, in Bayswater.

1891 Goal nets, invented by Liverpudlian J A Brodie, were used for the first time in an FA Cup Final.

1919 The Italian Fascist Party was formed by Benito Mussolini.

1925 Authorities in the state of Tennessee, USA, forbade the teaching of Darwinian theory in schools.

1956 Pakistan was declared an Islamic republic within the Commonwealth.

24 MARCH

1401 Tamerlane the Great captured Damascus.

1603 The crowns of England and Scotland were united when King James VI of Scotland succeeded to the English throne.

1877 The Oxford and Cambridge boat race ended in a dead heat, the only time this has happened.

1922 Only three of the 32 horses in the Grand National Steeplechase finished the race.

1942 The national loaf was introduced in Britain.

1976 Isabel Perón, president of Argentina, was deposed.

25 MARCH

National Day of Greece.

1306 Robert I 'the Bruce' was crowned king of Scots.

1609 English explorer Henry Hudson set off from Amsterdam, on behalf of the Dutch East India Company, in search of the North West Passage.

1807 The British parliament abolished the slave trade.

1843 A pedestrian tunnel was opened beneath the Thames in London, linking Wapping with Rotherhithe.

1876 In the first football international between Wales and Scotland, played in Glasgow, Scotland won 4–0.

1957 Six European countries (France, Belgium, Luxembourg, West Germany, Italy, and the Netherlands) signed the Treaty of Rome, establishing the European Community.

26 MARCH

1839 The annual rowing regatta at Henley-on-Thames was established.

1911 Tennessee Williams, American playwright who won the Pulitzer prize for his plays *A Streetcar Named Desire* and *Cat on a Hot Tin Roof* was born.

1920 The British special constables known as the Black and Tans arrived in Ireland.

1934 Driving tests were introduced in Britain.

1973 The first women were allowed on the floor of the London Stock Exchange.

1979 Israeli prime minister Menachem Begin and Egyptian president Anwar Sadat signed a peace treaty after two years of negotiations.

27 MARCH

1794 The United States Navy was formed.

1871 England and Scotland played their first rugby international, in Edinburgh; Scotland won.

1914 The first successful blood transfusion was performed, in a Brussels hospital.

1958 Nikita Khrushchev became leader of the Soviet Union.

1964 The ten Great Train Robbers who were caught were sentenced to a total of 307 years in prison.

1977 Pan Am and KLM jumbo jets collided on the runway at Tenerife airport, in the Canary Islands, killing 574 people.

28 MARCH

1910 The first seaplane took off near Marseille, S France.
1912 Both the Oxford and the Cambridge boats sank in the University boat race.
1930 The cities of Angora and Constantinople, in Turkey, changed their names to Ankara and Istanbul respectively.
1939 The Spanish Civil War came to an end as Madrid surrendered to General Franco.
1945 Germany dropped its last V2 bomb on Britain.
1979 The nuclear power station at Three Mile Island, Pennsylvania, suffered a meltdown in the core of one of its reactors.

29 MARCH

1461 Over 28,000 people are said to have been killed in the Battle of Towton, N Yorkshire; the Lancastrians under Henry VI were defeated.
1871 The Albert Hall, London, was opened by Queen Victoria.
1886 Coca Cola went on sale in the USA; it was marketed as a 'Brain Tonic' and claimed to relieve exhaustion.
1943 John Major, British prime minister, was born.
1973 The last US troops left Vietnam.
1974 US spacecraft *Mariner 10* took close-up photographs of the planet Mercury.

30 MARCH

1746 Francisco de Goya, Spanish painter, was born.
1775 The British parliament passed an Act forbidding its North American colonies to trade with anyone other than Britain.
1842 Ether was first used as an anaesthetic during surgery, by US doctor Crawford Long.
1856 The Crimean War was brought to an end by the signing of the Treaty of Paris.
1867 The USA bought Alaska from Russia for $7.2 million (oil had not yet been discovered).
1981 In Washington DC, USA, would-be assassin John Hinckley shot President Reagan in the chest.

31 MARCH

1596 René Descartes, French philosopher and mathematician, was born.

1889 In Paris, the Eiffel Tower, built for the Universal Exhibition, was inaugurated.

1896 The first zip fastener was patented in the USA by its inventor, Whitcomb Judson.

1959 Tibetan Buddhist leader the Dalai Lama fled from Chinese-occupied Tibet.

1973 Racehorse Red Rum set a record of 9 min 1.9 sec for the Grand National Steeplechase.

1986 Hampton Court Palace, near Richmond, SW London, was severely damaged by a fire which broke out in the south wing.

1 APRIL

All Fools' Day.

1578 William Harvey, English physician who explained the circulation of the blood, was born.

1939 Spanish Civil War effectively ended when USA recognized Franco's government.

1947 Britain's school-leaving age was raised to 15.

1960 The USA launched the world's first weather satellite, *Tiros I.*

1973 In Britain, Value Added Tax (VAT) replaced Purchase Tax and Selective Employment Tax.

1976 Max Ernst, German Surrealist painter, died.

2 APRIL

1792 The first mint was established in the USA.

1801 The British and Danish fleets met in the Battle of Copenhagen, during which Nelson put his telescope to his blind eye and ignored Admiral Parker's signal to stop fighting; the British fleet won.

1805 Hans Christian Andersen, Danish author, was born.

1849 Britain annexed the Punjab.

1979 Israeli prime minister Menachem Begin became the first Israeli leader to visit Cairo when he met Egyptian President Sadat.

1982 Argentina invaded the Falkland Islands.

3 APRIL

1721 Robert Walpole became the first prime minister of Britain.

1860 In the USA, the Pony Express came into operation, with despatch riders regularly making the 3,000 km/2,000 mi trip from St Joseph, Missouri to San Francisco, California.

1922	In the USSR, Stalin was appointed as general secretary of the Communist Party.
1930	Haile Selassie became emperor of Ethiopia.
1987	At an auction in Geneva, jewellery belonging to the late Duchess of Windsor raised over £31 million.
1993	Death of Dieter Plage, German wildlife photographer.

4 APRIL

National Day of Hungary.

1581	English navigator Francis Drake returned home after sailing around the world, and was knighted by Queen Elizabeth I.
1933	In the USA, 73 people died when the helium-filled airship *Akron* crashed into the sea off the New Jersey coast.
1934	'Cat's-eye' reflective studs were first used on roads near Bradford, Yorkshire.
1949	The North Atlantic Treaty Organization (NATO) was formed in Washington DC, USA; 11 countries signed the treaty.
1958	Members of the Campaign for Nuclear Disarmament (CND) held the first Aldermaston March, walking from Hyde Park Corner, London, to the Atomic Weapons Research Establishment at Aldermaston, Berkshire.
1968	Martin Luther King, US civil-rights leader, assassinated.

5 APRIL

1588	Birth of Thomas Hobbes, English philosopher, as the Spanish Armada was sighted approaching England.
1794	Georges Danton, French revolutionary leader, was guillotined.
1874	Johann Strauss's opera *Die Fledermaus* was first performed, in Vienna.
1955	British prime minister Winston Churchill resigned.
1964	Automatic, driverless trains began operating on the London Underground.
1976	Harold Wilson resigned as prime minister of Britain, and was succeeded by James Callaghan.

6 APRIL

1580	An earth tremor damaged several London churches, including the old St Paul's Cathedral.
1874	Harry Houdini, US escapologist, was born.

1896	The first modern Olympic Games began in Athens.
1909	US explorer Robert Peary became the first person to reach the North Pole.
1917	The USA declared war on Germany.
1965	*Early Bird*, the first commercial communications satellite, was launched by the USA.

7 APRIL

1770	William Wordsworth, English poet, was born.
1827	The first matches were sold in Stockton, England, by their inventor, chemist John Walker.
1853	Chloroform was used as an anaesthetic on Queen Victoria, during the birth of her eighth child, Prince Leopold.
1906	A major eruption of the Italian volcano, Vesuvius, took place.
1939	Italy invaded Albania.
1948	The World Health Organization (WHO) was established.

8 APRIL

1513	Spanish explorer Juan Ponce de Leon arrived in Florida and claimed it for Spain.
1838	Isambard Brunel's steamship *Great Western* set off on its first voyage, from Bristol to New York; the journey took 15 days.
1898	Lord Kitchener defeated Sudanese leader the Mahdi, at the Battle of Atbara.
1946	The League of Nations met for the last time.
1953	British colonial authorities in Kenya sentenced Jomo Kenyatta to seven years' imprisonment for allegedly organizing the Mau guerrillas.
1973	Death of Pablo Picasso, Spanish painter.

9 APRIL

1747	The Scottish Jacobite Lord Lovat was beheaded on Tower Hill, London, for high treason; he was the last man to be executed in this way in Britain.
1770	English navigator James Cook arrived in Botany Bay, Australia, the first European to do so.
1865	The American Civil War came to an end when Confederate general Robert E Lee surrendered to Union general Ulysses S Grant, at Appomatox, Virginia.

1869   The Hudson Bay Company agreed to transfer its territory to Canada.

1917   In France, during World War I, Canadian forces began the assault on Vimy Ridge, and the Battle of Arras began.

1969   The British supersonic aircraft *Concorde* made its first test flight, from Bristol to Fairford, Gloucestershire.

10 APRIL

1633   Bananas, never seen before in England, were on sale in a London shop.

1820   The first British settlers landed at Algoa Bay, South Africa.

1841   The US newspaper *New York Tribune* was first published.

1849   The safety pin was patented in the USA; unaware of this, a British inventor patented his own safety pin later the same year.

1864   Austrian Archduke Maximilian was made emperor of Mexico.

1972   Earthquakes in Iran killed over 3,000 people.

11 APRIL

1689   The coronation of William III and Mary II took place in London.

1713   The War of the Spanish Succession was ended by the signing of the Treaty of Utrecht; France ceded Newfoundland and Gibraltar to Britain.

1814   Napoleon abdicated and was exiled to the island of Elba; Louis XVIII became king of France.

1855   London's first pillar boxes were erected; there were just six of them, and they were painted green.

1945   Allied troops liberated the Nazi concentration camp at Buchenwald.

1961   Nazi war criminal Adolf Eichmann went on trial in Jerusalem after being kidnapped from Argentina, where he had fled after World War II.

12 APRIL

1204   Soldiers taking part in the Fourth Crusade under the direction of the Doge of Venice, captured the Byzantine city of Constantinople.

1606   The Union Jack was adopted as the official flag of England.

1782   The British fleet under Admiral Rodney defeated the French fleet in the Battle of the Saints in the West Indies.

| 1861 | The American Civil War began when Confederate troops fired on the Federal garrison at Fort Sumter. |

1861   The American Civil War began when Confederate troops fired on the Federal garrison at Fort Sumter.

1961   Soviet cosmonaut Yuri Gagarin became the first person to orbit the Earth.

1981   The US space shuttle *Columbia* was launched from Cape Canaveral.

13 APRIL

1668   English poet John Dryden became the first Poet Laureate.

1829   The British parliament passed the Catholic Emancipation Act, lifting restrictions imposed on Catholics at the time of Henry VIII.

1852   F W Woolworth, US founder of chain stores, was born.

1919   The Amritsar Massacre took place in the Punjab, India; British troops fired into a crowd of 10,000 which had gathered to protest at the arrest of two Indian Congress Party leaders, 379 people were killed and 1,200 wounded.

1936   Luton Town footballer Joe Payne set a goal-scoring record when he scored ten goals in one match against Bristol Rovers.

1980   Spanish golfer Severiano Ballesteros became the youngest-ever winner of the US Masters Tournament.

14 APRIL

Feast Day of St Anthony and St John.

1471   The Battle of Barnet took place in the Wars of the Roses, in which Yorkist forces defeated the Lancastrians, leading to the restoration of Edward IV.

1828   US lexicographer Noah Webster published his *American Dictionary of the English Language*.

1904   John Gielgud, English actor, was born.

1929   The first Monaco Grand Prix was held in Monte Carlo.

1931   The British Ministry of Transport published the first *Highway Code*.

1983   The first cordless telephone went on sale in Britain.

15 APRIL

1755   English lexicographer Dr Samuel Johnson published his *Dictionary*; he had taken eight years to compile it.

1865   Abraham Lincoln, 16th president of the USA, was assassinated.

1891   US inventor Thomas Edison gave a public demonstration of his kinetoscope, a moving-picture machine.

1912   Over 1,500 people died when the passenger liner *Titanic* sank
after colliding with an iceberg on its first voyage.

1922   Insulin was discovered by Canadian physiologist Frederick
Banting and J J R Macleod.

1942   The George Cross was awarded to the island of Malta, for bravery
under heavy attack by German and Italian forces during World
War II.

16 APRIL

1746   Charles Edward Stuart (Bonnie Prince Charlie) was defeated at
the Battle of Culloden.

1867   Wilbur Wright, US aviator, was born.

1883   Paul Kruger became president of South Africa.

1912   US pilot Harriet Quimby became the first woman to fly across
the English Channel.

1954   The first stock-car race meeting was held in Britain, at the Old
Kent Road stadium, London.

1972   The US spacecraft *Apollo 16* was launched.

17 APRIL

National Day of Syria.

1521   The Diet of Worms excommunicated German church reformer
Martin Luther.

1961   US troops and Cuban exiles failed in their attempt to invade
Cuba at the Bay of Pigs.

1957   Archbishop Makarios returned to Greece after over a year in
exile in the Seychelles.

1969   The age at which a person is eligible to vote in Britain was low-
ered from 21 to 18.

1975   The Cambodian communist Khmer Rouge captured the capital,
Pnomh Penh.

1980   Southern Rhodesia became Zimbabwe.

18 APRIL

1775   At the outbreak of the War of American Independence, US
patriot Paul Revere rode from Charleston to Lexington, warning
people as he went that British troops were on their way.

1881   The Natural History Museum in South Kensington, London,
was opened.

1906   An earthquake and the fire that followed it destroyed most of the city of San Francisco, and killed over 450 people.

1934 The first launderette, called a 'washeteria', was opened in Fort Worth, Texas.

1949 Eire proclaimed itself the Republic of Ireland.

1968 The old London Bridge was sold to a US company, who shipped it, stone by stone, to Arizona, where it was re-erected.

19 APRIL

1587 In the incident known as 'singeing the King of Spain's beard', English navigator Francis Drake sank the Spanish fleet in Cadiz harbour.

1775 The first battle in the War of American Independence took place at Lexington, Massachusetts.

1824 George Gordon Byron, English poet, died of malaria on his way to fight for Greek independence.

1958 Footballer Bobby Charlton played his first international match for England.

1956 US film actress Grace Kelly married Prince Rainier III of Monaco.

1972 Bangladesh joined the Commonwealth.

20 APRIL

1526 A Mogul army led by Babur defeated an Afghan army at the Battle of Panipat, taking the cities of Delhi and Agra.

1534 French explorer Jacques Cartier arrived on the coast of Labrador, North America.

1657 English admiral Robert Blake defeated the Spanish fleet in Santa Cruz Bay, off the Canary Islands.

1770 English navigator James Cook reached New South Wales, Australia.

1889 Adolf Hitler, German fascist dictator, was born.

1949 The Badminton Horse Trials were held for the first time, at Badminton, Gloucestershire.

21 APRIL

753 BC Traditionally, the date on which the city of Rome was founded.

1509 Henry VIII became king of England.

1960 The new city of Brasilia was declared the capital of Brazil, replacing Rio de Janeiro.

1964 BBC 2 began broadcasting.

1967   King Constantine II of Greece was removed in an army coup, and martial law was imposed.

1989   Over 100,000 Chinese students gathered in Tiananmen Square, ignoring government warnings of severe punishment.

22 APRIL

1500   Portuguese explorer Pedro Cabral claimed Brazil for Portugal.

1662   King Charles II granted a charter to the Royal Society of London, which became an important centre of scientific activity in England.

1838   The first steamship to cross the Atlantic, the British ship *Sirius*, arrived at New York; it made the crossing in 18 days.

1904   Robert Oppenheimer, US physicist who invented the atom bomb, was born.

1969   Sailor Robin Knox Johnston returned to Falmouth after a 312-day solo voyage around the world.

1972   The first people to row across the Pacific Ocean, Sylvia Cook and John Fairfax, arrived in Australia; they had been at sea for 362 days.

23 APRIL

Feast Day of St George and National Day of England.

1349   English king Edward III founded the Order of the Garter.

1564   William Shakespeare, English playwright and poet, was born.

1616   William Shakespeare died.

1661   Charles II was crowned king of Great Britain and Ireland.

1924   The British Empire Exhibition opened at Wembley.

1968   Britain's first decimal coins, the 5p and 10p, were issued in preparation for decimalization.

24 APRIL

1558   Mary, Queen of Scots married the French Dauphin.

1800   The US Library of Congress was founded in Washington, DC.

1895   US sailor Joshua Slocum set off from Boston, USA, to sail single-handed around the world; the voyage took just over three years.

1916   The Easter Rising – a Republican protest against British rule – took place in Dublin.

1949   Sweet-rationing in Britain came to an end.

1970   The Gambia was declared a republic within the Commonwealth.

25 APRIL

Feast Day of St Mark the Evangelist and Anzac Day in Australia.
1792 The guillotine was first used in Paris.
1859 Work began on the Suez Canal, supervised by the French engineer Ferdinand de Lesseps, who designed it.
1874 Guglielmo Marconi, Italian inventor and pioneer in the development of radio, was born.
1915 In World War I, Australian and New Zealand troops landed at Gallipoli.
1959 The St Lawrence Seaway was officially opened by Queen Elizabeth II and President Eisenhower, linking the Atlantic with ports on the Great Lakes.
1975 The first free elections for 50 years were held in Portugal, resulting in a precarious Socialist government.

26 APRIL

1923 The Duke of York and Elizabeth Bowes-Lyon, later King George VI and Queen Elizabeth, were married in Westminster Abbey.
1937 The Spanish town of Guernica was almost destroyed by German bombers acting in support of the Nationalists in the Spanish Civil War.
1957 English astronomer Patrick Moore presented the first broadcast of *The Sky at Night.*
1964 Tanganyika and Zanzibar merged to become the Republic of Tanzania.
1968 The largest underground nuclear device ever to be tested in the USA exploded in Nevada.
1986 Radioactive material was leaked from a damaged nuclear reactor at Chernobyl, Ukraine; the effects could be measured thousands of miles away.

27 APRIL

Feast Day of St Stephen.
1296 An English army, led by Edward I, defeated the Scots at the Battle of Dunbar.
1749 The first official performance of Handel's *Music for the Royal Fireworks* finished early due to the outbreak of fire.
1759 Mary Wollstonecraft Godwin, English feminist author, was born.
1937 King George VI performed the official opening of the National Maritime Museum at Greenwich.

1939   Conscription for men aged 20–21 was announced in Britain.

1947   Norwegian anthropologist Thor Heyerdahl set off from Callao, Peru, heading for Polynesia to prove his theory that the original Polynesian islanders could have come from Peru.

28 APRIL

1603   Queen Elizabeth I's funeral took place at Westminster Abbey.

1770   English navigator Captain James Cook and his crew, including the botanist Joseph Banks, landed in Australia, at the place which was later named Botany Bay.

1789   The crew of the ship *Bounty*, led by Fletcher Christian, mutinied against their captain, William Bligh.

1919   The League of Nations was founded.

1923   The first FA Cup Final was held at Wembley Stadium.

1969   French president General de Gaulle resigned.

29 APRIL

Feast Day of St Peter the Martyr and National Day of Japan.

1429   The Siege of Orléans was lifted by a French army under the leadership of Joan of Arc.

1884   Oxford University agreed to admit female students to examinations.

1899   'Duke' Ellington, US composer and bandleader, was born.

1913   Swedish-born US inventor Gideon Sundback patented the zip fastener in its modern form – earlier versions had not been successful.

1916   Republican rebels destroyed the Post Office in Dublin.

1945   The German army in Italy surrendered to the Allies under the British general Alexander.

30 APRIL

National Day of the Netherlands.

1789   George Washington became the first president of the USA.

1803   France sold Louisiana to the USA.

1902   Debussy's opera *Pelléas et Mélisande* had its first performance, in Paris.

1975   The Vietnam War ended, with the South surrendering unconditionally to the North.

1979   The Jubilee Line on the London Underground was officially opened.

1980   Queen Juliana of the Netherlands abdicated and was succeeded by her daughter, Beatrix.

1 MAY

May Day.

1517   In 'Evil May Day' riots in London, apprentices attacked foreign residents. Wolsey suppressed the rioters, of whom 60 were hanged.

1707   The Union of England and Scotland was proclaimed.

1851   Queen Victoria opened the Great Exhibition in Hyde Park, London.

1931   The Empire State Building, New York, was completed; it had cost $41 million to build.

1933   A telephone link between Britain and India was established.

1961   Betting shops became legal in Britain.

1994   Ayrton Senna, Brazilian racing driver, died on the racing track at San Marino, Italy.

2 MAY

1519   Leonardo da Vinci, Florentine artist and scientist, died.

1536   Queen Anne Boleyn was sent to the Tower of London.

1611   The *Authorized Version of the Bible* (King James Version) was first published.

1945   Germany surrendered to Allied forces.

1969   The passenger liner *Queen Elizabeth II* set off from Southampton on its first voyage.

1989   Martial law was imposed in China as the government took a firmer stand against pro-democracy demonstrators in Tiananmen Square.

3 MAY

1381   The weavers of Ghent, led by Philip van Artevelde, took Bruges; other Flemish towns revolted.

1493   Pope Alexander VI published the first bull *Inter cetera* dividing the New World between Spain and Portugal.

1497   A rising broke out in Cornwall, provoked by taxation; James Tutchet, Lord Audley, led an army of 15,000 from Taunton through the southern counties to attack London.

1808   A duel was fought from two hot-air balloons over Paris, the first of its kind.

1906 The Sinai Peninsula became Egyptian territory after Turkey renounced its claims.

1958 US President Eisenhower proposed demilitarization of Antarctica, subsequently accepted by the countries concerned.

4 MAY

1471 The Battle of Tewkesbury, the last battle in the Wars of the Roses, took place; the Yorkists defeated the Lancastrians.

1780 The first Derby was run at Epsom; the winner was *Diomed*.

1896 The first issue of the *Daily Mail* was published in London.

1926 The General Strike began in Britain, with almost half of the country's 6,000,000 trade-union members participating; it continued until 12 May.

1973 The world's tallest building, Sears Tower, Chicago, was completed.

1979 Margaret Thatcher became prime minister of Britain.

5 MAY

1525 The Peasants' Revolt in south Germany was suppressed and the Anabaptist preacher Thomas Münzer was hanged a few days later.

1762 The Treaty of St Petersburg was signed between Russia and Prussia; Russia restored all territory taken and formed an alliance with Prussia.

1818 Karl Marx, German philosopher and author, was born.

1821 Napoleon Bonaparte, French emperor, died in exile on the island of St Helena.

1863 In the American Civil War, Confederate troops defeated Federal forces at the Battle of Chancellorsville, but 'Stonewall' Jackson died of his wounds five days later.

1865 A revolt in San Domingo forced Spain to renounce sovereignty.

6 MAY

1527 The Sack of Rome, when imperialist troops under Charles, Duke of Bourbon (who was killed), mutinied, pillaging the city and killing some 4,000 of the inhabitants. Valuable art treasures were looted. Law was not restored until Feb 1528.

1626 Dutch settler Peter Minuit bought the island of Manhattan from native Americans for goods worth about $25.

1840 The Penny Black, the first postage stamp, was issued in Britain.

1856	Sigmund Freud, Austrian psychoanalyst, was born.
1910	George V became king of the United Kingdom on the death of Edward VII.
1994	The Channel Tunnel between Calais and Folkestone was officially opened by the Queen and President Mitterrand.

7 MAY

1793	The second partition of Poland was effected, with Russia taking Lithuania and W Ukraine, and Prussia taking Danzig, Thorn, Posen, Gnesen, and Kalisch.
1832	Greece became an independent kingdom.
1833	Johannes Brahms, German composer, was born.
1915	German forces sank the liner *Lusitania* off the Irish coast, with the loss of 1,198 lives; the USA was brought to the verge of war with Germany.
1928	Women's suffrage in Britain was reduced from the age of 30 to 21.
1954	Dien Bien Phu fell to Communist Vietnamese.

8 MAY

1559	Queen Elizabeth I of England signed the Act of Uniformity.
1886	The Presidential Succession law was passed in the USA, providing for succession to presidency in the event of the deaths of both the president and the vice-president.
1892	A ban was imposed on natives of the Congo, prohibiting them from collecting rubber and ivory other than for the state.
1902	On the Caribbean island of Martinique, the volcano Mount Pelée erupted, killing 30,000 people.
1926	David Attenborough, English naturalist and broadcaster, was born.
1950	Douglas MacArthur was appointed commander of UN forces in Korea.

9 MAY

1386	The Treaty of Windsor, between kings Richard and John, made a perpetual alliance between England and Portugal.
1695	The Scottish parliament met and enquired into the massacre of Glencoe.

1828	The British Test and Corporation Acts were repealed so that Catholic and Protestant Nonconformists could hold public office in Britain.

1828 The British Test and Corporation Acts were repealed so that Catholic and Protestant Nonconformists could hold public office in Britain.

1939 British prime minister Winston Churchill urged military alliance with USSR.

1940 RAF began night bombing of Germany.

1945 Russian troops took Prague.

10 MAY

994 The Danes devastated Anglesey.

1857 A revolt of Sepoys at Meerut began the Indian Mutiny against British rule.

1899 Fred Astaire, US dancer, was born.

1910 The British House of Commons resolved that the maximum life-time of parliament be reduced from seven to five years.

1916 Ernest Shackleton and companions reached South Georgia after sailing 1,300 km/800 mi in 16 days in an open boat to seek help for the remaining members of their party, marooned on Elephant Island, Antarctica.

1941 The House of Commons was destroyed in London's heaviest air raid.

11 MAY

973 Edgar crowned at Bath as King of all England; he then went to Chester, where eight Scottish and Welsh kings rowed him on the Dee.

1534 English king Henry VIII made peace with his nephew, James V of Scotland.

1812 British prime minister Spencer Perceval was assassinated in the House of Commons.

1824 British forces took Rangoon, Burma.

1949 Siam changed its name to Thailand.

1949 Israel was admitted to the United Nations.

12 MAY

1394 Malik Sarvar founded the Muslim kingdom of Jaunpur, on the middle Ganges.

1536 Sir Francis Weston, Mark Smeaton and other alleged lovers of Anne Boleyn were tried for treason; they were executed on the 17th.

1820	Florence Nightingale, English nursing pioneer, was born.
1961	United States of the Congo founded, with Léopoldville the federal capital.
1962	South African General Law Amendment Bill imposed the death penalty for sabotage.
1965	West Germany established diplomatic relations with Israel; Arab states broke off relations with Bonn.

13 MAY

1203	Byzantine emperor Alexius Comnenus seized Trebizond and established a new Greek empire there.
1265	Dante Alighieri, Italian poet, was born.
1607	Riots took place in Northamptonshire and other Midland counties of England in protest at widespread enclosure of common land.
1643	Oliver Cromwell defeated Royalists at Grantham.
1915	The names of emperors of Germany and Austria were struck off the roll of Knights of the Garter.
1927	'Black Friday' with the collapse of Germany's economic system.

14 MAY

1080	Walcher, Bishop of Durham and Earl of Northumberland was murdered; William (the Conqueror) consequently ravaged the area; he also invaded Scotland and built the castle at Newcastle-upon-Tyne.
1264	The English barons under Simon de Montfort defeated Henry III at the Battle of Lewes.
1610	Henry IV of France, assassinated by a religious fanatic, François Ravaillac.
1921	29 Fascists returned in Italian elections.
1946	Anti-Jewish pogrom in Kielce, Poland.
1948	As the British mandate in Palestine came to an end, a Jewish provisional government was formed in Israel with Chaim Weizmann as president and David Ben-Gurion as premier.

15 MAY

1567	Mary, Queen of Scots married Bothwell in Edinburgh.
1848	A communist rising began in Paris, after news of suppression of Polish revolt; workers overturned the government and set up a provisional administration which immediately collapsed.

1902	Portugal declared itself bankrupt.
1946	US President Truman signed a bill of credit for $3.75 billion for Britain.
1948	Egyptian troops intervened in Palestine on the side of the Arabs.
1957	Britain exploded the first British thermonuclear bomb in megaton range at Christmas Island, in the Central Pacific.

16 MAY

1220	Henry II laid the foundation stone of a new Lady Chapel at Westminster Abbey, thus beginning the new abbey-church (–1245).
1763	James Boswell first met Dr Samuel Johnson.
1770	The Dauphin of France (later Louis XVI) married Marie Antoinette, daughter of the empress Maria Theresa of Austria.
1804	Napoleon was declared emperor.
1905	Henry Fonda, US film actor, was born.
1949	Chinese Nationalists organized a Supreme Council under Chiang Kai-shek, which began to remove forces to Formosa.

17 MAY

1215	The English barons in revolt against King John took possession of London.
1527	Archbishop Warham began a secret inquiry at Greenwich into Henry VIII's marriage with Catherine of Aragon, the first step in divorce proceedings.
1885	Germany annexed Northern New Guinea and the Bismarck Archipelago.
1900	The Relief of Mafeking by British troops led by General Baden-Powell, against the besieging Boer forces.
1939	Sweden, Norway, and Finland rejected Germany's offer of non-aggression pacts, but Denmark, Estonia, and Latvia accepted.
1960	The Kariba Dam, Rhodesia, was opened.

18 MAY

1302	A French garrison was massacred in the 'Matins of Bruges', when the Flemings revolted against the French occupation.
1764	The British Parliament amended the Sugar Act from a commercial to a fiscal measure, to tax American colonists.
1878	Colombia granted a French company a nine-year concession to build the Panama Canal.

1936   An army revolt under Emilio Mola and Francisco Franco began the Spanish Civil War.

1940   At Japan's request Britain prohibited the passage of war materials for China passing through Burma.

1980   Mount St Helens, USA, erupted for the first time since 1857, devastating an area of 600 sq km/230 sq mi.

19 MAY

1585   English shipping in Spanish ports was confiscated as a reprisal for depredations across the Line; this served as a declaration of war on England.

1643   The Confederation of New England was formed by Connecticut, New Haven, Plymouth, and Massachusetts Bay.

1649   England was declared a Commonwealth.

1662   The Act of Uniformity gave consent to the revised English Prayer Book and denied the right to take up arms against the king; Presbyterianism in the Church was destroyed and many ministers who did not confirm were ejected. A Licensing Act forbade imports of literature contrary to Christian faith.

1930   White women were enfranchised in South Africa.

1964   The USA complained to Moscow about microphones concealed in its Moscow embassy.

20 MAY

1191   Richard I 'the Lion Heart' conquered Cyprus from its independent Greek ruler, then joined the Crusaders before Acre.

1506   Christopher Columbus, Genoese navigator, and discoverer of America, died in poverty in Valladolid, Spain.

1631   Flemish commander Count Tilly's imperialist army sacked Magdeburg; terrible carnage ensued and the city caught fire, leaving only the cathedral standing.

1941   German forces invaded Crete in the first airborne invasion of a country.

1944   Nazi officers attempted to assassinate Hitler at a staff meeting.

1946   A bill for nationalization of British coal mines passed the Commons stage.

21 MAY

1662   Charles II married Catherine de Braganza, daughter of John IV of Portugal.

1767	Townshend introduced taxes on imports of tea, glass, paper, and dyestuffs in American colonies to provide revenue for colonial administration.
1840	Britain claimed complete sovereignty over New Zealand.
1851	Gold was first discovered in Australia.
1894	The official opening of the Manchester Ship Canal took place.
1946	A world wheat shortage led to bread rationing in Britain.

22 MAY

853	A Greek expedition captured Damietta, in Egypt.
853	Olaf the White, son of the king of Norway, received the submission of Vikings and Danes in Ireland and made Dublin his capital.
1498	A death sentence was pronounced on Savonarola, former Prior of St Mark's and effective ruler of Florence, who had been excommunicated in June 1497 for attempting to seek the deposition of Pope Alexander VI.
1923	Stanley Baldwin formed a Conservative ministry, with Neville Chamberlain as Chancellor of the Exchequer.
1946	George Best, Irish footballer, was born.
1972	US President Richard Nixon visited Moscow to discuss arms limitations with Soviet President Leonid Brezhnev.

23 MAY

878	The Saxon king Alfred defeated the Danes at Edington; under the peace of Wedmore, their leader, Guthrum, was baptized as a Christian.
1430	Burgundian troops captured Joan of Arc and delivered her to the English.
1568	William of Orange with German mercenaries defeated a Spanish force under Count Aremberg at Heiligerlee; this action marked the beginning proper of the Revolt of the Netherlands.
1618	The Defenestration of Prague, when the Regents, Martinitz and Slawata, were overthrown by the Bohemian rebels, began the Thirty Years' War.
1926	France proclaimed the Lebanon a republic.
1933	Joan Collins, English actress, was born.

24 MAY

| 1530 | A list of heretical books was drawn up in London; Tyndale's Bible was burnt. |

1726 Voltaire landed in England on his liberation from the Bastille (he returned to France 1729).

1726 The first Circulating Library was opened by Allan Ramsay in Edinburgh.

1862 Westminster Bridge across the River Thames in London was opened.

1941 The British battleship HMS *Hood* was sunk by the Bismarck off Greenland.

1948 The USSR stopped road and rail traffic between Berlin and the West, forcing Western powers to organize airlifts.

25 MAY

1234 The Mongols took Kaifeng and destroyed the Chin dynasty.

1659 Richard Cromwell resigned; the Rump Parliament re-established the Commonwealth.

1694 The ministry in England was remodelled when William III dismissed Tories, except Godolphin and Danby, and introduced Whig Junta of Somers, Russell, Montague, and Wharton.

1703 Samuel Pepys, English diarist, died.

1914 The British House of Commons passed the Irish Home Rule Bill.

1961 US President Kennedy presented an extra-ordinary State of Union message to Congress for increased funds urgently needed for US space, defence, and air programmes.

26 MAY

1521 The Edict of Worms imposed on Martin Luther the ban of the Empire.

1798 Income tax was introduced in Britain, as a tax of 10% on all incomes over £200.

1805 Napoleon was crowned king of Italy in Milan Cathedral.

1846 Robert Peel repealed the Corn Laws (royal assent given 26 June), splitting the Conservative Party.

1865 The surrender of the last Confederate army at Shreveport, near New Orleans, ended the American Civil War.

1924 Calvin Coolidge signed a bill limiting immigration into the USA and entirely excluding the Japanese.

27 MAY

1063 Harold of Wessex began to conquer Wales.

1199 Pope Innocent III imposed the first direct papal taxation of Clergy.

1299	Peace was negotiated between Genoa and Venice, ending their war (since 1261) to control trade with the Byzantine Empire.
1719	Emperor Charles VI founded the Oriental Company in Vienna to compete with Dutch trade in the Orient.
1813	US forces occupied Fort St George, and the British abandoned the entire Niagara frontier.
1941	The German battleship *Bismarck* was sunk by the Royal Navy west of Brest.

28 MAY

1358	In France the uprising known as the Jacquerie broke out – the peasants were protesting at their impoverished state after the ravages of the Hundred Years' War.
1539	Royal assent was given to an Act (the Six Articles of Religion) 'abolishing diversity of opinions' in England, after Henry VIII personally intervened in the Lords' debate to argue with the Reforming bishops.
1932	The IJselmeer was formed in the Netherlands, by the completion of a dam which enclosed the former Zuider Zee.
1956	France ceded former French settlements in India to the Indian Union.
1959	Britain announced the removal of controls on imports of many consumer goods from the dollar area, with increased import quotas of other goods.
1961	The last journey of the *Orient Express* train, from Paris to Bucharest; it had been in operation for 78 years.

29 MAY

862	Riurick (of Jutland) founded the first dynasty of Princes of Russia at Novgorod.
1218	The Fifth Crusade landed outside Damietta, N Egypt.
1453	Mohammed II, founder of the Ottoman empire, captured Constantinople; the Byzantine emperor Constantine XI was killed and the Greek Empire finally extinguished. Constantinople became the Ottoman capital.
1458	Richard Neville, Earl of Warwick, defeated a Castilian fleet in the Channel.
1940	The first British forces were evacuated from Dunkirk.
1947	The Indian constituent assembly outlawed 'untouchability'.

30 MAY

1431 Joan of Arc was burnt as a heretic at Rouen, France.
1536 English king Henry VIII married Jane Seymour, his third wife.
1592 The Spanish defeated an English force under Sir John Norris at Cranon, Brittany.
1913 A peace treaty between Turkey and the Balkan states was signed in London.
1925 The shooting of Chinese students by municipal police in Shanghai and other incidents in Canton provoked a Chinese boycott of British goods.
1948 The British Citizenship Act conferred the status of British subjects on all Commonwealth citizens.

31 MAY

1287 The Genoese defeated the Venetian fleet off Acre and blockaded the coast of Outremer.
1902 The Peace of Vereeniging ended the Boer War, in which British casualties numbered 5,774 killed (and 16,000 deaths from disease) against 4,000 Boers killed in action.
1916 The Battle of Jutland began, in which Royal Navy losses exceeded those of the German fleet.
1930 Clint Eastwood, US film actor and director,was born.
1942 Czech patriots assassinated Gestapo leader Heydrich.
1961 South Africa became an independent republic outside the Commonwealth, with C R Swart as president.

1 JUNE

National Day of Tunisia.
836 Viking raiders sacked London.
1792 Kentucky became the 15th state of the USA.
1915 The first Zeppelin attack on London took place.
1946 Television licences were issued in Britain for the first time; they cost £2.
1957 ERNIE drew the first premium bond prizes in Britain.
1958 Iceland extended its fishery limits to 12 miles.

2 JUNE

National Day of Italy.
1627 The Duke of Buckingham sailed from Portsmouth with a fleet to aid the Huguenots in the defence of La Rochelle.

1780 The Gordon riots began in London, when Lord George Gordon headed a procession for presenting a petition to Parliament for repealing Catholic Relief act of 1778; Roman Catholic chapels were pillaged.

1793 The final overthrow of Girondins and arrest of Jacques Brissot began the Reign of Terror.

1916 The second battle of Ypres took place.

1949 Transjordan was renamed the Hashemite Kingdom of Jordan.

1953 The coronation of Queen Elizabeth II took place in Westminster Abbey.

3 JUNE

1098 The Crusaders took Antioch.

1162 Thomas à Becket was consecrated as Archbishop of Canterbury.

1665 The English fleet defeated the Dutch at the Battle of Lowestoft.

1942 US and Japanese naval forces began the Battle of Midway, in the Pacific.

1959 Singapore became self-governing.

1967 Arthur Ransome, English children's writer, died.

4 JUNE

1039 Gruffyd ap Llewelyn, king of Gwynned and Powys, defeated an English attack.

1210 King John embarked on an expedition to Ireland, enforcing his authority there.

1878 A secret Anglo-Turkish agreement was made to check Russian advance in Asia Minor, by which Britain promised to defend Turkey against further attack and Britain was allowed to occupy Cyprus.

1913 Emily Davidson, English suffragette, threw herself in front of the King's horse during the Derby.

1956 Egypt declared it would not extend the Suez Canal Company's concession after its expiry in 1968.

1959 US-owned sugar mills and plantations in Cuba were expropriated.

5 JUNE

National Day of Denmark.

1912 US marines landed in Cuba.

1916 HMS *Hampshire* sank off the Orkneys, with Lord Kitchener aboard.

1945	The Allied Control Commission assumed control throughout Germany, which was divided into four occupation zones.
1947	US Secretary of State George Marshall called for a European Recovery Programme (Marshall Aid).
1967	The Six-Day War broke out between Israel and the Arab states.
1970	Tonga became independent within the Commonwealth.

6 JUNE

National Day of Sweden.

1457	Polish forces took Marienburg; the Teutonic Knights then made Königsberg their headquarters.
1636	Puritan American colonist Roger Williams, banished from Massachusetts Bay Colony, founded Providence, Rhode Island, a colony with complete religious freedom.
1797	Napoleon Bonaparte founded the Ligurian Republic in Genoa.
1820	Caroline, Princess of Wales, whom George IV wished to divorce, triumphantly entered London, demanding her recognition as Queen.
1844	The Factory Act in Britain restricted female workers to a 12–hour day; children between eight and 13 years were limited to six-and-a-half hours.
1956	Bjorn Borg, Swedish tennis player, was born.

7 JUNE

1494	By the Treaty of Tordesillas, Spain and Portugal agreed to divide the New World between themselves: Portugal was to have all lands east of a line north and south drawn 370 leagues west of Cape Verde, Spain to have the rest.
1497	English king Henry VII defeated the Cornish rebels under Lord Audley at Blackheath.
1535	John Fisher, Bishop of Rochester, was tried for treason (he was executed on 22 June).
1672	Dutch Admiral de Ruyter was successful in action against the combined English and French fleets in Southwold Bay.
1832	The Reform Bill became law; over 140 seats were redistributed, and in the boroughs all antiquated forms of franchise were eliminated and the franchise was extended to include leaseholders paying minimum of £10 rent per annum, while in counties the 40-shilling freehold qualification was retained and certain leaseholders acquired the vote.
1848	Paul Gauguin, French painter, was born.

8 JUNE

1042 Harthacnut, King of England and Denmark, died; he was succeeded in England by his adopted heir, Edward the Confessor, and in Denmark by Magnus, King of Norway.

1536 The English parliament met and settled the succession on the future children of Henry VIII by Jane Seymour; the Princesses Mary and Elizabeth were declared illegitimate.

1934 Oswald Mosley addressed a mass meeting of the British Union of Fascists at Olympia.

1939 George VI visited the USA at the end of his tour of Canada; he was the first British monarch to do so.

1941 British and Free French Forces invaded Syria to prevent the establishment of Axis bases.

1965 US troops were authorized to engage in offensive operations in Vietnam.

9 JUNE

1572 A new Turkish fleet put to sea against Don John of Austria to complete the capture of Cyprus.

1788 English botanist Joseph Banks founded the Africa Association for arousing interest in exploration and trade.

1885 The Treaty of Tientsin between France and China recognized the French protectorate in Annam.

1893 Cole Porter, US composer of musicals, was born.

1934 Cartoon character Donald Duck first appeared.

1959 The USS *George Washington* was launched, the first submarine to be armed with ballistic missiles.

10 JUNE

1829 The Oxford team won the first-ever Oxford and Cambridge Boat Race.

1893 Alarmed at Belgian advances in the Congo, France sent an occupying force to forestall further annexations.

1899 US Congress appointed a canal commission to report on routes through Panama.

1922 Judy Garland, US film actress and singer, was born.

1942 The Czech village of Lidice was destroyed and every man in it killed in reprisal for the assassination of Nazi leader Richard Heydrich.

1943 The ball-point pen was patented in the USA.

11 JUNE

1509 Henry VIII married Catherine of Aragon, his first wife.

1727 George I became king of Great Britain.

1891 At an Anglo-Portuguese convention on territories north and south of Zambesi, Portugal assigned Barotseland to Britain; Nyasaland was subsequently proclaimed a British Protectorate.

1895 Britain annexed Togoland to block Transvaal's access to the sea.

1955 US President Eisenhower proposed financial and technical aid to all non-Communist countries to develop atomic energy.

1963 Constantine Karamanlis, the Greek premier, resigned in protest against King Paul's state visit to Britain.

12 JUNE

National Day of the Philippines.

1088 William II suppressed a revolt in England led by Odo of Bayeux, Bishop of Rochester, who was supporting Robert Curthose.

1667 The Dutch fleet under Admiral de Ruyter burned Sheerness, sailed up the River Medway, raided Chatham dockyard, and escaped with the royal barge, the *Royal Charles*; the nadir of English naval power.

1683 The Rye House Plot, to assassinate King Charles II and his brother James, Duke of York, was discovered.

1901 A Cuban convention making the country virtually a protectorate of the USA was incorporated in the Cuban constitution as a condition of the withdrawal of US troops.

1934 Political parties were banned in Bulgaria.

1964 Nelson Mandela and seven others were sentenced to life imprisonment for acts of sabotage in the Rivonia trial, Pretoria.

13 JUNE

1849 Communist riots in Paris were easily defeated and led to repressive legislation.

1866 The US 14th Amendment incorporated the Civil Rights Act and gave states the choice of Negro enfranchisement or reduced representation in Congress.

1900 The Boxer Rebellion began in China against Europeans.

1942 British forces lost 230 tanks in desert fighting.

1944 The first flying bomb was dropped on London.

1956 The last British troops left the Suez Canal base.

14 JUNE

1380 In the Peasants' Revolt, the rebels occupying London killed Archbishop Sudbury, the Chancellor, and Robert Hales, the Treasurer.

1645 In the English Civil War, Oliver Cromwell defeated the Royalists at the Battle of Naseby, Northamptonshire.

1800 Napoleon Bonaparte defeated an Austrian army at the Battle of Marengo and reconquered Italy.

1940 In World War II, German forces entered Paris.

1960 French President de Gaulle renewed his offer to the Algerian provisional government to negotiate a cease-fire, to which *Front de la Libération Nationale* agreed, but rejected subsequent French conditions.

1962 The European Space Research Organization was established at Paris.

15 JUNE

Official birthday of Queen Elizabeth II.

1520 Pope Leo X excommunicated Martin Luther by the bull *Exsurge*.

1658 The Mogul emperor Aurangzeb imprisoned his father the Shah, after winning a battle at Samgarh.

1672 The Sluices were opened in Holland to save Amsterdam from the French.

1855 Stamp duty on British newspapers was abolished.

1869 Celluloid was patented in the USA.

1977 Spain had its first general elections since 1936.

16 JUNE

1586 Mary, Queen of Scots recognized Philip II of Spain as her heir.

1779 Spain declared war on Britain (after France had undertaken to assist in the recovery of Gibraltar and Florida), and the siege of Gibraltar began.

1836 The formation of the London Working Men's Association began the Chartist Movement.

1871 The University Test Acts allowed students to enter Oxford and Cambridge without religious tests.

1972 Burglars were caught breaking into the Democratic Party head-quarters in the Watergate Building, Washington, DC, USA.

1977 Leonid Brezhnev became president of the USSR.

17 JUNE

National Day of Iceland.

1128 Henry I's daughter, Matilda, widow of Henry V, married Geoffrey Plantagenet of Anjou; she was recognized in England as her father's heir.

1579 Francis Drake proclaimed England's sovereignty over New Albion (California).

1617 James I met his Scottish parliament. His proposal that the Scottish lords should surrender to the Crown their hereditable jurisdictions met with vigorous opposition, but the five Articles of Religion, for introducing Anglican principles to Scottish worship were endorsed.

1703 John Wesley, English evangelist, was born.

1775 In the War of American Independence, British troops won a victory at Bunker Hill.

1940 Russian troops occupied the Baltic states.

18 JUNE

860 Vikings from Russia were repulsed in an attack on Constantinople.

1429 The French, led by Joan of Arc, defeated the English at the Battle of Patay.

1633 Charles I was crowned king of Scotland at Edinburgh.

1815 The Duke of Wellington and Gebhard von Blücher defeated Napoleon at the Battle of Waterloo.

1928 US aviator Amelia Earhart became the first woman to fly across the Atlantic.

1953 A republic was proclaimed in Egypt, with general M Neguib as president.

19 JUNE

1464 An ordinance of Louis XI in France created the *poste*, organizing relays of horses on the main roads for the king's business.

1754 The Anglo-French war broke out in North America when a force under George Washington skirmished with French troops near Fort Duquesne.

1769 Hyder Ali of Mysore compelled the British at Madras to sign a treaty of mutual assistance.

1809 Curwen's Act was passed in Britain, to prevent the sale of parliamentary seats, thus decreasing the number of seats which the British government could manipulate for its regular supporters.

1829 Robert Peel's Act was passed, to establish a new police force in London and its suburbs.

1867 Emperor Maximilian was executed in Mexico.

20 JUNE

840 Vikings sailed up the Seine as far as Rouen, for the first time.

1756 Over 140 British subjects were imprisoned in a cell ('The Black Hole of Calcutta'); only 23 came out alive.

1789 In France, the third estate took the Tennis Court oath, undertaking not to depart until a constitution was drawn up.

1791 Louis XVI attempted to leave France, but was turned back at Varennes and taken to Paris.

1837 On the death of William IV, Queen Victoria succeeded to the British throne.

1837 Hanover was automatically separated from Britain, as Salic Law forbids female succession, and the throne was taken by Ernest Augustus, Duke of Cumberland, the eldest surviving son of George III.

21 JUNE

1798 British general Gerard Lake defeated Irish rebels at Vinegar Hill and entered Wexford, ending the Irish Rebellion.

1813 The Duke of Wellington completely routed the French at Vittoria, forcing the Spanish king, Napoleon's brother Joseph, to return to France.

1827 Robert Peel reformed English criminal law, by reducing the number of capital offences, abolishing the immunity of the clergy from arrest in cases of felony, and by defining the law of offences against property in a simplified form.

1887 Britain annexed Zululand, blocking the attempt of Transvaal to gain communication with the coast.

1905 Jean-Paul Sartre, French philosopher, novelist, and playwright, was born.

1919 The German fleet was scuttled in Scapa Flow, in the Orkneys.

22 JUNE

1377 Richard II became king of England.

1527 Niccolò Machiavelli, Italian politician and diplomat, died.

1671 Turkey declared war on Poland.

1679 The Duke of Monmouth subdued an insurrection of Scottish Covenanters at Bothwell Bridge.

1826 The Pan-American Congress met in Panama under the influence of Simón Bolívar in an unsuccessful effort to unite the American Republics.

1907 The Northern Line was opened on the London Underground.

23 JUNE

National Day of Luxembourg.

1611 English navigator Henry Hudson and eight others were cast adrift by mutineers; the mutineers returned to England, but Hudson and his companions were never seen again.

1757 British troops under Robert Clive captured Plassey, in Bengal, and recovered Calcutta.

1934 Saudi Arabia and the Yemen signed a peace agreement after a war of six weeks.

1935 British foreign secretary Anthony Eden offered Benito Mussolini concessions over Abyssinia, which he rejected.

1951 Guy Burgess and Donald Maclean, 'missing diplomats', fled to the USSR.

1952 The US Air Force bombed hydroelectric plants in North Korea.

24 JUNE

1245 Pope Innocent sent John de Plano Carpinis, a friar minor, to the court of the Great Khan, at Karakorum; this embassy led to the establishment of Christian missions in China until c. 1368.

1314 Robert the Bruce defeated Edward II at Bannockburn and so completed his expulsion of the English from Scotland.

1559 The Elizabethan Prayer Book was first used.

1812 Napoleon crossed the River Niemen and entered Russian territory.

1917 The Russian Black Sea fleet mutinied at Sebastopol.

1956 Colonel Nasser was elected president of Egypt.

25 JUNE

1524 The Peasants' Revolt in southern Germany began at Stühlingen on the estates of Count von Lupfen. The rebels demanded the abolition of enclosures and feudal services.

1646 The surrender of Oxford to the Roundheads virtually signified the end of the English Civil War.

1788	Virginia became the 10th state of the USA.
1867	The first patent for barbed wire was taken out in Ohio, USA.
1876	US soldier George Custer and his 264 men were killed by Sioux Indians at the Battle of Little Big Horn, Montana.
1975	Mozambique achieved independence from Portugal.

26 JUNE

1483	Richard, Duke of Gloucester, began to rule as Richard III, having deposed his nephew, Edward V; the latter and his brother, Richard, Duke of York, were soon afterwards murdered in the Tower of London.
1519	Martin Luther's public disputation with Johann Eck on doctrine began at Leipzig.
1849	The British Navigation Acts were finally repealed.
1937	The Duke of Windsor married Mrs. Wallis Simpson in France.
1960	British Somaliland became independent; it joined Somalia on 27 June.
1962	The Portuguese in Mozambique required Indian nationals to leave within three months of release from internment camps.

27 JUNE

1771	Russia completed its conquest of the Crimea.
1801	Cairo fell to English forces.
1932	A Constitution was proclaimed in Siam.
1940	The USSR invaded Romania on the refusal of King Carol to cede Bessarabia and Bukovina; Romania appealed for German aid in vain.
1941	Hungary declared war on Russia.
1944	Allied forces took Cherbourg.

28 JUNE

1519	Charles I of Spain, Sicily, and Sardinia, was elected Holy Roman Emperor as Charles V.
1645	In the English Civil War, the Royalists lost Carlisle.
1914	Archduke Francis Ferdinand of Austria and his wife were assassinated at Sarajevo by Gavrilo Princip, a Bosnian revolutionary.
1919	Britain and the USA guaranteed France in event of an unprovoked German attack, which the USA later refused to ratify.
1950	North Korean forces captured Seoul.

1956 Sydney Silverman's bill for abolition of death penalty passed the Commons; it was defeated in the Lords, 10 July.

29 JUNE

1613 The Globe Theatre was destroyed by fire.
1900 Antoine de Saint-Exupéry, French author and aviator, was born.
1949 The USA completed its withdrawal of occupying forces from South Korea.
1949 British dock strike.
1949 The South African Citizenship Act suspended the automatic granting of citizenship to Commonwealth immigrants after five years, and imposed a ban on mixed marriages between Europeans and non-Europeans – the beginning of the Apartheid programme.
1954 Following the meeting of President Eisenhower and Winston Churchill in Washington the Potomac Charter, or six-point declaration of western policy, was issued.

30 JUNE

1574 William of Orange persuaded the Estates of Holland to open the dykes to hinder the Spanish siege of Leyden.
1596 English expedition under Lord Howard of Effingham and the Earl of Essex sacked Cadiz, ravaged the Spanish coast, and captured much booty. Philip II was thus prevented from sending an Armada against England.
1782 Spain completed its conquest of Florida.
1846 The Mormons under Brigham Young left Nauvoo City on trail for the Great Salt Lake.
1934 A Nazi purge took place in Germany with summary executions of Kurt von Schleicher, Ernst Roehm and other party leaders for an alleged plot against Hitler.
1965 An India–Pakistan cease-fire was signed.

1 JULY

National Day of Canada.
1751 The first volume of Diderot's *Encyclopédie* was published in Paris.
1838 Charles Darwin presented a paper to the Linnaean Society in London, on his theory of the evolution of species.

1916	The first Battle of the Somme began; more than 21,000 men were killed on the battle's first day.
1937	The telephone emergency service, 999, became operational in Britain.
1990	A state treaty establishing a unified economy and monetary system for East and West Germany went into effect.
1991	The Warsaw Pact, the last vestige of the Cold War era Soviet bloc, was formally disbanded.

2 JULY

1644	Oliver Cromwell defeated Prince Rupert at the Battle of Marston Moor, his first victory over the Royalists in the English Civil War.
1865	At a revivalist meeting at Whitechapel, London, William Booth formed the Salvation Army.
1900	The 2nd Olympic Games opened in Paris.
1956	Elvis Presley recorded 'Hound Dog' and 'Don't Be Cruel' in New York.
1964	President Johnson signed the US Civil Rights Bill prohibiting racial discrimination.
1990	Over a thousand Muslim pilgrims were killed when a stampede occurred in a pedestrian tunnel leading to the holy city of Mecca.

3 JULY

1608	French explorer Samuel Champlain founded Québec.
1905	In Odessa, over 6,000 people were killed by Russian troops to restore order during a general strike.
1954	Nearly nine years after the end of World War II, food rationing in Britain finally ended.
1962	Following a referendum, France proclaimed Algeria independent.
1976	An Israeli commando force rescued 103 hostages, who were being held at Entebbe airport, Uganda, from a hijacked aircraft.
1988	The USS *Vincennes*, patrolling the Gulf during the Iran–Iraq conflict, mistook an Iranian civil airliner for a bomber and shot it down, killing all 290 people on board.

4 JULY

Independence Day in the USA.

| 1776 | The American Declaration of Independence was adopted. |

1829 Britain's first regular scheduled bus service began running, between Marylebone Road and the Bank of England, in London.

1848 The *Communist Manifesto* was published by Karl Marx and Friedrich Engels.

1946 The Philippine Islands were given independence by the USA.

1968 Alec Rose landed at Portsmouth in *Lively Lady*, having sailed single-handed around the world.

1991 Colombia's president Cesar Gaviria Trujillo lifted the state of seige that had been in effect since 1984.

5 JULY

National Day of Venezuela.

1791 George Hammond was appointed the first British ambassador to the USA.

1946 A swimsuit designed by Louis Reard, called 'bikini', was first modelled at a Paris fashion show.

1948 Britain's National Health Service came into operation.

1965 Maria Callas, at the age of 41, gave her last stage performance singing *Tosca* at Covent Garden, London.

1969 The Rolling Stones gave a free concert in Hyde Park two days after the death of guitarist Brian Jones; it was attended by 250,000 people.

1980 Bjorn Borg won the Wimbledon singles championship for a record fifth consecutive time.

1989 Convicted for his involvement in the Iran-Contra affair, US Army Colonel Oliver North was fined $150,000 and given a suspended sentence.

6 JULY

National Day of Malawi.

1535 Sir Thomas More was beheaded on London's Tower Hill for treason.

1553 Mary I acceded to the throne, becoming the first queen to rule England in her own right.

1892 Britain's first non-white MP was elected – Dadabhai Naoraji won the Central Finsbury seat.

1928 The first all-talking feature film, *Lights of New York*, was presented at the Strand Theatre in New York City.

1965 The Beatles' film *A Hard Day's Night* was premiered in London, with royal attendance.

1988   An explosion aboard the North Sea oil rig *Piper Alpha* resulted in the loss of 166 lives.

7 JULY

1853   US naval officer Commodore Matthew Perry arrived in Japan, and persuaded her to open trade contacts with the West.

1927   Christopher Stone became the first 'disc jockey' on British radio when he presented his 'Record Round-up' from Savoy Hill.

1940   Ringo Starr, English drummer, one of The Beatles, was born.

1982   Queen Elizabeth II was woken by a strange man sitting on her bed in Buckingham Palace; the presence of the intruder, who merely asked her for a cigarette, raised concerns about Palace security.

1985   The unseeded 17-year-old Boris Becker became the youngest ever men's singles champion at Wimbledon.

1990   Martina Navratilova won a record ninth Wimbledon singles title.

8 JULY

1497   Portuguese navigator Vasco da Gama left Lisbon for a voyage on which he discovered the Cape route to India.

1709   Charles XII of Sweden was defeated by Peter the Great's army at the Battle of Poltava, crushing Sweden's territorial ambitions.

1884   The National Society for Prevention of Cruelty to Children (NSPCC) was founded in London.

1943   Jean Moulin, the French Resistance leader known as 'Max', was executed by the Gestapo.

1978   Reinhold Messner and Peter Habeler became the first to climb Everest entirely without oxygen.

1991   Iraq admitted to the UN that it had been conducting clandestine programmes to produce enriched uranium, a key element in nuclear weapons.

9 JULY

National Day of Argentina.

1816   Argentina declared independence from Spain at the Congress of Tucuman.

1877   The first Wimbledon Lawn Tennis championship was held at its original site at Worple Road.

1922   Johnny Weissmuller, aged 18, swam the 100 m in under a minute (58.6 sec).

1938 In anticipation of World War II, 35 million gas masks were issued to Britain's civilian population.

1984 Lightning struck York Minster Cathedral and set the roof on fire, destroying the south transept.

1991 The International Olympic Committee lifted a 21-year-old boycott on South Africa.

10 JULY

1553 Following the death of Edward VI, Lady Jane Grey was proclaimed queen of England.

1900 The Paris underground railway, the Metro, was opened.

1958 Britain's first parking meters were installed, in Mayfair, London.

1962 The US communications satellite *Telstar* was launched, bringing Europe the first live television from the USA.

1976 Seveso, in northern Italy, was covered by a cloud of toxic weedkiller leaked from a chemicals factory; crops and 40,000 animals died.

1985 The Greenpeace campaign ship *Rainbow Warrior* sank in Auckland, New Zealand, after two explosions tore its hull.

11 JULY

National Day of Mongolia.

1776 Captain Cook sailed from Plymouth in the *Resolution*, accompanied by the *Discovery*, on his last expedition.

1848 London's Waterloo Station was officially opened.

1950 *Andy Pandy*, the BBC's popular children's television programme, was first transmitted.

1975 Excavations at the tomb of Emperor Qin Shi Huangdi, near the ancient Chinese capital of Xi'an, uncovered an army of 8,000 life-size terracotta warriors dating from about 206 BC.

1977 In Britain, *Gay News* was fined £1,000 for publishing a poem which portrayed Jesus as homosexual.

1979 America's *Skylab I* returned to earth after 34,981 orbits and six years in space.

12 JULY

Orangeman's Day in Northern Ireland.

100 BC Gaius Julius Caesar, Roman emperor, was born.

1794 British admiral Horatio Nelson lost his right eye at the siege of Calvi, in Corsica.

1920 US President Wilson opened the Panama Canal.
1930 Australian batsman Don Bradman scored a record 334 runs – of which a record 309 were scored in one day – against England at Leeds.
1970 Thor Heyerdahl and his crew crossed the Atlantic in 57 days, in a papyrus boat.
1991 Hitoshi Igarashi, the Japanese translator of Salman Rushdie's *Satanic Verses*, was found stabbed to death in Tokyo.

13 JULY

1793 Jean Paul Marat, French revolutionary leader, was stabbed to death in his bath by Charlotte Corday.
1837 Queen Victoria became the first sovereign to move into Buckingham Palace.
1871 The first cat show was held, organized by Harrison Weir, at Crystal Palace, London.
1878 The Treaty of Berlin was signed, granting Bosnia-Herzegovina to Austria-Hungary, and gaining the independence of Romania, Serbia, and Montenegro from Turkey.
1930 The World Football Cup was first held in Uruguay; the hosts beat the 13 other competing countries.
1985 Two simultaneous 'Live Aid' concerts, one in London and one in Philadelphia, raised over £50 million for famine victims in Africa.

14 JULY

National Day of France (Bastille Day), and of Iraq.
1789 The Bastille was stormed by the citizens of Paris and razed to the ground as the French Revolution began.
1823 During a visit to Britain, King Kamehameha II of Hawaii and his queen died of measles.
1858 Emmeline Pankhurst, English suffragette, was born.
1867 Alfred Nobel demonstrated dynamite for the first time at a quarry in Redhill, Surrey.
1967 Abortion was legalized in Britain.
1972 Gary Glitter and the Glittermen (later called the Glitter Band) gave their first concert in Wiltshire.

15 JULY

Feast Day of St Swithin.
1099 Jerusalem was captured by the Crusaders with troops led by Godfrey and Robert of Flanders and Tancred of Normandy.

1606	Rembrandt, Dutch painter, was born.

1606 Rembrandt, Dutch painter, was born.

1869 Margarine was patented by Hippolyte Mege Mouries in Paris.

1948 Alcoholics Anonymous, in existence in the USA since 1935, was founded in London.

1965 *US Mariner* transmitted the first close-up pictures of Mars.

1990 In an ongoing campaign of violence, separatist Tamil Tigers massacred 168 Muslims in Colombo, the Sri Lankan capital.

16 JULY

622 Traditionally, the beginning of the Islamic Era, when Mohammed began his flight (the *Hejira*) from Mecca to Medina.

1661 Europe's first banknotes were issued, by the Bank of Stockholm.

1918 The last tsar of Russia, Nicholas II, along with his entire family, family doctor, servants, and even the pet dog, was murdered by Bolsheviks at Ekaterinburg.

1945 The first atomic bomb developed by Robert Oppenheimer and his team at Los Alamos was exploded in New Mexico.

1965 The Mont Blanc road tunnel, linking France with Italy, was opened.

1990 An earthquake struck the main Philippine island of Luzon, killing over 1,500 people.

17 JULY

1453 With the defeat of the English at the Battle of Castillon, the Hundred Years' War between France and England came to an end.

1841 The first issue of the humorous magazine *Punch* was published in London.

1945 The Potsdam Conference of Allied leaders Truman, Stalin, and Churchill (later replaced by Attlee) began.

1975 The US *Apollo* spacecraft and the Russian *Soyuz* craft successfully docked while in orbit.

1981 The Humber Estuary Bridge, the world's longest single-span structure, was officially opened by the Queen.

1990 Iraqi president Saddam Hussein threatened to use force against Kuwait and the United Arab Emirates, to stop them driving oil prices down by overproduction.

18 JULY

National Day of Spain.

64 The great fire began in Rome and lasted for nine days.

1918 Nelson Mandela, first black president of South Africa, was born.
1923 Under the Matrimonial Causes Bill, British women were given equal divorce rights with men.
1925 *Mein Kampf*, Hitler's political testament, was published.
1936 The Spanish Civil War began with an army revolt led by Francisco Franco against the Republican government.
1955 Disneyland, the 160-acre amusement park, opened near Anaheim, California.

19 JULY

1545 The *Mary Rose*, the pride of Henry VIII's battle fleet, keeled over and sank in the Solent with the loss of 700 lives. (The ship was raised 11 Oct 1982 to be taken to Portsmouth Dockyard.)
1837 Brunel's 70 m/236 ft steamship, the *Great Western,* was launched at Bristol.
1848 At a convention in Seneca Falls, New York, female rights campaigner Amelia Bloomer introduced 'bloomers' to the world.
1903 The first Tour de France cycle race was won by Maurice Garin.
1949 Laos gained independence.
1991 A major political scandal erupted in South Africa after the government admitted that it had made secret payments to the Zulu-based Inkatha Freedom Party.

20 JULY

National Day of Colombia.
1837 London's first railway station, Euston, was opened.
1845 Charles Sturt became the first European to enter Simpson's Desert in central Australia.
1885 Professional football was legalized in Britain.
1940 In the USA, Billboard published the first singles-record charts.
1944 German staff officer Colonel von Stauffenburg attempted to assassinate Hitler, in Rastenburg, Germany.
1975 After an 11-month journey, the US uncrewed *Viking 1* made a soft landing on Mars.

21 JULY

National Day of Belgium.
1798 The Battle of the Pyramids took place, in which Napoleon, soon after his invasion of Egypt, defeated an army of some 60,000 Mamelukes.

1861 The Confederates defeated the Union troops in the first Battle of Bull Run, in the American Civil War.

1897 London's Tate Gallery, built on the site of the Millbank Prison, was opened.

1960 Sirimavo Bandaranaika replaced her murdered husband as prime minister of Sri Lanka, becoming the first woman to hold this office.

1969 The lunar module *Apollo 11* landed on the Moon, and US astronauts Armstrong and Aldrin took their first exploratory walk.

1990 More than 150,000 people attended 'The Wall', a large-scale concert staged by rock performers in East Berlin to celebrate the dismantling of the Berlin Wall.

22 JULY

National Day of Poland.

1812 The Duke of Wellington defeated the French in the Battle of Salamanca, in Spain.

1822 Gregor Mendel, Austrian monk and botanist, whose theory of heredity became known as 'Mendelism', was born.

1933 Wiley Post completed the first around the world solo aeroplane flight – the journey took 7 days, 18 hrs and 49.5 min.

1934 US bank robber and 'public enemy no 1', John Dillinger, was gunned down by an FBI squad in Chicago.

1946 Bread rationing started in Britain.

1991 Prime Minister John Major unveiled the government's 'Citizen's Charter' aimed at improving public services.

23 JULY

National Day of Ethiopia and of The United Arab Republic.

1745 Charles Stuart, the Young Pretender, landed in the Hebrides.

1864 Dr Livingstone returned to England.

1940 The Local Defence Volunteers were renamed the Home Guard by Winston Churchill.

1952 King Farouk of Egypt was deposed by General Neguib.

1967 In the heat of the mountain stage of the Tour de France, British cyclist Tony Simpson, 29, collapsed and died.

1986 Prince Andrew married Lady Sarah Ferguson in Westminster Abbey, and was created Duke of York.

24 JULY

1534 Jacques Cartier landed at Gaspé in Canada and claimed the territory for France.

1824 The result of the world's first public opinion poll, on voters' intentions in the 1824 US Presidential election, was published in the *Harrisburg Pennsylvanian*.

1851 The window tax in Britain was abolished.

1925 A six-year-old girl became the first patient to be successfully treated with insulin, at Guy's Hospital, London.

1980 Peter Sellers, English comic actor, died.

1990 A Catholic nun and three policemen were killed by an IRA landmine hidden at the side of a road in County Armagh.

25 JULY

Feast Day of St Christopher.

1909 French aviator Louis Blériot made the first Channel crossing in an aeroplane which he had designed.

1917 Margarethe Zelle, the Dutch spy known as 'Mata Hari', was sentenced to death.

1943 Benito Mussolini was forced to resign as Dictator of Italy, bringing an end to the Fascist regime.

1948 Bread rationing in Britain ended.

1952 The European Coal and Steel Community, established by the treaty of Paris 1951, was ratified.

1978 The first test-tube baby in Britain was born – Louise Joy Brown, at Oldham General Hospital, Lancashire.

26 JULY

National Day of Liberia.

1745 The first recorded women's cricket match was played near Guildford, Surrey, between teams from Hambledon and Bramley.

1847 Liberia became the first African colony to secure independence.

1908 The US Federal Bureau of Investigation, concerned in particular with internal security, was founded.

1945 The Labour Party won a landslide victory in Britain's General Election.

1956 President Nasser of Egypt nationalized the Suez Canal which led to confrontation with Britain, France, and Israel.

1987 Cyclist Steve Roche became the first Irishman, and only the second non-continental European, to win the Tour de France.

27 JULY

1694 The Bank of England was founded by Act of Parliament.

1866 The *Great Eastern* arrived at Heart's Content in Newfoundland, having successfully laid the transatlantic telegraph cable.

1942 The Battle of El Alamein ended after 17 days, with the British having prevented the German and Italian advance into Egypt.

1953 The Korean armistice was signed at Panmujom, ending three years of war.

1985 Ugandan president Milton Obote was overthrown for a second time, this time by a coup led by brigadier Tito Okello.

1988 British pole-vault record holder Jeff Gutteridge was banned for life by the British Amateur Athletic Board for taking steroids.

28 JULY

National Day of Peru.

1786 The first potato arrived in Britain, brought from Colombia by Sir Thomas Harriot.

1794 Maximilien Robespierre and 19 other French Revolutionaries went to the guillotine.

1821 San Martin and his forces liberated Peru and proclaimed its independence from Spain.

1858 Fingerprints were first used as a means of identification by William Herschel, who later established a fingerprint register.

1868 The 14th Amendment to the US Constitution, dealing with citizens' rights of all races, was ratified.

1914 Austria-Hungary declared war on Serbia, beginning World War I.

29 JULY

1588 The Spanish Armada was defeated by the English fleet under Howard and Drake, off Plymouth.

1900 King Umberto I of Italy was assassinated by an anarchist and succeeded by Victor Emmanuel.

1948 The 14th Olympic Games opened in London – the first in 12 years, due to World War II.

1949 The first regular televised weather forecast was broadcast by the BBC.

1968 Pope Paul VI reaffirmed the Church's traditional teaching on (and condemnation of) birth control.

1981   The Prince of Wales married Lady Diana Spencer at London's St Paul's Cathedral; the televised ceremony was watched by over 700 million viewers around the world.

30 JULY

1793   Toronto (known as York until 1834) was founded by general John Simcoe.

1935   'Penguin' paperback books, founded by Allen Lane, went on sale in Britain.

1948   The world's first radar station was opened, to assist shipping at the port of Liverpool.

1963   Kim Philby, British intelligence officer from 1940 and Soviet agent from 1933, fled to the USSR.

1966   England won the Football World Cup in London, beating West Germany 4–2.

1990   Ian Gow, Conservative MP for Eastbourne, a close friend and personal advisor to prime minister Thatcher, was killed by a car bomb at his home.

31 JULY

1498   Columbus arrived at Trinidad on his third voyage.

1910   Dr Crippen was arrested aboard the SS *Montrose* as it was docking at Québec; charged with the murder of his wife, he was the first criminal to be caught by the use of radio.

1954   An Italian expedition, led by Ardito Desio, was the first to climb Mount Godwin-Austin (K2) in the Himalayas.

1965   Cigarette advertising on British television was banned.

1971   US astronauts David Scott and James Irwin entered their Lunar Roving Vehicle and went for a ride on the moon.

1991   At a superpower summit in Moscow, Presidents Bush and Gorbachev signed the Strategic Arms Reduction Treaty (START), and announced that they would be co-sponsoring a Middle East peace conference.

1 AUGUST

National Day of Switzerland.

1498   Christopher Columbus reached the American mainland, and named it Santa Isla, believing it to be an island.

1774   English chemist Joseph Priestley identified oxygen, which he called 'a new species of air'.

1778 The first savings bank was opened, in Hamburg, Germany.
1793 The kilogram was introduced in France as the first metric weight.
1834 Slavery was abolished throughout the British Empire.
1975 Thirty-five nations, including the USA and the USSR, signed the Helsinki Agreement on cooperation in human rights and other global issues.

2 AUGUST

1718 Britain, France, Austria, and Holland concluded the Quadruple Alliance against Spain, in an attempt to prevent Spain from annexing Sardinia and Sicily.
1875 Britain's first roller skating rink was opened to the public, in Belgravia, London.
1894 Death duties, now known as inheritance tax, were introduced in Britain.
1945 The Potsdam Conference, establishing the initial post-war treatment of Germany and demanding unconditional Japanese surrender, ended.
1980 Right-wing terrorists exploded a bomb in the crowded Bologna Railway Station, northern Italy, killing 84 people.
1990 Iraq invaded and annexed Kuwait, precipitating an international crisis.

3 AUGUST

1492 Christopher Columbus left Palos de la Frontera in Andalusia, Spain, on his first voyage of discovery.
1858 Lake Victoria, the source of the Nile, was discovered by the English explorer John Speke.
1904 A British expedition, led by Col Francis E Younghusband, became the first westerners to enter the 'Forbidden City' of Lhasa, Tibet.
1914 Germany declared war on France.
1958 The USS *Nautilus*, the first nuclear submarine, passed under the North Pole.
1963 The Beatles played The Cavern in their home town, Liverpool, for the last time.

4 AUGUST

1265 The Battle of Evesham took place, in which Simon de Montfort was defeated by Royalist forces led by the future king Edward I, during the Barons' War.

1792 Percy Bysshe Shelley, English poet, was born.

1870 The British Red Cross Society was founded.

1914 Britain declared war on Germany after the Germans had violated the Treaty of London, and World War I began.

1940 Italy invaded Kenya, the Sudan, and British Somaliland.

1966 In a US radio interview, John Lennon claimed that the Beatles were probably more popular than Jesus Christ; Beatles records were consequently banned in many US states and in South Africa.

5 AUGUST

1858 The first transatlantic cable was opened when Queen Victoria exchanged greetings with US President Buchanan.

1891 The first American Express traveller's cheque was cashed.

1924 The Turkish government abolished polygamy.

1962 ANC leader Nelson Mandela was arrested and given a life sentence on charges of attempting to overthrow the South African government.

1962 Marilyn Monroe, US film actress, died of an overdose of sleeping pills.

1963 The Test Ban Agreement was signed by the USA, the USSR, and the UK, contracting to test nuclear weapons only underground.

6 AUGUST

National Day of Bolivia.

1806 The Holy Roman Empire came to an end when Francis II renounced the crown, becoming Francis I, emperor of Austria.

1890 William Kemmler, a murderer, became the first to be executed in the electric chair, in Auburn Prison, New York.

1926 US swimmer Gertrude Ederle became the first woman to swim the English Channel, in 14 hr 34 min.

1945 An atomic bomb was dropped on the Japanese city of Hiroshima from a US Boeing B29 bomber.

1962 Jamaica became independent after being a British colony for 300 years.

1988 Russian ballerina Natalia Makarova danced again with the Kirov Ballet in London, 18 years after she defected to the West.

7 AUGUST

1711   The first race meeting was held at Ascot, established by Queen Anne.

1830   Louis Philippe was proclaimed 'Citizen King' (*Philippe Egalité*), for his support of the 1792 Revolution.

1840   The employment of climbing boys as chimney sweeps was prohibited by an Act of Parliament.

1926   Britain's first motor racing Grand Prix was held at Brooklands; the winning car averaged 71.61 mph.

1942   Guadalcanal, in the southern Solomon Islands, was assaulted by the US Marines in one of the most costly campaigns of World War II.

1960   The Ivory Coast (Côte d'Ivoire) achieved independence from France.

8 AUGUST

1786   Mont Blanc, Europe's tallest peak, was climbed for the first time by a doctor, Michael Galoniel Piccard, and his porter, Jacques Balmat; Swiss scientist Horace Saussure had offered a prize for the accomplishment of this feat.

1940   The Battle of Britain, which would continue into the following Oct, began.

1963   The Great Train Robbery, in which over £2.5 million was stolen, took place near Bletchley, Buckinghamshire.

1974   Richard Nixon became the first US president to resign from office in face of threats to impeach him for his implication in the Watergate scandal.

1988   The luckiest day of the decade, according to the Chinese, because the date – 8.8.88 – is a palindrome.

1991   Islamic Jihad released John McCarthy, a British journalist who had been held hostage since April 1986.

9 AUGUST

1842   The frontier between Canada and the USA was defined by the Webster-Ashburton treaty, signed by the USA and Britain.

1870   The British parliament passed The Married Women's Property Act, improving the situation of the nation's wives.

1912   An earthquake struck Turkey, in the area of Istanbul, killing 6,000 people and rendering 40,000 homeless.

1945   The second atom bomb of World War II was dropped on the Japanese city of Nagasaki.

· **1965** Singapore gained independence.
1979 Britain's first nudist beach was established in Brighton.

10 AUGUST

National Day of Ecuador.

1675 King Charles II laid the foundation stone of the Royal Observatory, Greenwich.

1846 The Smithsonian Institution was established in Washington, DC, to foster scientific research.

1889 The screw bottle top was patented by Dan Rylands of Hope Glass Works, Yorkshire.

1895 The first Promenade Concert was held at the Queen's Hall, London, conducted by Henry Wood.

1911 British MPs voted to receive salaries for the first time.

1966 *Orbiter I,* the first US lunar satellite, was launched.

11 AUGUST

1576 English navigator Martin Frobisher, on his search for the Northwest Passage, entered the bay in Canada now named after him.

1810 Severe earthquakes struck the Azores, causing the village of São Miguel to sink.

1877 Phobos and Deimos, the satellites or 'moons' of Mars, were discovered by US astronomer Asaph Hall.

1941 President Roosevelt and Winston Churchill signed the Atlantic Charter, largely to demonstrate public solidarity between the Allies.

1952 King Talal of Jordan was deposed because of mental illness, and his son, Crown Prince Hussein, succeeded to the throne.

1963 Canton was entered by Chinese general Chiang Kai-shek and his supporters.

12 AUGUST

1687 The Austro-Hungarians defeated the Turks at the Battle of Mohács, in Hungary, effectively ending Turkish expansion into Europe.

1851 The US schooner *America* won a race around the Isle of Wight, giving rise to the later America's Cup trophy.

1883 The quagga (a member of the horse family) in Amsterdam Zoo died, the last of this species in the world.

1898   Spain and the USA concluded an armistice over Cuba and other possessions.

1944   PLUTO ('pipe line under the ocean') began operating beneath the English Channel, supplying petrol to Allied forces in France.

1969   The world's first communications satellite was launched – America's *Echo*.

13 AUGUST

1521   Spanish conquistador Hernándo Cortés recaptured Tenochtitlán (Mexico City), and overthrew the Aztec empire.

1814   The Cape of Good Hope Province became a British colony when it was ceded by the Dutch (sold for £6 million).

1923   Kemal Atatürk was elected the first president of Turkey.

1964   The last hangings in Britain took place; two murderers were executed at Liverpool and Manchester.

1972   The last US troops left Vietnam.

1991   Prosecutors announced the discovery of one of the largest bank frauds in Japan's history, involving $2.5 billion in fraudulently obtained loans.

14 AUGUST

1678   The French repulsed William of Orange at the Battle of Mons, in Belgium.

1880   Cologne Cathedral was completed; it had been started in the 13th century.

1882   Cetewayo, King of Zululand, South Africa, was received by Queen Victoria.

1893   France became the first country to introduce vehicle registration plates.

1969   The first British troops were deployed in Northern Ireland to restore order.

1986   Pakistani politician Benazir Bhutto was arrested by President Zia and detained in prison for 30 days.

15 AUGUST

1769   Napoleon Bonaparte, French emperor, was born.

1947   India gained independence.

1948   The republic of South Korea was proclaimed.

1965   The National Guard was called in to quell race riots in Watts, Los Angeles, which left 28 dead and 676 injured.

1969 The Woodstock Music and Arts Fair began on a dairy farm in upstate New York. In the three days it lasted, 400,000 attended, two children were born, and three people died.

1987 Caning was officially banned in British schools (excluding independent schools).

16 AUGUST

1819 The Peterloo massacre took place in Manchester when militia opened fire on a crowd gathered to hear discussion of reform, killing 11 people.

1897 Endowed by the sugar merchant Henry Tate, the Tate Gallery, in London, was opened.

1934 US explorer Charles Beebe and engineer Otis Barton made a record-breaking dive to 923 m/3028 ft in their bathysphere (a spherical diving vessel) near Bermuda.

1958 Madonna, US rock singer, was born.

1960 Cyprus became an independent republic, with Archbishop Makarios as president.

1977 Elvis Presley, US rock singer, died.

17 AUGUST

National Day of Indonesia.

1833 The Canadian *Royal William*, the first steamship to cross the Atlantic entirely under power, set off from Nova Scotia.

1836 Under the Registration Act, the registration of births, deaths, and marriages was introduced in Britain.

1876 The first performance of Wagner's opera *Götterdämmerung* was given in Bayreuth, Germany.

1896 Gold was discovered at Bonanza Creek in Canada's Yukon Territory, leading to the great gold rush of 1898.

1976 Earthquakes and tidal waves in the Philippines resulted in the deaths of over 6,000 people.

1989 Electronic tagging was used for the first time in Britain, on Richard Hart, accused of theft.

18 AUGUST

1227 Genghis Khan, Mongol conqueror, who controlled the largest area of any individual in history, died.

1812 Napoleon's forces defeated the Russians at the Battle of Smolensk.

1866	The Treaty of Alliance forming the North German Confederation, under the leadership of Prussia, was signed.
1941	Britain's National Fire Service was established.
1960	The first oral contraceptive was marketed by the Searle Drug Company in the USA.
1964	South Africa was banned from participating in the Olympics because of its racial policies.

19 AUGUST

1274	The coronation of Edward I took place.
1796	France and Spain formed an alliance against Britain.
1897	Electric-powered cabs appeared in London; they proved to be uneconomical and were withdrawn in 1900.
1934	A plebiscite was held in Germany giving sole power to Adolf Hitler, the *Führer*.
1945	Bill Clinton, 42nd US president, was born.
1989	Poland became the first eastern European country to end one-party rule, when a coalition government was formed with Tadeuz Mazowiecki as prime minister.

20 AUGUST

1710	The French were defeated by the Austrians at the Battle of Saragossa.
1914	German forces occupied Brussels.
1924	Although considered the likely winner, British sprinter Eric Liddel refused to run in the 100m heats at the Paris Olympics because it fell on a Sunday.
1956	Calder Hall nuclear power plant, Britain's first nuclear power station, began operating.
1968	Russian troops invaded Czechoslovakia.
1977	The US *Voyager I* spacecraft was launched on its journey via Jupiter and Saturn to become the first artificial object to leave the solar system.

21 AUGUST

1808	The French forces, under General Junot, were defeated by Wellington at the Battle of Vimiero.
1901	The Cadillac Motor Company was formed in Detroit, Michigan, USA, named after the French explorer, Antoine Cadillac.
1911	Leonardo da Vinci's painting, the *Mona Lisa*, was stolen from the Louvre in Paris – it was recovered two years later.

1939   Civil Defence, to mitigate the effects of enemy attack, was started in Britain.

1959   Hawaii became the 50th state of the USA.

1991   An attempted coup d'état in the USSR failed; faced with international condemnation and popular protests led by Boris Yeltsin, the junta stepped down and Gorbachev was reinstated.

22 AUGUST

1642   The English Civil War began, between the supporters of Charles I and of Parliament, when the king raised his standard at Nottingham.

1788   The British settlement in Sierra Leone was founded, the purpose of which was to secure a home in Africa for freed slaves from England.

1846   New Mexico was annexed by the USA.

1864   The International Red Cross was founded by the Geneva Convention to assist the wounded and prisoners of war.

1910   Korea was annexed by Japan.

1985   Following an aborted take off, a British Airtours Boeing 737 burst into flames on the runway at Manchester Airport; 55 persons were killed.

23 AUGUST

National Day of Romania.

1813   The French were driven back by the Prussians under General von Bülow at the Battle of Grossbeeren.

1839   Hong Kong was taken by the British.

1914   The British Expeditionary Force fought its first battle at Mons, in the First World War.

1927   Nicola Sacco and Bartolomeo Vanzetti, two Italo-American anarchists, were falsely accused of robbery and murder, and were sent to the electric chair.

1940   The Blitz began as German bombers began an all-night raid on London.

1948   The World Council of Churches was founded.

24 AUGUST

Feast Day of St Bartholomew.

79   Mount Vesuvius erupted and buried the cities of Pompeii and Herculaneum in hot volcanic ash.

410	The Visigoths, led by Alaric, sacked Rome.
1572	Charles IX ordered the massacre of the Huguenots throughout France; in Paris thousands were killed in what became known as the Massacre of St Bartholomew.
1704	The French were defeated by the English and Dutch fleets at the Battle of Malaga.
1814	British forces captured Washington, DC and set the White House on fire.
1921	The Turkish army, led by Mustafa Kemal, drove back the Greeks at the Battle of the Sakkaria River.

25 AUGUST

National Day of Uruguay.

1919	The first daily scheduled flights started between London and Paris.
1931	Ramsay MacDonald formed a National Government.
1940	The RAF made the first air raid on Berlin.
1944	The Allies liberated Paris.
1960	The XVIIth Olympic Games opened in Rome.
1989	The US space probe *Voyager* reached Neptune; pictures of Triton, its moon, revealed the existence of two additional moons.

26 AUGUST

55 BC	Julius Caesar landed in Britain.
1346	King Edward III, aided by the Black Prince, his son, defeated the French at the Battle of Crécy.
1789	The French Assembly adopted the Declaration of the Rights of Man.
1883	Krakatoa, the island volcano, began erupting, killing thousands.
1920	Women in the USA were granted the right to vote.
1952	The USSR announced that it had successfully tested the ICBM (Intercontinental Ballistic Missile).

27 AUGUST

551 BC	Confucius, Chinese philosopher, was born.
1784	The first balloon ascent was made in Britain by James Tytler at Edinburgh.
1813	Napoleon defeated the Austrians at the Battle of Dresden.
1859	Edwin Drake was the first in the USA to strike oil – at Titusville, Pennsylvania.

1913 A Russian pilot, Lieutenant Peter Nesterov, became the first to perform the loop-the-loop.

1939 The first jet-propelled aircraft, the Heinkel 178, made its first flight.

28 AUGUST

1640 The Indian War in New England ended with the surrender of the Indians.

1850 The Channel telegraph cable was laid between Dover and Cap Gris Nez.

1914 The Battle of Heligoland Bight, the first major naval battle of World War I, was fought.

1945 US forces under General George Marshall landed in Japan.

1963 The massive (200,000 people) civil rights march from the American South ended in Washington, DC where Martin Luther King delivered his famous 'I have a dream' speech.

1988 The Yan Hee Polyclinic in Bangkok, Thailand, reported on a new slimming technique – overweight Thais were suppressing their appetites by sticking lettuce seeds in their ears and pressing them in ten times before meals.

29 AUGUST

1831 Michael Faraday successfully demonstrated the first electrical transformer at the Royal Institute, London.

1835 The city of Melbourne, Australia, was founded.

1842 The Treaty of Nanking was signed between the British and the Chinese, ending the Opium War, and leasing the Hong Kong territories to Britain.

1882 Australia defeated England at cricket for the first time; the *Sporting Times* published an 'obituary' for English cricket.

1966 At Candlestick Park, San Francisco, the Beatles played their last live concert.

1991 The Supreme Soviet voted to suspend formally all activities of the Communist Party.

30 AUGUST

1860 The first British tramway, operated by the Birkenhead Street Railway, was inaugurated by an American, George Francis Train.

1862 'Stonewall' Jackson led the Confederates to victory at the second Battle of Bull Run, in Virginia, during the American Civil War.

1901 Hubert Cecil Booth patented the vacuum cleaner.

1939 In anticipation of German bombing, the great evacuation of children from British cities began, four days before the outbreak of World War II.

1941 The seige of Leningrad by German forces began (ended in Jan 1943).

1963 To reduce the risk of accidental nuclear war, the 'Hotline' between the US President and the Soviet Premier was established.

31 AUGUST

National Day of Malaysia, and of Trinidad and Tobago.

1422 Henry VI, aged nine months, acceded as king.

1900 Coca Cola first went on sale in Britain.

1942 The German offensive was halted by the British at the Battle of Alam al-Halfa, marking the turning-point in the North African campaign.

1972 US swimmer Mark Spitz won five of the seven gold medals he achieved in total at the Munich Olympics.

1983 The USSR shot down a South Korean airliner, killing 269 people aboard.

1984 A tropical storm hit the Philippines, killing over 1,000 people.

1 SEPTEMBER

National Day of Libya.

70 The destruction of Jerusalem under Titus took place.

1853 The world's first triangular postage stamps were issued by the Cape of Good Hope.

1923 Nearly 200,000 people were killed in earthquakes in Tokyo and Yokohama.

1928 Albania was declared a kingdom, with Zog I as king.

1933 *The Shape of Things to Come*, the classic science fiction novel by H G Wells, was published.

1939 Germany invaded Poland, starting World War II.

2 SEPTEMBER

1666 The Great Fire of London started; it destroyed 13,000 buildings in four days.

1898 The British, led by Lord Kitchener, defeated the Sudanese at the Battle of Omdurman and re-occupied Khartoum, the capital.

1906 Roald Amundsen completed his sailing round Canada's Northwest Passage.

1939 Under the National Service Bill, men aged 19–41 were conscripted in Britain.

1958 China's first television station opened in Peking.

1987 The CD-video, combining digital sound with high-definition video, was launched by Philips.

3 SEPTEMBER

1783 Britain recognized US independence with the signing of a treaty in Paris.

1916 The first Zeppelin was shot down over England.

1930 Santo Domingo, in the Dominican Republic, was destroyed by a hurricane which killed 5,000 people.

1935 Malcolm Campbell reached a new world land speed record of 301.13 mph in *Bluebird* on Bonneville Salt Flats, Utah.

1939 Britain, New Zealand, Australia, and France declared war on Germany.

1976 The US spacecraft *Viking 2* landed on Mars and began sending pictures of the red planet to Earth.

4 SEPTEMBER

1886 Geronimo, the Apache chief, surrendered to the US army.

1909 The first Boy Scout rally was held at Crystal Palace, near London.

1940 The US Columbia Broadcasting System gave a demonstration of colour TV on station W2XAB.

1944 The Allies liberated Antwerp, Belgium.

1970 Natalia Makarova, of the Kirov Ballet, defected to the West.

1985 The wreck of the *Titanic* on the Atlantic seabed was photographed by remote control.

5 SEPTEMBER

1800 French troops surrendered Malta to the British, following Nelson's naval blockade.

1914 The first Battle of the Marne, during World War I, began.

1922 US aviator James Doolittle made the first US coast-to-coast flight in 21 hrs, 19 min.

1963 Christine Keeler, one of the women involved in the Profumo scandal, was arrested and charged with perjury.

1972   At the Olympic Games in Munich, terrorists of the Black September group seized Israeli athletes as hostages; nine of the Israelis, four of the terrorists, and one German policeman were killed.

1980   The world's longest road tunnel, the St Gotthard, was opened running 16 km/10 mi from Goschenen to Airolo, Switzerland.

6 SEPTEMBER

1522   Ferdinand Magellan's 17 surviving crew members reached the Spanish coast aboard the *Vittoria*, having completed the first circumnavigation of the world.

1852   Britain's first free lending library opened in Manchester.

1880   The first cricket test match in England was played between England and Australia at the Oval, London.

1941   Nazi Germany made the wearing of the yellow Star of David badges compulsory for all its Jewish citizens.

1975   A massive earthquake centred on Lice, Turkey, caused nearly 3,000 deaths.

1989   Due to a computer error, 41,000 Parisians received letters charging them with murder, extortion, and organized prostitution instead of traffic violations.

7 SEPTEMBER

National Day of Brazil.

1812   The Russians were defeated by Napoleon's forces at the Battle of Borodino, 70 mi west of Moscow.

1838   Grace Darling and her father rescued the crew of the *Forfarshire*, a steamer wrecked off the Northumberland coast; she subsequently became a national heroine.

1904   Francis Younghusband led a British expedition to Tibet, where a treaty was signed with the Dalai Lama.

1973   Jackie Stewart became world champion racing driver for the third consecutive year.

1986   Bishop Desmond Tutu was appointed Archbishop of Capetown, the first black head of South African Anglicans.

1991   Peace talks on the Yugoslav civil war opened in The Hague, the Netherlands, under EC sponsorship.

8 SEPTEMBER

1664   The Dutch colony of New Amsterdam was surrendered to the British who renamed it New York in 1669.

1886   Johannesburg, South Africa, was founded after the discovery of gold there.

1900   Parts of Texas, USA, were hit by a tornado and tidal waves, which caused over 6,000 deaths near Galveston.

1926   Germany was admitted to the League of Nations.

1951   The Treaty of Peace with Japan was signed by 49 nations in San Francisco.

1974   US President Ford fully pardoned Richard Nixon for his part in the Watergate affair.

9 SEPTEMBER

1513   The Scots were defeated by the English at the Battle of Flodden Field.

1835   Local government in Britain was constituted under the British Municipal Corporations Act.

1850   California became the 31st state of the USA.

1945   Palestinians attempted to hijack an El Al flight but were overpowered by security guards. The Israelis reluctantly handed over the failed hijackers at Heathrow, where the plane made its landing.

1975   Czech tennis player Martina Navratilova, aged 18, defected to the West, requesting political asylum in the USA.

1985   Massive earthquakes in Mexico left more than 4,700 dead and 30,000 injured.

10 SEPTEMBER

1823   Simón Bolívar, known as 'The Liberator', became the dictator of Peru.

1894   George Smith, a London cab driver, became the first person to be convicted for drunken driving; he was fined 20s (£1).

1919   The Treaty of Saint-Germain was signed; the new boundaries it set brought about the end of the Austrian Empire.

1945   Former Norwegian premier Vidkun Quisling, who had collaborated with the Germans during World War II, was sentenced to death.

1981   Picasso's *Guernica* was returned to Spain after 40 years in US custodianship; the artist had refused to show the painting in Spain before the restoration of democracy.

1989   Hungary opened its border to the West allowing thousands of East Germans to leave, much to the anger of the East German government.

11 SEPTEMBER

1777   American troops led by George Washington were defeated by the British at the Battle of Brandywine Creek, in the American War of Independence.

1841   The London to Brighton commuter express train began regular service, taking just 105 min.

1855   In the Crimean War, Sebastopol was taken by the Allies after capitulation by the Russians.

1951   Stravinsky's *The Rake's Progress* was performed for the first time, in Venice; the libretto was by W H Auden.

1973   A military junta, with US support, overthrew the elected government of Chile.

1978   Georgi Markov, a Bulgarian defector, was fatally stabbed by a poisoned umbrella point wielded by a Bulgarian secret agent in London.

12 SEPTEMBER

1609   Henry Hudson sailed the sloop *Half Moon* into New York Harbour and up to Albany to discover the river named after him.

1878   Cleopatra's Needle, the obelisk of Thothmes II, was erected on London's Embankment.

1888   Maurice Chevalier, French actor and entertainer, was born.

1910   Alice Stebbins Wells, a former social worker, became the world's first policewoman, appointed by the Los Angeles Police Department.

1940   The Lascaux Caves, France, containing prehistoric wall paintings, were discovered.

1974   A military coup deposed Emperor Haile Selassie of Ethiopia, the Lion of Judah.

13 SEPTEMBER

1788   New York became the capital of the USA (until 1789).

1845   The Knickerbocker Club, the first baseball club, was founded in New York.

1943   General Chiang Kai-shek was re-elected president of the Republic of China.

1956 Little Richard recorded 'Tutti Frutti' in Los Angeles with cleaned-up lyrics.

1957 *The Mousetrap* became Britain's longest running play, reaching its 1,998th performance.

1989 Britain's biggest ever banking computer error gave customers an extra £2 billion in a period of 30 min; 99.3 per cent of the money was reportedly returned.

14 SEPTEMBER

1759 *A Journey Through Europe, or the play of Geography,* the earliest dated English board game, went on sale, priced 8s (40p).

1812 Napoleon entered Moscow in his disastrous invasion of Russia.

1891 The first penalty kick taken in an English League football game was taken by Heath of Wolverhampton Wanderers against Accrington.

1901 Theodore Roosevelt became the 26th US president, 12 hours after the death of President McKinley who had been shot by an anarchist on 6 Sept.

1959 The Soviet *Lunik II* became the first spacecraft to land on the Moon.

1991 The South African government, the ANC, and the Inkatha Freedom Party signed a peace accord aimed at ending the factional violence in the black townships.

15 SEPTEMBER

National Day of Costa Rica and Battle of Britain Day.

1812 The Russians set fire to Moscow in order to halt the French occupation.

1830 The Manchester and Liverpool railway opened; during the ceremony, William Huskisson, MP, became the first person to be killed by a train.

1935 The Nuremberg laws were passed in Germany, outlawing Jews and making the swastika the country's official flag.

1964 The *Sun*, which became Britain's biggest selling newspaper, was first published.

1974 The civil war between Christians and Muslims in Beirut began.

1985 Tony Jacklin's European golf team won the Ryder Cup from the USA who had long dominated the competition.

16 SEPTEMBER

National Day of Mexico.

1847 The house in which Shakespeare was born in Stratford-upon-Avon became the first building in Britain to be purchased for preservation.

1963 Malaysia became independent and a mob of over 100,000 burned down the British Embassy.

1969 Biba, considered London's trendiest store in the 'swinging 60s', opened on Kensington High Street.

1976 The Episcopal Church in the USA approved the ordination of women to the priesthood.

1987 For the first time in South Africa, *Othello* was performed with a black actor, John Khani, playing the Moor.

1991 All Iran-Contra charges against Oliver North were dropped.

17 SEPTEMBER

1900 The Commonwealth of Australia, a federation of six colonies, was proclaimed.

1908 Lt Selfridge, on a test flight with Orville Wright, was killed when the plane crashed, becoming the first passenger to die in an air crash.

1931 The first long-playing record was demonstrated in New York by RCA-Victor, but the venture failed because of the high price of the players.

1939 Poland was invaded by the USSR.

1944 The British airborne invasion of Arnhem, Holland began as part of 'Operation Market Garden'.

1991 Estonia, Latvia, Lithuania, North and South Korea, the Marshall Islands, and Micronesia were admitted to the United Nations.

18 SEPTEMBER

National Day of Chile.

1851 The *New York Times* was first published.

1879 Blackpool's famous illuminations were switched on for the first time.

1910 The Chilean revolt against Spanish rule began.

1914 The Irish Home Rule Bill went into effect.

1931 Japan seized Manchuria and set up a puppet state called Manchukuo – it was returned to China in 1945 after World War II.

1981 France abolished execution by guillotine.

19 SEPTEMBER

1783 The Montgolfier brothers sent up the first balloon with live creatures aboard; passengers included a sheep, a rooster, and a duck.

1876 The US inventor Melville Bissell patented the first carpet sweeper.

1893 New Zealand became the first country to grant its female citizens the right to vote.

1945 Nazi campaigner William Joyce (called Lord Haw because of his upper class accent) was sentenced to hang for treason.

1960 A new dance craze began when Chubby Checker's 'The Twist' entered the US charts.

1960 The new Traffic Wardens issued the first 344 parking tickets in London.

20 SEPTEMBER

356 BC Alexander the Great was born.

451 The Romans defeated the Huns under Attila at Châlon-sur-Marne.

1928 The Fascist Party took over the supreme legislative body in Rome, replacing the Chamber of Deputies.

1961 Argentinian Antonio Abertondo started the first successful non-stop swim across the Channel and back, completed in 43 hr 5 min.

1966 The liner *Queen Elizabeth II* (QE2) was launched at Clydebank, Scotland.

1984 The US embassy in Beirut was attacked by a suicide bomber; explosives within a lorry were set off, killing 40 people.

21 SEPTEMBER

National Day of Malta.

1745 Bonnie Prince Charles and his Jacobite army defeated the English at the Battle of Prestonpans in Scotland.

1784 *The Pennsylvania Packet and General Advertiser*, the first successful US daily newspaper, was published.

1915 Stonehenge was sold at auction to Mr C H Chubb for £6,600. Mr Chubb presented it to the nation three years later.

1949 The Republic of Ireland beat England 2–0 at Goodison Park – England's first home defeat by a foreign football team.

1974 Over 8,000 people were killed by floods caused by hurricanes in Honduras.

1989 Hurricane Hugo struck the US coastal states of Georgia and South Carolina, causing widespread damage and loss of life.

22 SEPTEMBER

1792 France was declared a Republic.
1862 US President Lincoln issued the Emancipation Proclamation, ordering the freeing of slaves.
1955 Independent TV began operating; Britain's first commercial and first woman newsreader were transmitted.
1972 Idi Amin gave the 8,000 Asians in Uganda 48 hours to leave the country.
1980 The Solidarity movement in Poland was created, with Lech Walesa as its elected leader.
1989 An IRA bomb attack on the Royal Marines School of Music killed ten and injured twelve of the bandsmen.

23 SEPTEMBER

Feast Day of Saints Andrew, John, Peter and Antony, and National Day of Saudi Arabia.
1846 German astronomer Johann Galle discovered the planet Neptune.
1848 Chewing gum was first commercially produced in the USA by John Curtis in his home, and was called 'State of Maine Pure Spruce Gum'.
1912 *Cohen Collects a Debt*, the first of US film producer Mack Sennet's silent Keystone Cops films, was released.
1940 The George Cross and the George Medal for civilian acts of courage were instituted.
1973 Juan Perón was re-elected president of Argentina; he had been ousted in 1955.
1974 The world's first Ceefax teletext service was begun by the BBC.

24 SEPTEMBER

1852 French engineer Henri Giffaud made the first flight in a dirigible balloon, from Paris to Trappe.
1896 F Scott Fitzgerald, US novelist, was born.
1960 The first nuclear-powered aircraft carrier, the USS *Enterprise*, was launched at Newport, Virginia.
1975 British mountaineers Dougal Haston and Doug Scott became the first to reach Mt Everest's summit via the south-west face.

1980 The Iraqis blew up the Abadan oil refinery, turning the Iran–Iraq conflict into a full scale war.

1991 The Shiite Muslim Revolutionary Justice Organization freed British hostage Jack Mann, kidnapped in May 1989.

25 SEPTEMBER

1066 King Harold II defeated the king of Norway, Harald Hardrada, at the Battle of Stamford Bridge.

1513 Vasco Balboa, Spanish explorer, became the first European to sight the Pacific Ocean after crossing the Darien isthmus.

1818 The first blood transfusion using human blood, as opposed to earlier attempts with animal blood, took place at Guy's Hospital in London.

1909 The French battleship *Liberté* exploded in Toulon Harbour, killing 226 people.

1954 François Duvalier ('Papa' Doc) was elected president of Haiti.

1972 Norway voted against joining the EC in a referendum.

26 SEPTEMBER

1887 German-born US immigrant Emile Berliner patented the first gramophone.

1955 Frozen Birds Eye fish fingers first went on sale in Britain.

1961 Bob Dylan made his debut in New York's Greenwich Village, at Gerdie's Folk City.

1983 Alan Bond's *Australia II* won the America's Cup, the first non-US winner for 132 years.

1984 Britain agreed to transfer full sovereignty of Hong Kong to China in 1997.

1988 Canadian sprinter Ben Johnson was stripped of his gold medal in the 100 m at the Seoul Olympics after failing a drugs test.

27 SEPTEMBER

1821 Mexico achieved independence through the efforts of General Hubride, who declared himself Emperor Augustin I.

1826 The Stockton and Darlington Railway, the first passenger rail service, opened, with its first steam locomotive travelling at 10 mph.

1922 Constantine I, king of Greece, abdicated following the Greek defeat in Turkey.

1938 The 80,000-ton liner *Queen Elizabeth* was launched by the Queen Mother.

1939 Warsaw, the capital of Poland, surrendered to the German forces.
1968 The musical *Hair*, which took advantage of the end of British stage censorship by including a scene cast in the nude, had its first London performance.

28 SEPTEMBER

490 BC The Greeks defeated the Persians at the Battle of Marathon.
1864 The First International was founded in London, when Karl Marx proposed the formation of an International Working Men's Association.
1865 Elizabeth Garrett Anderson became the first qualified woman physician in Britain.
1894 Simon Marks and Tom Spencer opened their Penny Bazaar in Manchester, the first of what would become a nation-wide chain of stores.
1934 Brigitte Bardot, French film actress, was born.
1978 Pope John Paul I, pope for only 33 days, was found dead.

29 SEPTEMBER

1399 The first monarch to abdicate, Richard II, was replaced by Bolingbroke who ascended the throne as Henry IV.
1829 The first regular police force in London was inaugurated; the officers became known as 'bobbies' after Robert Peel, the Home Secretary who founded the modern police force.
1916 John D Rockefeller became the world's first billionaire during the share boom in the USA.
1944 Soviet troops entered Yugoslavia.
1950 The first automatic telephone answering machine was tested by the US Bell Telephone Company.
1991 Haiti's first freely elected president, Jean-Bertrand Aristide, was ousted in a military coup.

30 SEPTEMBER

National Day of Botswana.
1791 The first performance of Mozart's *Magic Flute* took place in Vienna.
1902 Rayon, or artificial silk, was patented.
1928 Alexander Fleming announced his discovery of penicillin.
1939 The USSR and Germany agreed on the partition of Poland.
1952 Cinerama, invented by Fred Waller, was first exhibited in New York.

1987   Keith Best, MP, was sentenced to four months in prison for trying to obtain British Telecom shares by deception.

1 OCTOBER

National Day of China, Nigeria, and Cyprus.

1843   The *News of the World*, Britain's most popular Sunday newspaper, was first published.

1908   The first Model T, produced in Detroit, Michigan, was introduced by Henry Ford.

1918   The Arab forces of Emir Faisal, with British officer T E Lawrence, captured Damascus from the Turks.

1936   General Francisco Franco took office as head of Spain's Nationalist government.

1949   The People's Republic of China was proclaimed, with Mao Tse Tung as its chairman.

1971   Disney World, the world's largest amusement resort, was opened in Florida.

2 OCTOBER

1608   The first telescope was demonstrated by the Dutch lens maker, Hans Lipperschey.

1836   Charles Darwin returned from his five-year survey of South American waters aboard the HMS *Beagle.*

1870   Rome became the capital of the newly unified Italy.

1901   The British Royal Navy's first submarine, built by Vickers, was launched at Barrow.

1909   The first rugby football match was played at Twickenham, between Harlequins and Richmond.

1983   Neil Kinnock was elected leader of Britain's Labour Party.

3 OCTOBER

1811   The first women's county cricket match began at Newington, between Hampshire and Surrey.

1906   SOS was established as an international distress signal, replacing the call sign CQD.

1929   The Kingdom of Serbs, Croats, and Slovenes was renamed Yugoslavia.

1952   The first British atomic bomb was detonated on the Monte Bello Islands, off W Australia.

1956   The Bolshoi Ballet performed in Britain, at Covent Garden, for the first time.

1990   East and West Germany were officially reunified, with Berlin as the capital.

4 OCTOBER

National Day of Lesotho.

1878   The first Chinese Embassy in Washington, DC was opened.

1905   Orville Wright became the first to fly an aircraft for over 33 minutes.

1957   The USSR's *Sputnik I*, the first space satellite, was launched.

1958   BOAC (now British Airways) began operating the first transatlantic passenger jet service.

1965   Pope Paul VI visited New York to address the UN, becoming the first pope to visit the USA.

1983   A world record speed of 663.5 mph was achieved by Richard Noble in his jet-powered car *Thrust II*, in Nevada.

5 OCTOBER

1880   The earliest 'ball pen',with its own ink supply and retractable tip, was patented by Alonzo T Cross.

1911   Italian troops occupied Tripoli, in Libya, during its war with Turkey.

1914   The first air battle took place between French and German aircraft during World War I; both sides suffered losses.

1930   The British airship *R101*, the world's largest dirigible at that time, crashed in France en route to India; the British air minister was among the 48 killed.

1936   The Jarrow march, of unemployed shipyard workers, started its southward journey to London.

1967   The first majority verdict by a jury in Britain was taken, in Brighton.

6 OCTOBER

1769   English naval explorer Captain James Cook, aboard the *Endeavour*, landed in New Zealand.

1883   The *Orient Express* completed its first run from Paris to Constantinople (now Istanbul) in nearly 78 hours.

1927   Warner Brothers' *Jazz Singer*, the first talking feature film (starring Al Jolson), premiered in New York.

1928   Nationalist general Chiang Kai-shek became president of China.

1968 The first three places in the US Grand Prix were taken by British drivers: Jackie Stewart, Graham Hill, and John Surtees.

1978 London Underground's first woman driver started work.

7 OCTOBER

1806 The first carbon paper was patented by its English inventor, Ralph Wedgwood.

1919 The Dutch airline KLM, the oldest existing airline, was established.

1931 Desmond Tutu, Archbishop of Cape Town, was born.

1949 The German Democratic Republic, or East Germany, was formed.

1958 The first photograph of the far side of the Moon was transmitted from the USSR's *Lunik I*.

1988 Grey whales trapped under ice in Alaska became the focus of an international rescue effort.

8 OCTOBER

1085 St Mark's Cathedral in Venice was consecrated.

1871 The Great Fire of Chicago started. It burned until the 11th, killing over 250 people and making 95,000 homeless.

1905 A permanent waving machine was first used on a woman's hair, by Charles Nessler.

1965 London's Post Office Tower, Britain's tallest building, opened.

1967 A breathalyser was used on a motorist for the first time, in Somerset.

1973 LBC (London Broadcasting), Britain's first legal commercial radio station, began transmitting.

9 OCTOBER

National Day of Uganda.

1470 Henry VI was restored to the throne after being deposed in 1461.

1779 The first Luddite riots, against the introduction of machinery for spinning cotton, began in Manchester.

1875 The Universal Postal Union was established, with headquarters in Berne, Switzerland.

1888 The massive marble Washington Monument, designed by Robert Mills, was opened.

1934 Alexander, king of Yugoslavia, and French foreign minister Louis Barthou were assassinated by Croatian terrorists in Marseilles.

1967 Ernesto 'Che' Guevara, Argentinian-born guerilla leader and revolutionary, was murdered in Bolivia.

10 OCTOBER

732 The Franks, under Charles Martel, defeated the Saracens at the Battle of Tours.

1886 The dinner jacket was first worn in New York by its creator at the Tuxedo Park Country Club, after which it was named.

1903 Mrs Emmeline Pankhurst formed the Women's Social and Political Union to fight for women's emancipation in Britain.

1911 China's Imperial Dynasty was forced to abdicate, and a republic was proclaimed, under Sun Yat-Sen.

1961 Following a volcanic eruption, the entire population of the South Atlantic island of Tristan da Cunha was evacuated to Britain.

1973 US vice president Spiro Agnew resigned after being fined US$10,000 for income tax evasion.

11 OCTOBER

1521 Pope Leo X conferred the title of 'Defender of the Faith' (*Fidei Difensor*) on Henry VIII for his book supporting Catholic principles.

1899 The Anglo-Boer War began.

1923 Rampant inflation in Germany caused the mark to drop to an exchange rate of 10,000,000,000 to the pound.

1968 The US spacecraft *Apollo 7* was launched from Cape Kennedy, with a crew of three.

1980 The Soviet *Salyut 6* returned to earth; its cosmonauts had been in space for a record 185 days.

1982 The *Mary Rose*, which had been the pride of Henry VIII's fleet until it sank in the Solent in 1545, was raised.

12 OCTOBER

1492 Columbus sighted his first land in discovering the New World, calling it San Salvador.

1901 US President Theodore Roosevelt renamed the Executive Mansion 'The White House'.

1935 Luciano Pavarotti, Italian operatic tenor, was born.

1948 The first Morris Minor, designed by Alec Issigonis, was produced at Cowley, Oxfordshire.

1984 During the Tory Party Conference at the Grand Hotel in Brighton, an IRA bomb exploded in the hotel in an attempt to murder the British Cabinet.

1986 Queen Elizabeth II became the first British monarch to visit China.

13 OCTOBER

1792 The cornerstone of the White House, Washington, DC, was laid by President George Washington.

1884 Greenwich was adapted as the universal time meridian of longitude from which standard times throughout the world are calculated.

1894 The first Merseyside 'derby' football match was played at Goodison Park between Liverpool and Everton, with Everton winning 3–0.

1904 Sigmund Freud's *The Interpretation of Dreams* was published.

1923 Ankara replaced Istanbul as the capital of Turkey.

1988 The Cardinal of Turin confirmed reports that the Shroud of Turin, believed to carry the imprint of Christ's face, had been scientifically dated to the Middle Ages.

14 OCTOBER

National Day of Madagascar.

1066 The Battle of Hastings was fought on Senlac Hill, where King Harold was slain as William the Conqueror's troops routed the English army.

1884 Photographic film was patented by US entrepreuner and inventor George Eastman.

1920 Oxford degrees were conferred on women for the first time.

1947 The first supersonic flight (670 mph) was made in California by Charles Yeagar in his *Bell XI* rocket plane.

1971 The US spacecraft *Mariner 9* transmitted the first close-up TV pictures of Mars to Earth.

1982 A mass wedding took place in Seoul, South Korea, when 5,837 couples were married simultaneously.

15 OCTOBER

1581 The first major ballet was staged at the request of Catherine de' Medici at the palace in Paris.

1582 The Gregorian calendar was adopted in Italy, Spain, Portugal, and France; 5 Oct became 15 Oct.

1915   In World War I, Bulgaria allied itself with the Central European Powers.

1917   Mata Hari, Dutch spy, was shot in Paris, having been found guilty of espionage for the Germans.

1928   The German airship *Graf Zeppelin*, captained by Hugo Eckener, completed its first transatlantic flight.

1961   The human-rights organization Amnesty International was established in London.

16 OCTOBER

1815   Napoleon was exiled to the Atlantic island of St Helena.

1902   The first detention centre housing young offenders was opened in Borstal, Kent.

1946   Nazi war criminals, including von Ribbentrop, Rosenberg, and Streicher, were hanged at Nuremberg.

1964   Labour Party leader Harold Wilson became prime minister.

1978   Cardinal Karol Wojtyla was elected Pope John Paul II – the first non-Italian pope since 1542.

1987   Southern England was hit by hurricane force winds, causing 19 deaths and hundreds of millions of pounds' worth of damage.

17 OCTOBER

1651   Charles II, defeated by Cromwell at Worcester, fled to France, destitute and friendless.

1777   British commander General Burgoyne surrendered to General Horatio Gates at Saratoga, a victory for the American colonists.

1914   An earthquake struck Greece and Asia Minor, killing over 3,000 people.

1931   US gangster Al Capone was sentenced to 11 years in prison for income-tax evasion, the only charge that could be sustained against him.

1956   Calder Hall, Britain's first nuclear power station, was opened.

1959   The South African De Beers diamond firm announced that synthetic industrial diamonds had been produced.

18 OCTOBER

1697   Canaletto, Italian painter, was born.

1887   Russia transferred Alaska to the USA for $7.2 million.

1922   The British Broadcasting Company (later Corporation) was officially formed.

1977 Germany's anti-terrorist squad stormed a hijacked Lufthansa aircraft at Mogadishu Airport, Somalia, killing three of the four Palestinian hijackers and freeing all of the hostages.

1989 Following a wave of pro-democracy demonstrations in East Germany, Erich Honecker was replaced as head of state by Egon Krenz.

1989 With the end of Communist rule, Hungary was proclaimed a free republic.

19 OCTOBER

1781 Lord Cornwallis surrendered to General Washington at Yorktown, Virginia, marking the end of the American War of Independence.

1860 The first company to manufacture internal combustion engines was formed in Florence.

1872 The Holtermann nugget was mined at Hill End, New South Wales; weighing 630lbs, it was the largest gold-bearing nugget ever found.

1987 Wall Street was struck by 'Black Monday', during which millions were wiped out on stock markets around the world.

1987 Jacqueline du Pré, British cellist, died of multiple sclerosis.

1989 After serving 14 years in prison for the IRA Guildford and Woolwich bombings, the 'Guildford Four' had their convictions quashed.

20 OCTOBER

1714 The coronation of King George I took place.

1822 The *Sunday Times* was first published.

1827 The Battle of Navarino, off the coast of Greece, ended with the combined British, French, and Russian fleets completely destroying the Egyptian and Turkish fleets.

1935 Mao Zedong's Long March ended in Yenan, north China.

1968 Jacqueline Kennedy, widow of US president Kennedy, married Greek millionaire Aristotle Onassis.

1973 The Sydney Opera House, designed by Danish architect John Utzon, was opened to the public.

21 OCTOBER

1805 The British defeated the Franco-Spanish fleet at the Battle of Trafalgar.

1934 Mao Zedong's Long March, with his 100,000-strong Communist army, began.

1950 Tibet was occupied by Chinese forces.

1966 The Welsh village of Aberfan was engulfed by a collapsed slagheap, killing 144, including 116 children.

1984 Niki Lauda became world motor-racing champion for the third time.

1991 Jesse Turner, an American who had been held hostage in Lebanon for just under five years, was freed by his captors.

22 OCTOBER

1797 The first parachute jump was made by André-Jacques Garnerin from a balloon above the Parc Monceau, Paris.

1909 French aviator Elise Deroche became the first woman to make a solo flight.

1910 Dr Hawley Crippen was found guilty of poisoning his wife and was sentenced to be hanged on 23 October 1910.

1935 Haiti was struck by a hurricane, causing over 2,000 deaths.

1962 US President Kennedy announced that Soviet missile bases had been installed in Cuba.

1987 The first volume of the Gutenberg Bible was sold at auction in New York for $5.39 million/£3.26 million – a record price for a printed book.

23 OCTOBER

1642 The Battle of Edgehill, in the Cotswolds, took place – the first major conflict of the English Civil War.

1942 The Battle of El Alamein, in Egypt, began.

1946 The first meeting of the United Nations General Assembly took place in New York.

1956 The Hungarian revolt against Soviet leadership began, in which thousands of demonstrators called for the withdrawal of Soviet forces.

1970 Gary Gabelich achieved the world land speed record of 631.367mph, in his rocket-engine car on Bonneville Salt Flats, Utah.

1987 Former British champion jockey Lester Piggott was sentenced to three years in prison for tax evasion.

24 OCTOBER

National Day of Zambia and United Nations Day.

1857 The first football club was formed by a group of Cambridge University Old Boys meeting in Sheffield.

1901 Mrs Ann Edson Taylor braved a descent over Niagara Falls in a padded barrel to help pay the mortgage.

1945 The United Nations charter came into force.

1977 Saudi Arabia purchased the transatlantic liner *France* for use as a floating luxury hotel.

1987 Heavyweight boxing champion Frank Bruno knocked out Joe Bugner in Britain's most hyped boxing match held at White Hart Lane, London.

1989 US television preacher Jim Bakker was sentenced to 45 years in prison and fined $500,000/£272,000 for his multi-million dollar scam.

25 OCTOBER

1415 The English army, led by King Henry V, defeated the French at the Battle of Agincourt, during the Hundred Years' War.

1839 *Bradshaw's Railway Guide*, the world's first railway timetable, was published in Manchester.

1854 Lord Cardigan led the Charge of the Light Brigade during the Battle of Balaclava in the Crimean War.

1961 The British satirical magazine *Private Eye* was first published.

1971 Taiwan was expelled from the UN to allow the admission of the People's Republic of China.

1983 Over 2,000 US troops invaded Grenada.

26 OCTOBER

National Day of Iran and of Austria.

1860 Italian unification leader Giuseppe Garibaldi proclaimed Victor Emmanuel king of Italy.

1927 Duke Ellington and his orchestra recorded the jazz classic, 'Creole Love Song'.

1929 T W Evans of Miami, Florida, became the first woman to give birth aboard an aircraft.

1956 The UN's International Atomic Energy Agency was formed.

1965 Queen Elizabeth presented the Beatles with their MBEs at Buckingham Palace.

1985 A US infant, known as Baby Fae, was given a baboon's heart to replace her malformed one.

27 OCTOBER

1662 Charles II sold Dunkirk to Louis XIV for 2.5 million livres.
1901 In Paris, a 'getaway car' was used for the first time, when thieves robbed a shop and sped away.
1904 The first section of New York City's subway system was opened.
1936 Mrs Wallis Simpson was granted a divorce from her second husband, leaving her free to marry King Edward VIII.
1939 John Cleese, English actor and comedian, was born.
1971 The Republic of Congo changed its name to the Republic of Zaire.

28 OCTOBER

1636 Harvard University, the first in the USA, was founded.
1831 English chemist and physicist Michael Faraday demonstrated the first dynamo.
1886 The Statue of Liberty, designed by Auguste Bartholdi, was presented by France to the USA to mark the 100th anniversary of the Declaration of Independence.
1914 George Eastman, of Eastman Kodak Company, announced the introduction of a colour photographic process.
1971 By a margin of 112 votes, the House of Commons backed prime minister Heath's decision to apply for EEC membership.
1982 Felipe González became Spain's first Socialist prime minister, with a sweeping electoral victory.

29 OCTOBER

National Day of Turkey.
1618 Sir Walter Raleigh, English navigator, courtier, and once favourite of Elizabeth I, was beheaded at Whitehall for treason.
1863 The International Red Cross was founded by Swiss philanthropist Henri Dunant.
1929 The Wall Street crash known as 'Black Tuesday' took place, leading to the Great Depression.
1964 The union of Tanganyika and Zanzibar was announced, adopting the name of Tanzania.
1982 In Australia, Lindy Chamberlain was sentenced to life imprisonment for the murder of her nine-week-old baby who, she claimed, had been carried off by a dingo.

1991   Vietnam formally approved a plan to repatriate forcibly tens of thousands of Vietnamese refugees living in camps in Hong Kong.

30 OCTOBER

1650   'Quakers', the more common name for the Society of Friends, came into being during a court case, at which George Fox, the founder, told the magistrate to 'quake and tremble at the word of God'.

1911   P'u-Yi, the boy emperor of China aged five, granted a new constitution, officially ending three centuries of Manchu domination over China.

1918   The Republic of Czechoslovakia was proclaimed.

1925   The Scottish inventor John Baird made the first televised transmission of a moving object (a 15-year-old office boy).

1938   US actor Orson Welles' radio production of *The War of the Worlds* by H G Wells caused panic in the USA.

1988   Sun Myung Moon, head of the Unification Church, conducted the marriage of 6,516 couples in a Seoul factory; the couples had first met the day before.

31 OCTOBER

All Hallows' Eve (Halloween).

1902   The first telegraph cable across the Pacific Ocean was completed.

1940   The Battle of Britain ended.

1951   Zebra crossings came into effect in Britain.

1952   At Eniwetok Atoll, in the Pacific, the USA detonated the first hydrogen bomb.

1971   An IRA bomb exploded at the top of the Post Office Tower, London.

1982   The Thames barrier, part of London's flood defences, was raised for the first time.

1 NOVEMBER

Feast Day of All Saints and National Day of Algeria.

1848   The first W H Smith railway bookstall opened, at Euston Station, London.

1914   The British ships *Good Hope* and *Monmouth* were sunk by the Germans, at the Battle of Coronel.

1940   A prehistoric painting was discovered in a cave in Lascaux in the Dordogne, France.

1950 Two Puerto Rican nationalists attempted to assassinate US President Truman.

1959 The first stretch of the M1 motorway was opened.

1972 Orissa, India, was struck by a tidal wave which killed 10,000 people and left 5 million homeless.

2 NOVEMBER

Feast Day of All Souls.

1785 The first insubmersible lifeboat was patented by Lionel Lakin, a London coach builder.

1871 The 'Rogues Gallery' was started, when photographs of all prisoners in Britain were first taken.

1930 Ras Tafari, King of Ethiopia, was crowned emperor Haile Selassie ('Might of the Trinity').

1957 With eight simultaneous hits in the UK Top 30 chart, Elvis Presley set an all-time record.

1960 A British jury acquitted Penguin Books of obscenity in the matter of publishing D H Lawrence's *Lady Chatterley's Lover*.

1990 Ivana Trump filed for divorce from unfaithful US millionaire Donald Trump.

3 NOVEMBER

National Day of Panama.

1493 Christopher Columbus, on his second voyage of discovery, sighted Dominica, in the West Indies.

1706 A violent earthquake occurred in the Abruzzi, Italy, killing some 15,000 inhabitants.

1942 British troops, led by Field Marshal Montgomery, broke through Rommel's front line in Africa.

1957 The Russian dog, Laika, became the first in space aboard *Sputnik II*.

1975 The North Sea pipeline, the first to be built underwater, was officially opened by Queen Elizabeth II.

1993 A mystery woman paid a record 5 million Swiss francs (£2.2m) for an envelope with two stamps sent from Mauritius to a Bordeaux wine exporter in 1847.

4 NOVEMBER

1605 Guy Fawkes, a Roman Catholic convert and conspirator in the Gunpowder Plot, was arrested in parliament's cellar.

1862   US inventor Richard Gatling patented the rapid-fire, or machine, gun.
1922   British archaeologist Howard Carter discovered the tomb of the Egyptian pharaoh Tutankhamun.
1946   UNESCO was established, with headquarters in Paris.
1979   Iranian students stormed the US Embassy in Tehran and held over 60 staff and US marines hostage.
1980   Ronald Reagan was elected 40th US president.

5 NOVEMBER

Guy Fawkes' Night
1912   The British Board of Film Censors was appointed.
1919   Rudolph Valentino, the archetypal romantic screen lover, married actress Jean Acker; the marriage lasted less than six hours.
1927   Britain's first automatic traffic lights began functioning, in Wolverhampton.
1968   Richard Nixon was elected 37th US president.
1990   Rabbi Meir Kahane, founder of the militant Jewish Defence League and Israel's extremist anti-Arab Kach party, was assassinated in a New York City hotel.
1991   Robert Maxwell, British publishing and newspaper proprietor, drowned under mysterious circumstances in the Canary Islands.

6 NOVEMBER

1860   Abraham Lincoln was elected 16th US president.
1869   Diamonds were discovered at Kimberley, in Cape Province, South Africa.
1932   In general elections held in Germany, the Nazis emerged as the largest party.
1956   Construction of the Kariba High Dam, on the Zambezi River between Zambia and Zimbabwe, began.
1975   UK punk rock group, the Sex Pistols, gave their first public performance at London's St Martin's College of Art; college authorities cut the concert short – after 10 minutes.
1988   Six thousand US Defense Department computers were crippled by a virus; the culprit was the 23-year-old son of the head of the country's computer security agency.

7 NOVEMBER

National Day of Russia.

1783 The last public hanging in England took place when John Austin, a forger, was executed at Tyburn.

1867 Marie Curie, Polish physicist, who discovered polonium and radium 1898, was born.

1916 Jeanette Rankin, of the state of Montana, became the first woman member of US Congress.

1917 The Bolshevik Revolution, led by Lenin, overthrew Prime Minister Alexander Kerensky's government.

1988 In Las Vegas, 'Sugar' Ray Lewis knocked out Canadian Donny Londe, completing his collection of world titles at five different weights.

1990 Mary Robinson became the Irish Republic's first woman prime minister.

8 NOVEMBER

1793 The Louvre was opened to the public by the Revolutionary government, although only part of the collection could be viewed.

1895 Wilhelm Röntgen discovered X-rays during an experiment at the University of Wurzburg.

1922 Christiaan Barnard, South African heart transplant pioneer, was born.

1958 *Melody Maker* published the first British album charts.

1987 An IRA bomb went off in Enniskillen, Co Fermanagh, shortly before a Remembrance Day service, killing 11 people.

1991 EC foreign ministers, meeting in Rome, imposed an economic embargo on Yugoslavia in an effort to halt the civil war there.

9 NOVEMBER

National Day of Cambodia.

1837 Moses Montefiore became the first Jew to be knighted in England.

1859 Flogging in the British army was abolished.

1908 Britain's first woman mayor, Elizabeth Garrett Anderson, was elected at Aldeburgh.

1953 Dylan Thomas, Welsh poet, died in America, age 39.

1965 Capital punishment was abolished in Britain.

1988 Gary Kasparov became world chess champion after beating Anatoly Karpov, who had held the title for ten years, in Moscow.

10 NOVEMBER

1728   Oliver Goldsmith, Irish playwright and novelist, was born.

1775   The Continental Congress authorized the creation of the 'Continental Marines', now known as the US Marines.

1871   Henry Morton Stanley, who had been sent to track down missing explorer David Livingstone, met him at Ujiji, on Lake Tanganyika.

1938   Kristallnacht, or 'night of (broken) glass', took place when Nazis burned 267 synagogues and destroyed thousands of Jewish homes and businesses in Germany.

1928   Hirohito was crowned emperor of Japan, at the age of 27.

1989   Bulldozers began demolishing the 28-year-old Berlin Wall, following the government's announcement that it would allow free travel between East and West Germany.

11 NOVEMBER

1918   The armistice was signed between the Allies and Germany in Compeigne, France, effectively ending World War I.

1921   The British Legion held its first Poppy Day to raise money for wounded World War I veterans.

1940   The Willys-Overland Company launched a four-wheel drive vehicle for the US Army, named 'Jeep' after GP (general purpose).

1952   The first video recorder was demonstrated in Beverly Hills, California, by its inventors John Mullin and Wayne Johnson.

1965   Ian Smith, prime minister of Rhodesia, unilaterally declared his country's independence from Britain.

1975   Angola gained independence from Portugal.

12 NOVEMBER

1660   English author John Bunyan was arrested for preaching without a licence; refusing to give up preaching, he remained in jail for 12 years.

1859   Jules Léotard, the daring young man on the flying trapeze, made his debut at the Cirque Napoléon, in Paris.

1912   The remains of English explorer Robert Scott and his companions were found in Antarctica.

1918   The Republic of Austria was declared, thus ending the Habsburg dynasty.

1974   For the first time since the 1840s, a salmon was caught in the Thames.

1981 The US shuttle *Columbia* became the first reusable crewed space-craft, by making its second trip.

13 NOVEMBER

1851 The telegraph service between London and Paris began operating.
1907 The first helicopter rose 2 m/6.5 ft above ground in Normandy.
1916 In World War I, the Battle of the Somme ended, having caused the deaths of some 60,000 allied soldiers.
1970 A cyclone and tidal waves struck East Pakistan, killing over 500,000 people.
1985 The Columbian volcano Nevado del Ruiz, dormant since 1845, erupted, killing over 20,000 people.
1987 With a view to encouraging 'safe sex', or AIDS prevention, the BBC screened its first condom commercial (without a brand name).

14 NOVEMBER

1896 The speed limit for motor vehicles in Britain was raised from 4 mph to 14 mph.
1925 An exhibition of Surrealist art opened in Paris, including works by Max Ernst, Man Ray, Joan Miró, and Pablo Picasso.
1940 Enemy bombing destroyed Coventry's medieval cathedral.
1963 The island of Surtsey off Iceland was 'born' by the eruption of an underwater volcano.
1973 Bobby Moore made his 108th (and final) international appearance for England, against Italy at Wembley.
1991 Prince Sihanouk, Cambodia's former head of state, returned to Phnom Penh after nearly 13 years in exile to head the country's interim government.

15 NOVEMBER

1837 Pitman's system of shorthand was published, under the title *Stenographic Sound-Hand*.
1899 Winston Churchill was captured by the Boers while covering the war as a reporter for the *Morning Post*.
1956 *Love Me Tender*, the first film starring Elvis Presley, premiered in New York.
1968 The Cunard liner *Queen Elizabeth* ended her final transatlantic journey.

1983   An independent Turkish Republic of Northern Cyprus was unilaterally proclaimed, recognized only by Turkey.

1985   UK and Irish premiers, Margaret Thatcher and Garret Fitzerald,
signed the Anglo-Irish Agreement in Dublin.

16 NOVEMBER

1824   Australian explorer Hamilton Hume discovered the Murray
River, the longest river in Australia.

1869   The Suez Canal, which had taken ten years to build, was formally opened.

1913   The first volume of *Remembrance of Things Past*, the classic auto-
biographical novel by Marcel Proust, was published in Paris.

1928   In London, obscenity charges were brought against Radclyffe
Hall's crusading lesbian novel *The Well of Loneliness*.

1965   The USSR launched *Venus III*, an unmanned spacecraft that successfully landed on Venus.

1993   Amid the tears of its employees and sympathizers, Vladimir
Lenin's mausoleum was closed by the Russian authorities; it was
the first site in Moscow linked to Lenin to be shut down.

17 NOVEMBER

1800   The US Congress met for the first time, in Washington, DC.

1880   The first three British women to graduate received their
Bachelor of Arts degrees from the University of London.

1922   The last sultan of Turkey was deposed by Kemal Atatürk.

1970   The USSR's *Luna 17* landed on the Sea of Rains on the moon, and
released the first moonwalker vehicle.

1970   Stephanie Rahn became the *Sun* newspaper's first Page Three
girl.

1988   Benazir Bhutto was elected prime minister of Pakistan, becoming the first female leader of a Muslim state.

18 NOVEMBER

1477   William Caxton's *The Dictes or Sayinges of the Philosophres* was
published – the first printed book in England bearing a date.

1626   St Peter's in Rome was consecrated.

1928   The first experimental sound cartoon, *Steamboat Willie*, starring
Mickey Mouse, was screened in the USA.

1977   President Anwar Sadat became the first Egyptian leader to visit
Israel and to address the *Knesset* (parliament).

1987 A fire broke out at London's King's Cross underground station, killing 30 people.

1991 The Shiite Muslim faction Islamic Jihad freed Church of England envoy Terry Waite (held since Jan 1987) and US university professor Thomas Sutherland (held since June 1985).

19 NOVEMBER

1493 On his second voyage to the New World, Columbus discovered Puerto Rico.

1850 Alfred Tennyson was appointed Poet Laureate.

1863 President Lincoln delivered his famous Gettysburg address, after the American Civil War.

1942 The Red Army counter-attacked and surrounded the German army at Stalingrad.

1969 Brazilian footballer Pelé scored his 1,000th goal in his 909th first-class match.

1987 A record price for a car was reached when a 1931 Bugatti Royale was sold at auction for £5.5 million.

20 NOVEMBER

1759 The British fleet under Admiral Hawke defeated the French at the Battle of Quiberon Bay, thwarting an invasion of England.

1899 Edwin Powell Hubble, US astronomer, was born.

1944 The lights of Piccadilly, the Strand, and Fleet Street were switched back on after five years of blackout.

1945 The Nuremberg trials of 24 chief Nazi war criminals by an international military tribunal began.

1979 Anthony Blunt, Surveyor of the Queen's Pictures, was stripped of his knighthood when his past work as a double agent was made public.

1980 The solar-powered *Solar Challenger* was flown for the first time, entirely under solar power.

21 NOVEMBER

1783 François de Rozier and the Marquis d'Arlandres made the first human flight when they lifted off from the Bois de Boulogne, Paris, in a hot-air balloon built by the Montgolfier brothers.

1918 The German High Seas Fleet surrendered to the Allies.

1934 Cole Porter's *Anything Goes* was first performed in New York.

1953	The discovery of the Piltdown Man skull by Charles Dawson in Sussex in 1912 was finally revealed as a hoax.
1974	In Birmingham, 20 people were killed and 200 injured by IRA bomb explosions.
1990	Leaders of NATO and Warsaw Pact member states signed the Charter of Paris and a treaty on Conventional Forces in Europe, bringing an end to the Cold War.

22 NOVEMBER

National Day of Lebanon.

1497	Portuguese navigator Vasco da Gama rounded the Cape of Good Hope in his search for a route to India.
1938	The first coelacanth, a prehistoric fish believed to be extinct, was caught off the South African coast.
1946	Biro ball point pens went on sale in Britain, invented by Hungarian journalist László Biro.
1963	John F Kennedy, 35th US president, was assassinated in Dallas, Texas, allegedly by Lee Harvey Oswald.
1986	Mike Tyson, aged 20, defeated Trevor Berbick in Las Vegas, becoming the youngest-ever heavyweight boxing champion.
1990	Prime minister Margaret Thatcher, who had led Britain since 1979, announced her resignation.

23 NOVEMBER

1852	Britain's first pillar boxes were erected, at St Helier, Jersey.
1889	The first juke box was installed in the Palais Royal Saloon in San Francisco.
1906	Italian operatic tenor Enrico Caruso was fined $10 for sexual harassment.
1921	US President Warren Harding banned doctors from prescribing beer, eliminating a loophole in the prohibition law.
1963	The first episode of the BBC TV serial *Dr Who* was broadcast, with William Hartnell as Dr Who and Anna Ford as his female companion.
1980	A violent earthquake struck Southern Italy, killing over 4,000 people.

24 NOVEMBER

1642	Dutch navigator Abel Tasman discovered Van Dieman's Land which he named after his captain, but it was later renamed Tasmania.

1859	Darwin's *The Origin of Species* was published.
1963	Lee Harvey Oswald, charged with the assassination of John F Kennedy, was shot while in police custody by Jack Ruby, a strip-club owner.
1989	Czech politician Alexander Dubček made his first public appearance in over 20 years, speaking at a pro-democracy rally in Prague.
1991	Freddie Mercury, English rock singer, died of AIDS.
1993	The last 14 bottles of Scotch whisky salvaged from the SS *Politician*, wrecked in 1941 and the inspiration of the book and film, *Whisky Galore*, were sold at auction for £11,462 at Christie's.

25 NOVEMBER

1884	Evaporated milk was patented by John Mayenberg of St Louis, Missouri.
1937	An inter-regional spelling competition became the first British quiz programme to be broadcast.
1952	The longest-running play, *The Mousetrap* by Agatha Christie, opened in London, at the Ambassador's Theatre.
1969	In protest against Britain's involvement in Biafra and support of US involvement in Vietnam, John Lennon returned his MBE.
1975	Surinam, formerly called Dutch Guiana, became a fully independent republic.
1991	Winston Silcott became the first of the 'Tottenham Three', convicted for the 1985 killing of a policeman in Tottenham, North London, to have his conviction overturned.

26 NOVEMBER

1703	England was hit by severe gales, known as the Great Storm, in which 8,000 people died.
1789	The American holiday of Thanksgiving was celebrated nationally for the first time.
1906	President Theodore Roosevelt returned to Washington after a trip to Central America, becoming the first US president to travel abroad while in office.
1942	The Soviet forces counter-attacked at Stalingrad, ending the siege and forcing General von Paulus's Sixth Army to retreat.
1949	India became a federal republic within the Commonwealth.
1966	French president Charles de Gaulle opened the world's first tidal power station in Brittany.

27 NOVEMBER

1095 Pope Urban began to preach the First Crusade at Clermont, France.

1582 William Shakespeare, aged 18, married Anne Hathaway.

1914 Britain's first policewomen went on duty, at Grantham, Lincolnshire.

1967 French president Charles de Gaulle rejected British entry into the Common Market.

1970 The Gay Liberation Front held its first demonstration in London.

1975 Ross McWhirter, British editor with his twin brother, of *The Guinness Book of Records*, was killed by an IRA bomb.

28 NOVEMBER

1520 Portuguese navigator Ferdinand Magellan sailed through the Straits at the tip of South America and reached an ocean which he named the Pacific.

1660 The Royal Society was chartered in London.

1905 The Irish political party Sinn Fein was founded by Arthur Griffith in Dublin.

1909 In France, a law was passed allowing women eight weeks' maternity leave.

1948 Edwin Land's first polaroid cameras went on sale in Boston.

1993 The Northern Ireland peace process and prime minister John Major's credibility were dealt a blow when secret government contacts with the IRA were publicly disclosed.

29 NOVEMBER

1864 The Sand Creek massacre took place when over 150 Cheyenne and Arapaho Indians – who had surrendered and were disarmed – were killed by US cavalry.

1898 C S Lewis, English scholar and writer, was born.

1929 US admiral Richard Byrd became the first man to fly over the South Pole, with his pilot Bernt Balchen.

1945 Yugoslavia was proclaimed a Federal People's Republic, under Tito's leadership.

1947 The UN approved Britain's plan for a partition of Palestine.

1990 The UN Security Council, at the urging of the USA, authorized the use of force against Iraq if it did not withdraw totally from Kuwait by 15 January 1991.

30 NOVEMBER

National Day of Scotland.

1840   Napoleon I's remains were returned from St Helena to Paris.

1872   The first international football match was played, Scotland vs England (drawing 0–0).

1914   Charlie Chaplin made his film debut in *Making a Living*, a Mack Sennett one-reeler, without his trademark moustache and cane.

1936   The Crystal Palace at Sydenham, designed by Joseph Paxton and originally constructed in Hyde Park to house the Great Exhibition of 1851, burned down.

1939   The USSR invaded Finland.

1988   PLO leader Yasser Arafat attempted to enter the USA to address the UN General Assembly, but was refused a visa.

1 DECEMBER

World AIDS Day.

1919   US-born Lady Nancy Astor became the first woman to take her seat in the House of Commons, as MP for the Sutton division of Plymouth.

1925   The Locarno Pact was signed in London, guaranteeing peace and frontiers in Europe.

1939   *Gone with the Wind* premiered in New York.

1942   The Beveridge Report on Social Security, which formed the basis of the welfare state in Britain, was issued.

1953   The first issue of Hugh Hefner's *Playboy* magazine was published; the centre-spread nude featured Marilyn Monroe.

1989   Pope John Paul II and Mikhail Gorbachev met in Rome, ending 70 years of hostility between the Vatican and the USSR.

2 DECEMBER

1697   St Paul's Cathedral, rebuilt by Sir Christopher Wren, was opened.

1823   US President James Monroe proclaimed the Monroe Doctrine, warning that any further European colonial ambitions in the western hemisphere would be considered threats to US peace and security.

1901   In the USA, King Camp Gillette patented a safety razor with a double-edged disposable blade.

1942   The first nuclear chain reaction took place at the University of Chicago, under physicists Enrico Fermi and Arthur Compton.

1988 In Bangladesh, a cyclone killed thousands of people and left five million homeless.

1990 West German chancellor Helmut Kohl was elected chancellor of a united Germany.

3 DECEMBER

1910 Neon lighting was displayed for the first time at the Paris Motor Show.

1917 The Quebec Bridge, the world's longest cantilever, over the St Lawrence River, was opened – 87 lives were lost during its construction.

1961 At the Museum of Modern Art in New York, Henri Matisse's painting *Le Bateau*, which had been hanging upside-down for 46 days, was hung the right way up.

1967 At Groote Schurr Hospital, Cape Town, Dr Christiaan Barnard carried out the world's first heart transplant.

1984 A chemical leakage at a pesticide factory in Bhopal, India caused the deaths of over 2,500 people and blinded many thousands.

1993 Frank Zappa, US composer and guitarist, died.

4 DECEMBER

1154 The only Englishman to become a pope, Nicholas Breakspear, became Adrian IV.

1791 Britain's oldest Sunday paper, the *Observer*, was first published.

1798 William Pitt the Younger first introduced income tax in Britain, to finance the wars with revolutionary France.

1808 Napoleon abolished the Inquisition in Spain.

1829 Under British rule, suttee (whereby a widow commits suicide by joining her husband's funeral pyre) was made illegal in India.

1991 News correspondent Terry Anderson, the longest-held Western hostage in Lebanon (2,454 days in captivity), was freed by Islamic Jihad.

5 DECEMBER

National Day of Thailand.

1766 James Christie, founder of the famous auctioneers, held his first sale in London.

1901 Walt Disney, US filmmaker and animator, was born.

1904 The Russian fleet was destroyed by the Japanese at Port Arthur, during the Russo-Japanese War.

1908 The first American football game in which players were numbered was played, at Pittsburgh.
1933 Prohibition was repealed in the USA after more than 13 years.
1958 Britain's first motorway, the Preston by-pass, was opened by prime minister Macmillan.

6 DECEMBER

National Day of Finland.
1492 Columbus discovered Hispaniola, now Haiti and the Dominican Republic.
1774 Austria became the first nation to introduce a state education system.
1877 With a recording of himself reciting 'Mary Had a Little Lamb' Thomas Edison demonstrated the first gramophone, in New Jersey, USA.
1907 In Monongah, West Virginia 361 people were killed in America's worst mine disaster.
1926 Mussolini introduced a tax on bachelors.
1990 Saddam Hussein announced that he would free all of the 2,000 foreign hostages held in Iraq and occupied Kuwait.

7 DECEMBER

1732 The original Covent Garden Theatre Royal (now the Royal Opera House) was opened.
1787 Delaware became the first state of the USA.
1907 At London's National Sporting Club, Eugene Corri became the first referee to officiate from inside a boxing ring.
1941 The Japanese attacked the US fleet in Pearl Harbor.
1982 The first execution by lethal injection took place at Fort Worth Prison, Texas.
1988 An earthquake in Armenia killed thousands and caused widespread destruction.

8 DECEMBER

1854 Pope Pius IX declared the dogma of the Immaculate Conception of the Blessed Virgin Mary to be an article of faith.
1863 Tom King of England defeated American John Heenan, becoming the first world heavyweight champion.
1941 The USA, Britain, and Australia declared war on Japan, one day after the attack on Pearl Harbor.

1980 John Lennon, British rock singer and songwriter, was shot dead in New York by a fan.

1987 US President Reagan and Soviet President Gorbachev signed the Intermediate Nuclear Forces treaty in Washington, DC, the first nuclear arms reduction agreement.

1991 The leaders of Russia, Byelorussia, and the Ukraine signed an agreement forming a 'Commonwealth of Independent States' to replace the USSR; the decision was denounced by President Gorbachev as unconstitutional.

9 DECEMBER

National Day of Tanzania.

1783 The first executions at Newgate Prison took place.

1868 Gladstone was elected prime minister of Britain, beginning the first of his four terms.

1886 Clarence Birdseye, US inventor of deep-freezing process, was born.

1955 Sugar Ray Robinson knocked out Carl Olson, regaining his world middleweight boxing title.

1960 The first episode of *Coronation Street* was screened on ITV.

1990 Lech Walesa, leader of the once-outlawed Solidarity labour movement, was elected president of Poland.

10 DECEMBER

1768 The Royal Academy of Arts was founded in London by George III, with Joshua Reynolds as its first president.

1845 Pneumatic tyres were patented by Scottish civil engineer Robert Thompson.

1898 Cuba became independent of Spain following the Spanish-American War.

1901 Nobel prizes were first awarded.

1941 The Royal Naval battleships *Prince of Wales* and *Repulse* were sunk by Japanese aircraft in the Battle of Malaya.

1991 The leaders of the 12 EC nations ended their two-day summit and agreed on the treaty of Maastricht, pledging closer political and economic union.

11 DECEMBER

1769 Edward Beran of London patented venetian blinds.

1844 Nitrous oxide, or laughing gas, was first used for a tooth extraction.

1894 The first motor show opened in Paris, with nine exhibitors.

1941 Germany and Italy declared war on the USA.

1987 Charlie Chaplin's trademark cane and bowler hat were sold at Christie's for £82,500.

1991 Salman Rushdie, under an Islamic death sentence for blasphemy, made his first public appearance since 1989 in New York, at a dinner marking the 200th anniversary of the First Amendment (which guarantees freedom of speech).

12 DECEMBER

National Day of Kenya.

1896 Guglielmo Marconi gave the first public demonstration of radio at Toynbee Hall, London.

1915 The first all-metal aircraft, the German Junkers J1, made its first flight.

1925 The world's first motel, in San Luis Obispo, California, opened.

1955 Bill Haley and the Comets recorded 'See You Later Alligator' at Decca Recording Studios, New York.

1955 British engineer Christopher Cockerell patented the first hovercraft.

1989 US billionairess Leona Helmsley, dubbed the 'Queen of Greed', was fined $7 million and sentenced to four years in prison for tax evasion.

13 DECEMBER

1577 Francis Drake began his journey from Plymouth in the *Golden Hind* that was to take him around the world.

1642 Dutch navigator Abel Tasman discovered New Zealand.

1903 Moulds for ice cream cones were patented by Italo Marcione of New York.

1904 The Metropolitan Underground railway in London went electric.

1967 A military coup replaced the monarchy in Greece, sending King Constantine II into exile.

1973 Due to the Arab oil embargo and the coalminers' slowdown, the British government ordered a three-day working week.

14 DECEMBER

1900   Professor Max Planck of Berlin University revealed his revolutionary Quantum Theory.

1911   A Norwegian expedition led by Roald Amundsen became the first to reach the South Pole – 35 days ahead of Captain Scott.

1918   For the first time in Britain women (over 30) voted in a general election.

1959   Archbishop Makarios was elected Cyprus' first president.

1962   US *Mariner II* sent the first close-up pictures of the planet Venus back to Earth.

1990   After 30 years in exile, ANC president Oliver Tambo returned to South Africa.

15 DECEMBER

1654   A meteorological office established in Tuscany began recording daily temperature readings.

1791   The Bill of Rights' ten amendments became part of the US Constitution.

1916   In World War I, the first Battle of Verdun ended; over 700,000 German and Allied soldiers died in the action.

1939   Nylon was first produced commercially in Delaware, USA.

1961   Nazi official Adolph Eichmann was found guilty of crimes against the Jewish people and sentenced to death, after a trial in Jerusalem.

1992   Bettino Craxi, the leader of Italy's Socialist Party, was informed that he was under investigation in a burgeoning corruption scandal that had racked the northern city of Milan.

16 DECEMBER

1653   Oliver Cromwell became Lord Protector of England.

1773   The Boston Tea Party, a protest against British taxation, took place off Griffin's Wharf in Boston harbour.

1838   The Zulu chief Dingaan was defeated by a small force of Boers at Blood River – celebrated in South Africa as 'Dingaan's Day'.

1850   The first immigrant ship, the Charlotte Jane, arrived at Lyttleton, New Zealand.

1944   The Battle of the Bulge, in the Ardennes, began with a strong counter-attack by the Germans under General von Rundstedt.

1991   The UN General Assembly voted to repeal its 1975 resolution equating Zionism with racism.

17 DECEMBER

1843   *A Christmas Carol* by Charles Dickens was published.
1892   Tchaikovsky's *The Nutcracker* was first performed, in St Petersburg by the Russian Imperial Ballet.
1903   Orville Wright made the first successful controlled flight in a powered aircraft, at Kill Devil Hill, near Kitty Hawk, North Carolina, USA.
1973   Thirty-one people were killed at Rome airport after Arab guerillas hijacked a German airliner.
1986   At Papworth Hospital, Cambridge, Davina Thompson became the world's first recipient of a heart, lungs, and liver transplant.
1992   Israel deported over 400 Palestinians to Lebanese territory in an unprecedented mass expulsion of suspected militants.

18 DECEMBER

1865   The USA officially abolished slavery with the ratification of the 13th Amendment.
1903   The Panama Canal Zone was acquired 'in perpetuity' by the USA, for an annual rent.
1912   The immigration of illiterate persons to the USA was prohibited by Congress.
1912   The discovery of the Piltdown Man in East Sussex was announced; it was proved to be a hoax in 1953.
1969   The death penalty for murder was abolished in Britain.
1979   The sound barrier on land was broken for the first time by Stanley Barrett, driving at 739.6 mph, in California.

19 DECEMBER

1562   The Battle of Dreux was fought between the Huguenots and the Catholics, beginning the French Wars of Religion.
1842   Hawaii's independence was recognized by the USA.
1955   'Blue Suede Shoes' was recorded by Carl Perkins in Memphis, Tennessee.
1957   An air service between London and Moscow was inaugurated.
1984   Britain and China signed an agreement in Beijing, in which Britain agreed to transfer full sovereignty of Hong Kong to China in 1997.

1991   Bob Hawke was deposed as Australia's prime minister by his parliamentary colleagues and replaced by Paul Keating.

20 DECEMBER

1860   South Carolina seceded from the American Union, and joined the Confederacy.
1915   The ANZACS, Australian and New Zealand forces with British troops were evacuated from Gallipoli, after their expedition against the Turks went seriously wrong.
1933   *Flying Down to Rio*, the first film to feature Fred Astaire and Ginger Rogers, was first shown in New York.
1957   Elvis Presley, at the height of his stardom, received his draft papers.
1989   General Noriega, Panama's former dictator, was overthrown by a US invasion force invited by the new civilian government.
1990   Soviet foreign minister Shevardnadze resigned, complaining of conservative attacks on his policies.

21 DECEMBER

1620   The Pilgrim Fathers, aboard the *Mayflower*, landed at Plymouth Rock, Massachusetts.
1879   Joseph Stalin, Soviet leader, was born.
1937   Walt Disney's *Snow White and the Seven Dwarfs* was shown in Los Angeles; the first full-length animated talking picture.
1958   Charles de Gaulle became president of France.
1988   A Pan Am jet blew up in mid-flight and crashed in Lockerbie, Scotland, killing all 259 passengers aboard and 11 people on the ground; the terrorist bomb had been concealed within a radio.
1990   In a German television interview, Saddam Hussein declared that he would not withdraw from Kuwait by the UN deadline.

22 DECEMBER

1715   James Stuart, the 'Old Pretender', landed at Petershead after his exile in France.
1894   Alfred Dreyfus, the French officer who was falsely convicted for selling military secrets, was sent to Devil's Island.
1895   German physicist Wilhelm Röntgen made the first X-ray, of his wife's hand.

…es Davis became the first US soldier to die in Vietnam, while
…involvement was still limited to the provision of military
…dvisers.

1989 Romanian dictator Nicolae Ceausescu was overthrown in a bloody revolutionary coup.

1991 Eleven of the 12 Soviet republics (excluding Georgia) agreed, in Alma Ata, Kazakhstan, on the creation of a Commonwealth of Independent States.

23 DECEMBER

1834 English architect Joseph Hansom patented his 'safety cab', better known as the Hansom cab.

1888 Following a quarrel with Paul Gauguin, Dutch painter Vincent van Gogh cut off part of his own earlobe.

1922 The BBC began daily news broadcasts.

1986 Dick Rutan and Jeana Yeager made the first non-stop flight around the world without refuelling, piloting the US plane *Voyager*.

1965 A 70-mph speed limit was introduced in Britain.

1990 Elections in Yugoslavia ended, leaving four of its six republics with non-Communist governments.

24 DECEMBER

1814 The War of 1812 between the USA and Britain was brought to an end with the signing of the Treaty of Ghent.

1871 Verdi's *Aïda* was first performed in Cairo.

1914 The first air raid on Britain was made when a German airplane dropped a bomb on the grounds of a rectory in Dover.

1951 Libya achieved independence as the United Kingdom of Libya, under King Idris.

1965 A meteorite landed on Leicestershire; it weighed about 45 kg 100lbs.

1979 Afghanistan was invaded by Soviet troops as the Kabul government fell.

25 DECEMBER

Christmas Day.

800 Charlemagne was crowned first Holy Roman Emperor in Rome by Pope Leo III.

1066 William the Conqueror was crowned king of England at Westminster Abbey.
1914 During World War I, British and German troops observed an unofficial truce, even playing football together on the Western Front's 'no man's land'.
1972 The Nicaraguan capital Managua was devastated by an earthquake which killed over 10,000 people.
1989 Dissident playwright Vaclav Havel was elected president of Czechoslovakia.
1991 Unable to maintain control over a disintegrating Soviet Union, Mikhail Gorbachev announced his resignation as president.

26 DECEMBER

Boxing Day and Feast Day of St Stephen.
1898 Marie and Pierre Curie discovered radium.
1908 Texan boxer 'Galveston Jack' Johnson knocked out Tommy Burns in Sydney, Australia, to become the first black boxer to win the world heavyweight title.
1943 The German battlecruiser *Scharnhorst* was sunk in the North Sea, during the Battle of North Cape.
1956 Fidel Castro attempted a secret landing in Cuba to overthrow the Batista regime; all but 11 of his supporters were killed.
1959 The first charity walk took place, along Icknield Way, in aid of the World Refugee Fund.
1991 The Soviet Union's parliament formally voted the country out of existence.

27 DECEMBER

1703 The Methuen Treaty was signed between Portugal and England, giving preference to the import of Portuguese wines into England.
1831 Charles Darwin set sail in the *Beagle* on his voyage of scientific discovery.
1904 James Barrie's *Peter Pan* premiered in London.
1927 Defeated in his struggle for power against Stalin, Leon Trotsky was expelled from the Communist Party.
1965 The BP oil rig *Sea Gem* capsized in the North Sea, with the loss of 13 lives.
1978 With the adoption of a new constitution, Spain became a democracy after 40 years of dictatorship.

28 DECEMBER

1836   Mexico's independence was recognized by Spain.

1879   The central portion of the Tay Bridge, Scotland, collapsed as a train was passing over it, killing 75 people.

1908   An earthquake killed over 75,000 at Messina in Sicily.

1926   The highest recorded cricket innings score of 1,107 runs was hit by Victoria, against New South Wales, in Melbourne.

1937   The Irish Free State became the Republic of Ireland when a new constitution established the country as a sovereign state under the name of Eire.

1989   Alexander Dubček, who had been expelled from the Communist Party in 1970, was elected speaker of the Czech parliament.

29 DECEMBER

1170   St Thomas à Becket, the 40th archbishop of Canterbury, was murdered in his own cathedral by four knights acting on Henry II's orders.

1860   HMS *Warrior*, Britain's first seagoing iron-clad warship, was launched.

1890   The massacre at Wounded Knee, the last major battle between Native American Indians and US troops, took place.

1895   The Jameson Raid from Mafikeng into Transvaal, which attempted to overthrow Kruger's Boer government, started.

1911   Sun Yat-sen became the first president of a republican China, following the Revolution.

1989   Following Hong Kong's decision to forcibly repatriate some Vietnamese refugees, thousands of Vietnamese 'boat people' battled with riot police.

30 DECEMBER

1460   At the Battle of Wakefield, in the Wars of the Roses, the Duke of York was defeated and killed by the Lancastrians.

1887   A petition to Queen Victoria with over one million names of women appealing for public houses to be closed on Sundays was handed to the home secretary.

1919   Lincoln's Inn, one of the four legal societies in London, admitted the first female bar student.

1922   The Union of Soviet Socialist Republics was formed.

1947 King Michael of Romania abdicated in favour of a Communist Republic.
1988 Colonel Oliver North subpoenaed President Reagan and Vice President Bush to testify at the Irangate hearings.

31 DECEMBER

New Year's Eve.

1687 The first Huguenots set sail from France for the Cape of Good Hope, where they would later create the South African wine industry with the vines they took with them on the voyage.
1695 The window tax was imposed in Britain, which resulted in many being bricked up.
1891 New York's new Immigration Depot was opened at Ellis Island, to provide improved facilities for the massive numbers of arrivals.
1923 The chimes of Big Ben were first broadcast by the BBC.
1960 The farthing coin, which had been in use in Britain since the 13th century, ceased to be legal tender.
1990 Titleholder Gary Kasparov of the USSR won the world chess championship match against his countryman Anatoly Karpov.

CHRONOLOGIES

AFRICA

14 million BC	Africa, which is considered the 'cradle continent', probably produced the first humanlike creatures.
3–5 million BC	Direct line of descent of modern humans was established in E Africa.
15,000	Agriculture first practised in Egypt.
10,000–2000	The originally fertile Sahara became a barrier desert between north and south.
5450–2500	Era of Saharan rock and cave paintings.
7th C BC – AD 6th C	Assyria, Persia, Greece, Rome, and Byzantium in turn made conquests in N Africa. Meroe: the Egyptian and Negro tradition met in the Nubian kingdom of Kush.
320 BC AD 50	The kingdom of Axum flourished in Ethiopia and gave rise to the later legend of Prester John.
AD 640	Islamic expansion began in N, E, and Central Africa.
300–1500	Period of the great medieval states: Ghana, Mali, Songhai, Benin, Ife, and the culture of Great Zimbabwe.
12th–15th C	Period of the Arab travellers: for example, Ibn Batuta; and of trade, for example, Kilwa.
1488	Diaz rounded the Cape of Good Hope.
15th–16th C	European sea trade in gold, ivory, timber, and pepper.
17th–19th C	Height of the Atlantic and Indian Ocean slave trade which provided cheap African labour for plantations in the Americas.
18th–19th C	European travellers in Africa: Park, Livingstone, Stanley, Speke, Mary Kingsley.
19th C	Colonial wars against well-organized native states: Ashanti, Dahomey, Zululand.
1880–90	Peak of European colonization in the 'scramble for Africa'.
1899–1902	South African War, the first large-scale war between whites in Africa.
1920	League of Nations mandate system introduced the idea of European trusteeship.

1936	Italy's conquest of Ethiopia.
1942	World War II reached its turning point in the Battles of Alamein.
1951	Libya became the first independent state to be declared by the United Nations.
1954–62	The fight for independence in Algeria precipitated the end of the French Fourth Republic 1958.
1957	Ghana became independent, the first of the revived black nation states.
1952–60	Mau-Mau movement in Kenya began the ousting of white settlers south of the Sahara.
1963	Organization of African Unity (OAU) founded.
1967–70	Revolt of Biafra within the federation of Nigeria constituted the first civil war in a modern black state.
1975	Mozambique's independence led to the end of dictatorship in Portugal.
1979	Zimbabwe's achievement of independence left South Africa as the last white-ruled state in Africa.
1980	Future of the OAU doubtful due to division over Western Sahara and Libyan aggression towards Chad. Extensive food shortages in many parts of Central and East Africa.
1984	Increasing internal disaster in South Africa leading to violence between black population and minority white groups.
1988	Peace treaty between Angola, South Africa, and Cuba leading to Namibia's independence.
1990	Namibia declared independent. South Africa's African National Congress (ANC) party leader Nelson Mandela freed.
1991	North African states oppose Iraq on Kuwait invasion. Ethiopia's communist regime collapses.
1992	New constitution in South Africa leading to all-races majority rule approved by whites-only referendum. Southern Africa experienced the worst drought of the 20th century.
1994	Nelson Mandela was elected president in the first South African free election.

AGE OF THE GREAT VOYAGES

1253–55	Willem van Ruysbroeck of France travelled overland to the capital of the Mongolian empire at Karakorum.
1260–69	The Venetian travellers Nicolo and Maffeo Polo explored central Asia and China.
1271	Marco Polo joined the next expedition to China and stayed there in the service of the Khan until 1292. His written account of his experiences did much to inspire European interest in travel.
1325	Giovanni di Montecorvino became the first European to visit Tibet, during his travels across Asia.
1325–55	Ibn Battutah, an Arab of Tangier, travelled extensively in central Africa, Arabia, and Indonesia.
1340s	Europeans possibly reached Senegal by sea.
1405–33	Zheng He led Chinese exploration south of China and in the Indian Ocean as far west as Africa.
c.1430s	Arab merchants began to gain knowledge of the interior of southern Africa.
1440–60	Prince Henry the Navigator of Portugal sponsored voyages by Portuguese explorers to expand his country's wealth and power.
1440s	Inca explorers started to move outward along the Pacific coast.
1445	A Portuguese expedition under Dinas Dias sailed down the African coast as far as Senegal.
1481–95	King John II of Portugal made discovery of routes to India a priority for Portuguese explorers.
1487	Bartolomeu Dias, a Portuguese explorer, rounded the Cape of Good Hope (then known as the Cape of Storms) and proved a sea voyage to India was possible.
1492	Christopher Columbus, attempting to reach China from the west, landed in the Bahamas and Hispaniola instead, becoming the first European in the 'West Indies'.
1493–94	Columbus travelled again to the Caribbean.
1497	Vasco da Gama reached India via the Cape and the East African coast.
1497	John Cabot sailed westwards from Ireland and landed on Newfoundland. He disappeared on a second voyage a year later.

1498	Columbus travelled to Trinidad and Venezuela.
1499	Amerigo Vespucci explored the northern part of the South American continent. The area was named 'America' in about 1507.
1500	Pedro Alvarez Cabral ran into the Brazilian coast while heading for India.
1506–08	New maps, such as that of Ruysch, attempted to incorporate knowledge gained from European explorations.
1519–22	One ship of a fleet captained by Magellan achieved the first circumnavigation of the globe – although Magellan died en route in 1521. The 'Age of Discovery' is often considered to end at this point.
1534	Jacques Cartier navigated the St Lawrence River while searching for a North West Passage.
1553	Willoughby attempted to sail north of Russia to reach China (the North East passage). Other attempts followed.
1577–80	Sir Francis Drake circumnavigated the globe and explored up and down the coast of California.
1610s	Accounts of landings on the Australian coast started to circulate late in Europe.
1642	A Dutch sailor, Abel Tasman, explored New Zealand and Tasmania. Later he also sailed along the north coast of Australia.

AMERICAN REVOLUTION

1773	A government tax on tea led Massachusetts citizens disguised as North American Indians to board British ships carrying tea and throw it into Boston harbour, the Boston Tea Party.
1774–75	The First Continental Congress was held in Philadelphia to call for civil disobedience in reply to British measures such as the Intolerable Acts, which closed the port of Boston and quartered British troops in private homes.
1775	Hostilities began at Lexington and Concord, Massachusetts.
19 April	The first shots were fired when British troops, sent to seize illegal military stores and arrest rebel leaders John Hancock and Samuel Adams, were attacked by the local militia (minutemen).
10 May	Fort Ticonderoga, New York, was captured from the British.

17 June	The colonists were defeated in the first battle of the Revolution, the Battle of Bunker Hill (which actually took place on Breed's Hill, nearby); George Washington was appointed colonial commander in chief soon afterwards.
1776 4 July	The Second Continental Congress issued the Declaration of Independence, which specified some of the colonists' grievances and proclaimed an independent government.
27 Aug	Washington was defeated at Long Island and was forced to evacuate New York and retire to Pennsylvania.
26 Dec	Washington recrossed the Delaware River and defeated the British at Trenton, New Jersey.
1777 3 Jan	Washington defeated the British at Princeton, New Jersey.
11 Sept– 4 Oct	British general William Howe defeated Washington at Brandywine and Germantown and occupied Philadelphia.
17 Oct	British general John Burgoyne surrendered at Saratoga, New York, and was therefore unable to link up with Howe.
1777–78	Washington wintered at Valley Forge, Pennsylvania, enduring harsh conditions and seeing many of his troops leave to return to their families.
1778	France, with the support of its ally Spain, entered the war on the US side (John Paul Jones led a French-sponsored naval unit).
1780 12 May	The British captured Charleston, South Carolina, one of a series of British victories in the South, but alienated support by enforcing conscription.
1781 19 Oct	British general Charles Cornwallis, besieged in Yorktown, Virginia, by Washington and the French fleet, surrendered.
1782	Peace negotiations opened.
1783 3 Sept	The Treaty of Paris recognized American independence.

ANCIENT EGYPT

5000 BC	Egyptian culture already well established in the Nile Valley, with Neolithic farming villages.
3200	Menes united Lower Egypt (the delta) with his own kingdom of Upper Egypt.
2800	The architect Imhotep built the step pyramid at Sakkara.

c. 2600	Old Kingdom reached the height of its power and the kings of the 4th dynasty built the pyramids at El Gîza.
c. 2200–1800	Middle Kingdom, under which the unity lost towards the end of the Old Kingdom was restored.
1730	Invading Asian Hyksos people established their kingdom in the Nile Delta.
c. 1580	New Kingdom established by the 18th dynasty following the eviction of the Hyksos, with its capital at Thebes. The high point of ancient Egyptian civilization under the pharaohs Thothmes, Hatshepsut, Amenhotep, Ikhnaton (who moved the capital to Akhetaton), and Tutankhamen.
c. 1321	19th dynasty: Ramses I built a temple at Karnak, Ramses II the temple at Abu Simbel.
1191	Ramses III defeated the Indo-European Sea Peoples, but after him there was decline, and power within the country passed from the pharaohs to the priests of Ammon.
1090–663	Late New Kingdom: during this period Egypt was often divided between two or more dynasties; the nobles became virtually independent.
8th–7th C	Brief interlude of rule by kings from Nubia.
666	The Assyrians under Ashurbanipal occupied Thebes.
663–609	Psammetichus I restored Egypt's independence and unity.
525	Egypt was conquered by Cambyses and became a Persian province.
c. 405–340	Period of independence.
332	Conquest by Alexander the Great. On the division of his empire, Egypt went to one of his generals, Ptolemy I, and his descendants, the Macedonian dynasty.
30	Death of Cleopatra, last of the Macedonians, and conquest by the Roman emperor Augustus; Egypt became a province of the Roman empire.
AD 641	Conquest by the Arabs; the Christianity of later Roman rule was for the most part replaced by Islam.

ANCIENT GREECE

c.1600–1200 BC	The first Greek civilization, known as Mycenaean, owed much to the Minoan civilization of Crete and may have been produced by the intermarriage of Greek-speaking invaders with the original inhabitants.
c. 1300	A new wave of invasions began. The Achaeans overran Greece and Crete, destroying the Minoan and Mycenaean civilizations and penetrating Asia Minor.
By 1000	Aeolians, Ionians and Dorians had settled in the area that is now Greece. Many independent city states, such as Sparta and Athens, had developed.
c. 800–500	During the Archaic Period, Ionian Greeks led the development of philosophy, science, and lyric poetry. The Greeks became great sea traders, and founded colonies around the coasts of the Mediterranean and the Black Sea, from Asia Minor in the east to Spain in the west.
776	The first Olympic games held.
594	The laws of Solon took the first step towards a more democratic society.
c. 560–510	The so-called 'tyranny' of the Pisistratids in Athens was typical of a pre-democratic stage that many Greek cities passed through after overturning aristocratic rule.
545	From this date the Ionian cities in Asia Minor fell under the dominion of the Persian Empire.
507	Cleisthenes, ruler of Athens, is credited with the establishment of democracy. Other cities followed this lead, but Sparta remained unique, a state in which a ruling race, organized on military lines, dominated the surrounding population.
500–338	The Classical Period in ancient Greece.
499–494	The Ionian cities, aided by Athens, revolted unsuccessfully against the Persians.
490	Darius of Persia invaded Greece only to be defeated by the Athenians at Marathon and forced to withdraw.
480	Another invasion by the Persian emperor Xerxes, after being delayed by the heroic defence of Thermopylae by 300 Spartans, was defeated at sea off Salamis.
479	The Persians defeated on land at Plataea.
478	The Ionian cities, now liberated, formed a naval alliance with Athens, the Delian League.

455–429	Under Pericles, the democratic leader of Athens, drama, sculpture, and architecture were at their peak.
433	The Parthenon in Athens was completed.
431–404	The Peloponnesian War destroyed the political power of Athens, but Athenian thought and culture remained influential. Sparta became the leading Greek power.
370	The philosopher Plato opened his Academy in Athens.
338	Phillip II of Macedon (359–336 BC) took advantage of the wars between the city states and conquered Greece.
336–323	Rule of Phillip's son, Alexander the Great. Alexander overthrew the Persian Empire, conquered Syria and Egypt, and invaded the Punjab. After his death, his empire was divided among his generals, but his conquests had spread Greek culture across the known world.
280	Achaeon League of 12 Greek city states formed in an attempt to maintain their independence against Macedon, Egypt, and Rome.
146	Greece became part of the Roman Empire. Under Roman rule Greece remained a cultural centre and Hellenistic culture remained influential.

ANCIENT ROME

753 BC	According to tradition, Rome was founded.
510	The Etruscan dynasty of the Tarquins was expelled and a republic established, with power concentrated in patrician hands.
450	Publication of the law code contained in the Twelve Tables.
396	Capture of Etruscan Veii, 15 km/9 mi N of Rome.
387	Rome sacked by Gauls.
367	Plebeians gained the right to be consuls (the two chief magistrates, elected annually).
343–290	Sabines to the N, and the Samnites to the SE, were conquered.
338	Cities of Latium formed into a league under Roman control.
280–272	Greek cities in S Italy subdued.
264–241	First Punic War against Carthage, ending in a Roman victory and the annexation of Sicily.
238	Sardinia seized from Carthage.
226–222	Roman conquest of Cisalpine Gaul (Lombardy, Italy). More

	conflict with Carthage, which was attempting to conquer Spain.
218	Second Punic War. Hannibal crossed the Alps and invaded Italy, winning a series of brilliant victories.
202	Victory of General Scipio Africanus Major over Hannibal at Zama was followed by the surrender of Carthage and relinquishing of its Spanish colonies.
188	Peace of Apamea confined the rule of the Seleucid king Antiochus the Great to Asia.
168	Final defeat of Macedon by Rome.
146	After a revolt, Greece became in effect a Roman province. Carthage was destroyed and its territory annexed.
133	Tiberius Gracchus suggested agrarian reforms and was murdered by the senatorial party. Roman province of Asia formed from the kingdom of Pergamum, bequeathed to Rome by the Attalid dynasty.
123	Tiberius' policy adopted by his brother Gaius Gracchus, who was likewise murdered.
91–88	Social War: revolt by the Italian cities forced Rome to grant citizenship to all Italians.
87	While Sulla was repelling an invasion of Greece by King Mithridates of Pontus (in Asia Minor), Marius seized power.
82–79	Sulla returned and established a dictatorship ruled by terror.
70	Sulla's constitutional changes were reversed by Pompey and Crassus.
66–63	Pompey defeated Mithridates and annexed Syria.
60	The First Triumvirate was formed, an alliance between Pompey and the democratic leaders Crassus and Caesar.
51	Caesar conquered Gaul as far as the Rhine.
49	Caesar crossed the Rubicon, returned to Italy, and a civil war between him and Pompey's senatorial party began.
48	Pompey defeated at Pharsalus.
44	Caesar's dictatorship ended by his assassination.
43	Second Triumvirate formed by Octavian, Mark Antony, and Lepidus.
32	War between Octavian and Mark Antony.
31	Mark Antony defeated at Actium.
30	Egypt was annexed after the deaths of Mark Antony and Cleopatra.
27	Octavian took the name Augustus. He was by now absolute ruler, though in title he was only 'princeps' (first citizen).

AD 14	Augustus died. Tiberius proclaimed as his successor.
43	Claudius added Britain to the empire.
70	Jerusalem sacked by Titus.
96–180	The empire enjoyed a golden age under the Flavian and Antonine emperors Nerva, Trajan, Hadrian, Antoninus Pius, and Marcus Aurelius Antoninus.
115	Trajan conquered Parthia, achieving the peak of Roman territorial expansion.
180	Marcus Aurelius died, and a century of war and disorder followed, with a succession of generals being put on the throne by their armies.
212	Caracalla granted citizenship to the communities of the empire.
284–305	Diocletian reorganized the empire, dividing power between himself and three others (the Tetrarchy).
313	Constantine the Great recognized the Christians' right to freedom of worship by the Edict of Milan.
330	Constantine made Constantinople his new imperial capital.
395	The empire divided into eastern and western parts.
410	Visigoths sacked Rome. Roman legions withdrew from Britain.
451–52	Huns raided Gaul and Italy.
455	Vandals sacked Rome.
476	Last Western emperor, Romulus Augustulus, deposed.

ANTARCTIC EXPLORATION

1773–74	English explorer James Cook first sailed in Antarctic seas, but exploration was difficult before the development of iron ships able to withstand ice pressure.
1819–21	Antarctica was circumnavigated by Russian explorer Fabian Bellingshausen.
1823	British navigator James Weddell sailed into the sea now named after him.
1841–42	Scottish explorer James Ross sighted the Great Ice Barrier now named after him.
1895	Norwegian explorer Carsten Borchgrevink was one of the first landing party on the continent.
1898	Borchgrevink's British expedition first wintered in Antarctica.
1901–04	English explorer Robert Scott first penetrated the interior of the continent.

1907–08	English explorer Ernest Shackleton came within 182 km/113 mi of the Pole.
1911	Norwegian explorer Roald Amundsen reached the Pole, 14 Dec, overland with dogs.
1912	Scott reached the Pole, 18 Jan, initially aided by ponies.
1928–29	US naval officer Richard Byrd made the first flight to the Pole.
1935	US explorer Lincoln Ellsworth (1880–1951) first flew across Antarctica.
1946–48	US explorer Finn Ronne's expedition proved the Antarctic to be one continent.
1957–58	English explorer Vivian Fuchs made the first overland crossing.
1959	A Soviet expedition crossed from the West Ice Shelf to the Pole; the International Antarctic Treaty suspended all territorial claims, reserving an area south of 60°S latitude for peaceful purposes.
1961–62	The Bentley Trench was discovered, which suggested that there may be an Atlantic–Pacific link beneath the continent.
1966–67	Specially protected areas were established internationally for animals and plants.
1979	Fossils of apelike humanoids resembling E Africa's Proconsul were found 500 km/300 mi from the Pole.
1980	International Convention on the exploitation of resources – oil, gas, fish, and krill.
1982	The first circumnavigation of Earth (2 Sept 1979–29 Aug 1982) via the Poles was completed by English explorers Ranulph Fiennes and Charles Burton.
1990	The longest unmechanized crossing (6,100 km/3,182 mi) was made by a six-person international team, using only skis and dogs.
1991	The Antarctic Treaty imposing a 50-year ban on mining activity was secured.
1992–93	Norwegian lawyer Erling Kagge skiied unassisted to South Pole from Berkner Island in Weddell Sea; Ranulph Fiennes and Michael Stroud crossed Antarctic continent on foot, unassisted, but had to be rescued before reaching ultimate destination of Scott's Base.

ARCTIC EXPLORATION

60,000–35,000 BC	Ancestors of the Inuit and American Indians began migration from Siberia to North America by the 'lost' land bridge of Beringia.
320	Pytheas, a Greek sailor contemporary with Alexander the Great, possibly reached Iceland.
AD 9th–10th C	Vikings colonized Iceland and Greenland, which then had a much warmer climate.
c. 1000	Norwegian sailor Leif Ericsson reached Baffin Island (NE of Canada) and Labrador.
1497	Genoese pilot Giovanni Caboto first sought the North-west Passage as a trade route around North America for Henry VII of England.
1553	English navigator Richard Chancellor tried to find the Northeast Passage around Siberia and first established direct English trade with Russia.
1576	English sailor Martin Frobisher reached Frobisher Bay, but found only 'fools' gold' (iron pyrites) for Elizabeth I of England.
1594–97	Dutch navigator Willem Barents made three expeditions in search of the Northeast Passage.
1607	English navigator Henry Hudson failed to cross the Arctic Ocean, but his reports of whales started the northern whaling industry.
1670	Hudson's Bay Company started the fur trade in Canada.
1728	Danish navigator Vitus Bering passed the Bering Strait.
1829–33	Scottish explorer John Ross discovered the North Magnetic Pole.
1845	The mysterious disappearance of English explorer John Franklin's expedition to the Northwest Passage stimulated further exploration.
1878–79	Swedish navigator Nils Nordensköld was the first European to discover the Northeast Passage.
1893–96	Norwegian explorer Fridtjof Nansen's ship *Fram* drifted across the Arctic while locked in the ice, proving that no Arctic continent existed.
1903–06	Norwegian explorer Roald Amundsen sailed through the Northwest Passage.
1909	US explorers Robert Peary, Matt Henson, and four Inuit reached the North Pole on 2 April.

1926	US explorers Richard Byrd and Floyd Bennett flew to the Pole on 9 May.
1926	Italian aviator Umberto Nobile and Amundsen crossed the Pole (Spitzbergen–Alaska) in the airship *Norge* on 12 May.
1954	Scandinavian Airlines launched the first regular commercial flights over the short-cut polar route.
1958	The US submarine *Nautilus* crossed the Pole beneath the ice.
1960	From this date a Soviet nuclear-powered icebreaker kept open a 4,000 km/2,500 mi Asia–Europe passage along the north coast of Siberia for 150 days a year.
1969	Wally Herbert of the British Transarctic Expedition made the first surface crossing, by dog sled, of the Arctic Ocean (Alaska–Spitzbergen).
1977	The Soviet icebreaker *Arktika* made the first surface voyage to the Pole.
1982	English explorers Ranulph Fiennes and Charles Burton completed the first circumnavigation of the Earth via the Poles, 2 Sept 1979–29 Aug 1982.
1988	Canadian and Soviet skiers attempted the first overland crossing from the USSR to Canada via the Pole.

ASIA

2800–2200 BC	Sage kings, earliest Chinese legendary dynasty; civilization spread to all of China.
2500–1500	Indus Valley civilization.
AD 563	Birth of the Buddha.
551	Birth of Confucius.
215	Great Wall of China begun.
320–550	Gupta dynasty in India.
1192	First Muslim kingdom of India established.
1279	Kublai Khan became emperor of China; Marco Polo visited.
1395	Tamerlane defeated the Golden Horde.
1526	Babur established Mogul empire in N India.
1600s	British East India Company chartered.
1757	Clive defeated the nawab of Bengal at Plassey.
1839–42	Opium War between Britain and China ended with ceding of Hong Kong to Britain and opening of treaty ports in China.

1854	US Commodore Perry forced Japanese shogun to grant commercial treaty.
1857–58	Sepoy Rebellion in India.
1894–95	Sino-Japanese War.
1912	Qin dynasty overthrown in republican revolution in China.
1931	Japan invaded China.
1941	Japan attacked US fleet at Pearl Harbor.
1947	India and Pakistan gained independence.
1949	Chiang Kai-shek forced by Chinese communists to flee to Taiwan, where he set up a US-backed Republic of China.
1950–53	Korean War.
1954	End of French colonialism in Indochina: Vietnam was divided into the communist north and the noncommunist south.
1955	US sent to advise South Vietnam against Vietcong communist insurgents, backed by North Vietnam and China.
1965	US troops sent to support South Vietnamese government in large numbers.
1971	East Pakistan declared independence as Bangladesh.
1975	Fall of South Vietnam to North Vietnam. Khmer Rouge seized power in Cambodia.
1976	Death of Mao Zedong.
1980	Trial of Gang of Four (including Mao's widow Jiang Qing).
1980s	Japan became world's richest nation.
1986	Agreement between British and Chinese governments on future 1997 administration of Hong Kong.
1989	Prodemocracy demonstrations in China bloodily repressed by government troops.

AUSTRALIA

c. 40–50,000 BC	Aboriginal immigration from SE Asia via Indonesian Archipelago.
AD 1605–06	First recorded European sightings of Australia include Dutch ship *Duyfken* off Cape York.
1616	Dutchman Dirck Hartog lands at Shark Bay, WA.
1642	Dutch navigator Abel Tasman discovers Tasmania, naming it Van Diemen's Land.
1688	British pirate William Dampier lands on N coast of WA.

1770	Captain Cook explores E coast of Australia and claims it as a British possession to be named New South Wales.
1788	First Fleet arrives at Sydney Cove and colony established with Arthur Phillip as first governor.
1797	First merino sheep brought to the colony.
1803	Matthew Flinders completes circumnavigation of Australia.
1804	Extensive settlement in Van Diemen's Land causes racial trouble with 50 Aborigines killed. Riots at Castle Hill, NSW, by Irish convicts.
1808	Rum Rebellion, Governor Bligh deposed.
1810	Lachlan Macquarie appointed governor of NSW.
1813	Blue Mountains crossed by Blaxland, Wentworth and Lawson.
1825	Van Diemen's Land made a separate colony.
1826	Colony established in Western Australia.
1830	Sturt completes exploration of the Murray River.
1835	John Batman buys land on the site of Melbourne from local Aborigines.
1836	Settlement of South Australia as a separate colony begins.
1841	E J Eyre completes crossing from Fowlers Bay, SA, to King George Sound, WA.
1848	Ludwig Leichhardt vanishes while attempting to cross Australia from E to W and Edmund Kennedy killed by Aborigines while exploring Cape York Peninsula.
1850	Transportation of convicts to NSW stopped.
1851	Port Phillip District becomes a separate colony named Victoria. Discovery of gold near Bathurst, NSW, and at Clunes, Victoria, begins the gold rushes.
1852	University of Sydney founded.
1854	Eureka Stockade at Ballarat, Victoria.
1855	Responsible government for NSW, Victoria, and Tasmania.
1856	Victoria introduces world's first secret ballot. Responsible government for South Australia.
1859	Queensland gains responsible government and becomes a separate colony.
1861	Burke and Wills die in central Australia on return journey from the Gulf of Carpentaria. Anti-Chinese riots at Lambing Flat, NSW. First Melbourne Cup run.
1862	John McDouall Stuart crosses Australia S to N.
1870	Construction of Overland Telegraph started.

1876	Truganini, claimed to be the last of the full-blooded Tasmanian Aborigines, dies.
1877	First England versus Australia cricket test in Melbourne.
1880	Ned Kelly captured and hanged.
1883	Lead and zinc discovered at Broken Hill.
1890	Maritime and shearers' strikes. Responsible government in Western Australia.
1890s	Economic depression and the development of the Australian Labor Party.
1894	Women given the vote in SA.
1899	Australian troops leave for the Boer War.
1900	Commonwealth of Australia Constitution Act passed by the British Parliament. Bubonic plague outbreak in Sydney.
1901	Commonwealth of Australia comes into effect on 1 Jan with Edmund Barton as the first prime minister. Population at federation is 3,773,801.
1904	J C Watson becomes Australia's first Labor prime minister.
1905	*The Story of Ned Kelly*, claimed to be the world's first full-length feature film, is produced.
1908	Invalid and old-age pensions introduced.
1911	Site for national capital chosen (named Canberra two years later).
1914	Australia enters World War I. German cruiser *Emden* sunk by HMAS *Sydney*.
1915	Australian and New Zealand troops adopt code name of ANZACs. Gallipoli campaign. Federal income tax introduced.
1916	Australian troops fight in Palestine and France. Referendum on introduction of conscription defeated.
1918	World War I ends.
1919	11,552 die in influenza epidemic.
1926	Council for Scientific and Industrial Research (now CSIRO) established.
1927	First parliament in Canberra opened by the Duke of York (later King George VI). Australian Council of Trade Unions (ACTU) created.
1929	Dame Nellie Melba gives final Australian performance.
1930	Effects of the worldwide Depression felt in Australia. Don Bradman scores 334 in cricket test in England.
1932	Sydney Harbour Bridge opened. Australian Broadcasting Commission (now Corporation) formed.

1939	Beginning of World War II.
1940	Australians in action in North Africa and Middle East.
1941	ALP under John Curtin takes office. War declared on Japan.
1942	War in the Pacific. Darwin bombed. Japanese submarines in Sydney Harbour. Allied headquarters established in Australia under General Douglas MacArthur. Battle of the Coral Sea. Kokoda Trail.
1945	End of World War II.
1948–75	Two million new immigrants, the majority from Europe.
1950–53	Australian forces fight in Korean War.
1951	Referendum to ban Communist Party fails. ANZUS treaty signed.
1954	First visit of Queen Elizabeth II.
1956	ALP split – formation of the DLP. Olympic Games in Melbourne.
1960	First Adelaide Arts Festival.
1961	Radio telescope built at Parkes, NSW.
1964	Collision between HMAS *Melbourne* and HMAS *Voyager*.
1965–72	Australian troops in alliance with US forces in Vietnam War.
1966	Menzies resigns after record term as prime minister. Visit of US President Johnson. Japan takes greatest percentage of Australian exports.
1967	Prime minister Holt drowns. Referendum gives the Commonwealth the right to legislate concerning Aborigines.
1972	ALP under Whitlam gains power.
1973	Sydney Opera House opened. Patrick White wins Nobel prize for literature.
1974	Cyclone Tracy destroys Darwin.
1975	Trust territory of Papua New Guinea becomes independent. Dismissal of Whitlam government by Governor-General Sir John Kerr.
1976	First Vietnamese boat people arrive beginning increased Asian immigration.
1977	Granville rail disaster in Sydney.
1979	Start of uranium mining in the Northern Territory.
1983	Hawke Labor government wins office. Yacht *Australia II* wins America's Cup.
1986	Census records population of 15,602,156.
1987	Resignation of Qld Premier Joh Bjelke-Petersen.

1988	Celebration of bicentennial of European settlement accompanied by Aboriginal protest. New Parliament House in Canberra opened.
1989	Earthquake affects Newcastle, NSW.
1990	Hawke wins record 4th term as Labor prime minister.
1991	Paul Keating successfully challenged Hawke for the Labor Party leadership. He consequently replaced Hawke as prime minister.
1992	Keating's popularity in decline as economic problems continued.
1993	Labor Party won general election, entering fifth term of office.

BYZANTINE EMPIRE

330	Emperor Constantine converted to Christianity and moved his capital to Constantinople.
395	The Roman Empire was divided into eastern and western halves.
476	The Western Empire was overrun by barbarian invaders.
527–565	Emperor Justinian I temporarily recovered Italy, N Africa, and parts of Spain.
7th–8th C	Syria, Egypt, and N Africa were lost to the Muslims, who twice besieged Constantinople (673–77, 718), but the Christian Byzantines maintained their hold on Anatolia.
8th–11th C	The Iconoclastic controversy brought the emperors into conflict with the papacy, and in 1054 the Greek Orthodox Church broke with the Roman.
867–1056	Under the Macedonian dynasty the Byzantine Empire reached the height of its prosperity; the Bulgars proved a formidable danger, but after a long struggle were finally crushed in 1018 by Basil II ('the Bulgar-Slayer'). After Basil's death the Byzantine Empire declined because of internal factions.
1071–73	The Seljuk Turks conquered most of Anatolia.
1204	The Fourth Crusade sacked Constantinople and set Baldwin of Flanders (1171–1205) on the throne of the new Latin (W European) Empire.
1261	The Greeks recaptured the Latin (W European) Empire and restored the Byzantine Empire, but it maintained a precarious existence.
1453	The Turks captured Constantinople and founded the Ottoman Empire.

CANADA

c. 35,000 BC	People arrived in North America from Asia by way of Beringia.
c. 2000	Inuit (Eskimos) began settling Arctic coast from Siberia E to Greenland.
c. AD 1000	Vikings, including Leif Ericsson, landed in NE Canada, and started settlements that did not survive.
1497	John Cabot landed on Cape Breton Island.
1534	Jacques Cartier reached the Gulf of St Lawrence.
1603	Samuel Champlain began his exploration of Canada.
1608	Champlain founded Québec.
1759	James Wolfe captured Québec.
1763	France ceded Canada to Britain under the Treaty of Paris.
1775–83	American Revolution caused Loyalist influx to New Brunswick and Ontario.
1791	Canada divided into English-speaking Upper Canada (much of modern Ontario) and French-speaking Lower Canada (much of modern Québec and mainland Newfoundland).
1793	Alexander Mackenzie reached the Pacific by land.
1812–14	War of 1812 between Britain and the USA. US invasions repelled by both provinces.
1837	Rebellions led by William Lyon Mackenzie in Upper Canada and Louis Joseph Papineau in Lower Canada.
1840	Upper and Lower Canada united to form the Province of Canada.
1867	British North America Act created the Dominion of Canada (Ontario, Québec, Nova Scotia, and New Brunswick).
1869	Uprising, led by Louis Riel, against the Canadian government and the threat of a flood of white settlers into Rupert's Land.
1870	Manitoba created (from part of Rupert's Land) and joined confederation. North West (later Northwest) Territories created.
1871	British Columbia entered confederation.
1873	Prince Edward Island entered confederation.
1885	Northwest Rebellion crushed and leader Louis Riel hanged. Canadian Pacific Railway completed.
1905	Alberta and Saskatchewan formed from the Northwest Territories and entered confederation.
1914–18	World War I – Canadian troops at 2nd Battle of Ypres, Vimy Ridge, Passchendaele, the Somme, and Cambrai.

| 1931 | Canada became an independent nation. Norway renounced its claim to the Sverdrup Islands, confirming Canadian sovereignty in the entire Arctic Archipelago north of the Canadian mainland. |

1931   Canada became an independent nation. Norway renounced its claim to the Sverdrup Islands, confirming Canadian sovereignty in the entire Arctic Archipelago north of the Canadian mainland.

1939–45 World War II – Canadian participation in all theatres.

1949   Newfoundland joined the confederation.

1950–53 Korean War – Canada participated in United Nations force, and subsequently in almost all UN peacekeeping operations.

1957   Progressive Conservatives returned to power after 22 years in opposition.

1961   NDP formed.

1963   Liberals elected under Lester Pearson.

1968   Pearson succeeded by Pierre Trudeau.

1979   Joe Clark, leader of the Progressive Conservatives, formed a minority government; defeated on budget proposals.

1980   Liberals under Trudeau returned with a large majority. Québec referendum rejected demand for independence.

1982   Canada Act removed Britain's last legal control over Canadian affairs; 'patriation' of Canada's constitution.

1983   Clark replaced as leader of the Progressive Conservatives by Brian Mulroney.

1984   Trudeau retired and was succeeded as Liberal leader and prime minister by John Turner. Progressive Conser-vatives won the federal election with a large majority, and Mulroney became prime minister.

1988   Conservatives re-elected with reduced majority on platform of free trade with the USA.

1989   Free-trade agreement signed. Turner resigned as Liberal Party leader, and Ed Broadbent as NDP leader.

1990   Collapse of Meech Lake accord. Canada joined the coalition opposing Iraq's invasion of Kuwait.

1992   Gradual withdrawal of Canadian forces in Europe announced. Self-governing homeland for Inuit approved. Constitutional reform package, the Charlottetown Accord, rejected in national referendum.

1993   Feb: Mulroney resigned leadership of Conservative Party. June: Kim Campbell, the new party leader, became prime minister. North American Free Trade Agreement (NAFTA) with USA and Mexico ratified. Oct: Conservatives defeated in general election. Liberal leader Jean Chretien became prime minister. Dec: Kim Campbell resigned Conservative Party leadership.

CHINA

500,000 BC	The oldest human remains found in China were those of 'Peking man' (*Sinanthropus pekinensis*, later known as *Homo erectus*).
25,000	Humans of the Upper Palaeolithic modern type (*Homo sapiens sapiens*) inhabited the region.
5000	A simple Neolithic agricultural society was established.
c. 2800– c. 2200	The **Sage kings**, a period of agricultural development, known only from legend.
c. 2200– c. 1500	The **Xia dynasty**, a Bronze Age early civilization, with further agricultural developments, including irrigation, and the first known use of writing in this area.
c. 1500– c. 1066	The **Shang dynasty** is the first of which we have documentary evidence. Writing became well developed; bronze vases survive in ceremonial burials. The first Chinese calendar was made.
c. 1066– 221	During the **Zhou dynasty**, the feudal structure of society broke down in a period of political upheaval, though iron, money, and written laws were all in use, and philosophers like Confucius flourished. The dynasty ended in the 'Warring States' period (403–221 BC), with the country divided into small kingdoms.
221–206	The **Qin dynasty** corresponds to the reign of Shi Huangdi, who curbed the feudal nobility and introduced orderly bureaucratic government; he had roads and canals built and began the Great Wall of China to keep out invaders from the north.
206 BC– AD 220	The **Han dynasty** was a long period of peace, during which territory was incorporated, the keeping of historical records was systematized, and an extensive civil service set up. Art and literature flourished, and Buddhism was introduced. The first census was taken in AD 2, registering a population of 57 million. Chinese caravans traded with the Parthians.
220–581	The area was divided into **Three Kingdoms**: the Wei, Shu, and Wu. Confucianism was superseded by Buddhism and Taoism; glass was introduced from the West. After prolonged fighting, the Wei became the most powerful kingdom, eventually founding the Western **Jin dynasty** (265–316), which expanded to take over from the barbarian invaders who ruled much of China at that time, but from 316 to 581 (the Northern

and Southern dynasties era) lost the territory they had gained to the Tatar invaders from the north.

581–618   Reunification came with the **Sui dynasty**: the government was reinstated, the barbarian invasions stopped, and the Great Wall refortified.

618–907   During the **Tang dynasty** the system of government became more highly developed and centralized, and the empire covered most of SE and much of central Asia. Scul-pture, painting, and poetry flourished again, Buddhism spread (8th century), and trade relations were established with the Islamic world and the Byzantine Empire.

907–960   The period known as the **Five Dynasties and Ten Kingdoms** was characterized by war, economic depression, and loss of territory in N China, central Asia, and Korea, but printing was developed, including the first use of paper money, and porcelain was traded to Islamic lands.

960–   The **Song dynasty** was a period of calm and creativity.
1279   Central government was restored, and movable type was invented. At the end of the dynasty, the northern and western frontiers were neglected, and Mongol invasions took place. The Venetian traveller Marco Polo visited the court of the Great Khan in 1275. NE China was controlled by the Liao (945–1125) and Jin (1126–1235) dynasties.

1279–   The **Yuan dynasty** saw the beginning of Mongol rule in
1368   China, with Kublai Khan on the throne in Beijing 1293; there were widespread revolts. Marco Polo served the Kublai Khan.

1368–   The Mongols were expelled by the first of the native Chinese
1644   **Ming dynasty**, who expanded the empire. Chinese ships sailed to the Sunda Islands 1403, Ceylon 1408, and the Red Sea 1430. Mongolia was captured by the second Ming emperor. Architecture developed and Beijing flourished as the new capital. Portuguese explorers reached Macao 1516 and Canton 1517; other Europeans followed. Chinese porcelain arrived in Europe 1580. The Jesuits reached Beijing 1600.

1644–   The last of the dynasties was the **Manchu**, who were non-
1912   Chinese nomads from Manchuria. Initially trade and culture flourished, but during the 19th century it seemed that China would be partitioned among the US and European imperialist nations, since all trade was conducted through treaty ports in their control. The Boxer Rebellion 1900 against Western influence was suppressed by European troops.

1911–12	Revolution broke out, and the infant emperor Henry P'u-i was deposed.
1912	Abdication of the emperor and his government. China became a republic. First parliament met. General Yuan Shih-K'ai became president. Formation of the Guomin-dang (National People's Party), led by Sun Yat-sen.
1913	Second revolution in Nanjing suppressed.
1916–26	Republic divided by warlordism.
1917	Sun Yat-sen became supreme commander of forces in the S. China entered World War I in an attempt to have treaties with Japan annulled and German treaty ports returned. Very few of these aims were achieved.
1918	Sun Yat-sen resigned and reorganized the Guomindang.
1919	Demonstration of Beijing students led to May 4th movement.
1921	Chinese Communist Party founded in Shanghai. Military government abolished by rump parliament and Sun Yat-sen elected president of new government.
1923	Beginnings of cooperation between Guomindang and communists in order to re-unite China. Guomindang manifesto stated 'Three People's Principles' were platform of the party.
1925	Sun Yat-sen died.
1926	Revolutionary Army led by Chiang Kai-shek attacked warlords in N and central regions. It then took Hengzhou, which became the seat of the National Government Nov.
1927	Shanghai and Nanjing fell to the Revolutionary Army. Chiang Kai-shek broke with the Communist Party and liquidated communists in Shanghai. National Govern-ment formed in Nanjing. Suppression of communists and peasant rebellions.
1928	Chiang Kai-shek's forces took Beijing and the unification of China was complete. The Guomindang became the basis for a one-party state. Communist Party created a Red Army in Hunan.
1930–34	Chiang Kai-shek's 'bandit encirclement' campaigns against the communists.
1931	Mukden incident gave pretext for Japanese imperial forces to attack and capture Manchuria.
1932	Japanese set up puppet state of Manchukuo with former emperor P'u-i as head of state. Japanese forces occupied Shanghai.

1933	Armistice with Japan.
1934–35	Red Army undertook Long March from Jiangxi and Fujian provinces in the S to Yan'an in the N.
1935	Mao Zedong became effective head of the Chinese Communist Party in Yan'an.
1937	Marco Polo Bridge incident provided pretext for further Japanese aggression. The interior of China was attacked, Beijing fell, and the capital was moved to Chongqing.
1937–45	Sino-Japanese War. Chiang Kai-shek isolated, but received help from Western powers after Britain and USA entered the war against Japan. Guomindang and communists upheld uneasy truce throughout war.
1943	Chiang Kai-shek met Churchill and Roosevelt in Cairo.
1945	Japanese surrendered in China.
1946	Open warfare between Guomindang, led by Chiang Kai-shek, and communists led by Mao Zedong.
1947	USA failed to organize reconciliation between the two sides. New constitution proclaimed.
1948	Communist took Shanxi and Henan.
1949 Jan	Chiang Kai-shek forced to resign presidency.
1949 Sept	Communists took Beijing. People's Republic of China pro claimed by Mao Zedong.
1954	Soviet-style constitution adopted.
1956–57	Hundred Flowers Movement encouraged criticism of the government.
1958–60	Great Leap Forward commune experiment to achieve 'true communism'.
1960	Withdrawal of Soviet technical advisers.
1962	Sino-Indian border war.
1962–65	Economic recovery programme under Liu Shaoqi; Maoist 'socialist education movement' rectification campaign.
1966–69	Great Proletarian Cultural Revolution; Liu Shaoqi overthrown.
1969	Ussuri River border clashes with USSR.
1970–76	Reconstruction under Mao and Zhou Enlai.
1971	Entry into United Nations.
1972	US president Nixon visited Beijing.
1975	New state constitution. Unveiling of Zhou's 'Four Modernizations' programme.
1976	Deaths of Zhou Enlai and Mao Zedong; appointment of Hua Guofeng as prime minister and Communist Party chair. Vice Premier Deng Xiaoping in hiding. Gang of Four arrested.

1977	Rehabilitation of Deng Xiaoping.
1979	Economic reforms introduced. Diplomatic relations opened with USA. Punitive invasion of Vietnam.
1980	Zhao Ziyang appointed prime minister.
1981	Hu Yaobang succeeded Hua Guofeng as party chair. Imprisonment of Gang of Four.
1982	New state constitution adopted.
1984	'Enterprise management' reforms for industrial sector.
1986	Student prodemocracy demonstrations.
1987	Hu was replaced as party leader by Zhao, with Li Peng as prime minister. Deng left Politburo but remained influential.
1988	Yang Shangkun replaced Li Xiannian as state president. Economic reforms encountered increasing problems; inflation rocketed.
1989	Over 2,000 killed in prodemocracy student demonstrations in Tiananmen Square; international sanctions imposed.
1991	March: European Community and Japanese sanctions lifted. May: normal relations with USSR resumed. Sept: UK prime minister John Major visited Beijing. Nov: relations with Vietnam normalized.
1992	China promised to sign 1968 Nuclear Non-Proliferation Treaty. Historic visit by Japan's emperor.
1993	Jiang Zemin, Chinese Communist Party general secretary, replaced Yang Shangkun as president.

ENGLAND

AD 43	Roman invasion.
5th–7th C	Anglo-Saxons overran all England except Cornwall and Cumberland, forming independent kingdoms including Northumbria, Mercia, Kent, and Wessex.
c. 597	England converted to Christianity by St Augustine.
829	Egbert of Wessex accepted as overlord of all England.
878	Alfred ceded N and E England to the Danish invaders but kept them out of Wessex.
1066	Norman Conquest; England passed into French hands under William the Conqueror.
1172	Henry II became king of Ireland and established a colony there.
1215	King John forced to sign Magna Carta.
1284	Conquest of Wales, begun by the Normans, completed by Edward I.

1295	Model Parliament set up.
1338–1453	Hundred Years' War with France enabled parliament to secure control of taxation and, by impeachment, of the king's choice of ministers.
1348–49	Black Death killed about 30% of the population.
1381	Social upheaval led to the Peasants' Revolt, which was brutally repressed.
1399	Richard II deposed by Parliament for absolutism.
1414	Lollard revolt repressed.
1455–85	Wars of the Roses.
1497	Henry VII ended the power of the feudal nobility with the suppression of the Yorkist revolts.
1529	Henry VIII became head of the Church of England after breaking with Rome.
1536–43	Acts of Union united England and Wales after conquest.
1547	Edward VI adopted Protestant doctrines.
1553	Reversion to Roman Catholicism under Mary I.
1558	Elizabeth I adopted a religious compromise.
1588	Attempted invasion of England by the Spanish Armada.
1603	James I united the English and Scottish crowns; parliamentary dissidence increased.
1642–52	Civil War between royalists and parliamentarians, resulting in victory for Parliament.
1649	Charles I executed and the Commonwealth set up.
1653	Oliver Cromwell appointed Lord Protector.
1660	Restoration of Charles II.
1685	Monmouth's rebellion.
1688	William of Orange invited to take the throne; flight of James II.
1707	Act of Union between England and Scotland under Queen Anne, after which the countries became known as Great Britain.

For further history, see United Kingdom.

EUROPE

3000 BC	Bronze Age civilizations: Minoan, Mycenaean.
1000	Iron Age.
6th–4th C	Greek civilization at its height; Alexander the Great advances eastwards to India.
3rd C	Rome in control of the Italian peninsula.

146	Greece a Roman province, and Carthage destroyed.
1st C	Augustus made the Rhine and Danube the Roman Empire's northern frontiers; see Celts .
AD 1st C	Britain brought within the Roman Empire
2nd C	Roman Empire ceased to expand.
4th C	Christianity the established religion of the Roman Empire, which halved into E and W empires (see Byzantine empires).
4th–6th C	W Europe overrun by Anglo Saxons, Franks, Goths, Lombards. W Roman empire fell 476. Middle Ages begin; feudalism prevails.
7th–8th C	Christendom threatened by the Moors (Muslim Arabs) via the Mediterranean countries.
800	Charlemagne given title of emperor by the Pope; Holy Roman empire begins.
1073	Gregory VII began 200 years of conflict between the powers of the empire and papacy.
1096–1272	Crusades to take Jerusalem.
12th C	Setting up of German, Flemish, and Italian city states, which in the 14th–15th centuries fostered the Renaissance.
1453	Byzantine empire falls to the Turks.
16th–17th C	Dominated by rivalry of France and the Habsburgs, the Protestant Reformation, and the Catholic Counter Reformation.
17th C	Absolute monarchy came to prevail (Louis XIV) in Europe, although in Britain supremacy of Parliament established by Civil War.
18th C	War of the Austrian Succession and Seven Years' War ended in the loss of the French colonial empire to Britain and the establishment of Prussia as Europe's military power.
1789–95	French Revolution led to the Revolutionary and Napoleonic wars.
1821–29	Greek War of Independence marked the end of Turkish control of the Balkans.
1848	Year of revolutions.
1914–1918	World War I arose from the Balkan question, Franco–German rivalry, and colonial differences; it destroyed the Austrian, Russian, and Turkish empires and paved the way for the Russian Revolution and the formation of the USSR.
1933	Hitler came to power in a defeated, impoverished Germany. His geopolitical aggression caused World War II.

1939–45   World War II resulted in decline of European colonial rule in Africa and Asia; emergence of Soviet power, and most of Western Europe under the military aegis of the USA (NATO); the Cold War begins.

1957   Establishment of the European Economic Community, the 'Common Market'.

1973   Enlargement of the European Community to include Britain, Denmark, and the Irish Republic.

1979   First direct elections to the European Parliament.

1989–90   Beginning of democratization of Eastern bloc, including USSR, Poland, Romania, Czechoslovakia, East Germany, Lithuania. Unification of Germany.

1991   Baltic republics of Estonia, Latvia, and Lithuania regain independence; other Soviet republics follow.

1992   European Community becomes a single market.

FRANCE

5th C BC   France, then called **Gaul** (*Gallia* by the Romans) was invaded by Celtic peoples.

57–51   Conquest by the Roman general Julius Caesar.

AD 1st–   During Roman rule the inhabitants of France accepted Roman
5th C   civilization and the Latin language. As the empire declined, Germanic tribes overran the country and settled.

481–511   A Frankish chief, Clovis, brought the other tribes under his rule, accepted Christianity, and made Paris the capital.

511–751   Under Clovis' successors, the Merovingians, the country sank into anarchy.

741–68   Unity was restored by Pepin, founder of the Carolingian dynasty.

768–814   Charlemagne made France the centre of the Holy Roman Empire.

912   The province of Normandy was granted as a duchy to the Viking leader Rollo, whose invading Norsemen had settled here.

987   The first king of the House of Capet assumed the crown. Under Charlemagne's weak successors the great nobles had become semi-independent. The Capets established rule in the district around Paris but were surrounded by vassals stronger than themselves.

11th–13th C	The power of the Capetian dynasty was gradually extended, with the support of the church and the towns-people.
1337–1453	In the Hundred Years' War Charles VII expelled the English from France, aided by Joan of Arc.
1483	Burgundy and Brittany were annexed. Through the policies of Louis XI the restoration of the royal power was achieved.
1503–1697	Charles VIII's Italian wars initiated a struggle with Spain for supremacy in W Europe that lasted for two centuries.
1562–98	Protestantism (Huguenot) was adopted by a party of the nobles for political reasons; the result was a succession of civil wars, fought under religious slogans.
1589–1610	Henry IV restored peace, established religious toleration, and made the monarchy absolute.
1634–48	The ministers Richelieu and Mazarin, by their intervention in the Thirty Years' War, secured Alsace and made France the leading power in Europe.
1643–1763	Louis XIV embarked on an aggressive policy that united Europe against him; in his reign began the conflict with Britain that lost France its colonies in Canada and India in the War of the Spanish Succession (1701–14), War of the Austrian Succession (1756–58), and Seven Years' War (1756–63).
1789–99	The French Revolution abolished feudalism and absolute monarchy, but failed to establish democracy.
1799–1815	Napoleon's military dictatorship was aided by foreign wars (1792–1802, 1803–15). The Bourbon monarchy was restored 1814 with Louis XVIII.
1830	Charles X's attempt to substitute absolute for limited monarchy provoked a revolution, which placed his cousin, Louis Philippe, on the throne.
1848	In the Feb revolution Louis Philippe was overthrown and the Second Republic set up.
1852–70	The president of the republic, Louis Napoleon, Napoleon I's nephew, restored the empire 1852, with the title of Napoleon III. His expansionist foreign policy ended in defeat in the Franco-Prussian War and the foundation of the Third Republic.
1863–1946	France colonized Indochina, parts of N Africa, and the S Pacific.
1914	France entered World War I.

1936–37	A radical-socialist-communist Popular Front alliance introduced many social reforms.
1939	France entered World War II.
1940	The German invasion allowed the extreme right to set up a puppet dictatorship under Pétain in Vichy, but resistance was maintained by the *maquis* and the Free French under de Gaulle.
1944	Liberation from the Nazis.
1944–46	Provisional government headed by General Charles de Gaulle; start of Fourth Republic.
1954	Indochina achieved independence.
1956	Morocco and Tunisia achieved independence.
1957	Entry into European Economic Community.
1958	Recall of de Gaulle after Algerian crisis; start of Fifth Republic.
1959	De Gaulle became president.
1962	Algeria achieved independence.
1966	France withdrew from military wing of NATO.
1968	'May events' uprising of students and workers.
1969	De Gaulle resigned after referendum defeat; Georges Pompidou became president.
1974	Giscard d'Estaing elected president.
1981	François Mitterrand elected Fifth Republic's first socialist president.
1986	'Cohabitation' experiment, with the conservative Jacques Chirac as prime minister.
1988	Mitterrand re-elected. Moderate socialist Michel Rocard became prime minister. Matignon Accord on future of New Caledonia approved by referendum.
1989	Greens gained 11% of vote in elections to European Parliament.
1991	French forces were part of the US-led coalition in the Gulf War. Edith Cresson became prime minister; Mitterrand's popularity rating fell rapidly.
1992	March: Socialist Party humiliated in regional and local elections; Greens and National Front polled strongly. April: Cresson replaced by Pierre Bérégovoy. Sept: referendum narrowly endorsed Maastricht Treaty.
1993	March: Socialist Party suffered heavy defeat in National Assembly elections. Edouard Balladur appointed prime minister; 'cohabitation' government re-established. May: Bérégovoy committed suicide. Michel Rocard appointed PS leader.

GERMANY

BC–AD 4th C	The W Germanic peoples, originating in Scandinavia, moved into the region between the rivers Rhine, Elbe, and Danube, where they were confined by the Roman Empire.
496	The Frankish king Clovis conquered the Alemanni.
768–814	The reign of Holy Roman Emperor Charlemagne, who extended his authority over Germany and imposed Christianity on the Saxons.
814–919	After Charlemagne's death Germany was separated from France under its own kings while the local officials or dukes became virtually independent.
919–1002	Central power was restored by the Saxon dynasty. Otto I, who in 962 revived the title of emperor, began colonizing the Slav lands east of the river Elbe.
1075–1250	A feud between emperors and popes enabled the Germanic princes to recover their independence.
12th C	German expansion eastwards (the *Drang nach Osten*) into lands between the Elbe and the Oder.
1157	Frederick Barbarossa annexed Silesia from Poland.
1493–1519	A temporary revival of imperial power took place under Maximilian I.
1521	The Diet of Worms at which Charles V confronted the Protestant Martin Luther. The Reformation increased Germany's disunity.
1618–48	The Thirty Years' War reduced the empire to a mere name and destroyed Germany's economic and cultural life.
1740–86	The rise of Brandenburg-Prussia as a military power, which had begun in the 17th century, reached its height under Frederick II.
1806	The French emperor Napoleon united W Germany in the Confederation of the Rhine and introduced the ideas and reforms of the French Revolution; his reforms were subsequently imitated in Prussia. The Holy Roman Empire was abolished.
1848	Ideas of democracy and national unity inspired the unsuccessful revolutions of 1848.
1867	The North German Confederation, under the leadership of Prussia, was formed.
1871	Under Chancellor Bismarck's leadership, the German Empire was formed after victorious wars with Austria and France. William I of Prussia became emperor.

1914–18	World War I: Germany and other Central Powers at war with Britain, France, and Russia.
1918	A revolution overthrew the monarchy; the social democrats seized power and established the democratic **Weimar Republic**.
1922–23	Rampant inflation. In 1922 one dollar was worth 50 marks; in 1923 one dollar was worth 2.5 trillion marks.
1929–33	The economic crisis brought Germany close to revolution, until in 1933 the reaction manoeuvred the Nazis into power with Adolf Hitler as chancellor.
1933–39	At home the Nazis solved the unemployment problem by a vast rearmament programme; they suspended the democratic constitution and ruthlessly destroyed all opposition. Abroad, the policy of geopolitical aggression led to war.
1939–45	World War II: Germany (from 1940 in an alliance known as the Axis with Italy and Japan) attacked and occupied neighbouring countries, but was defeated by the Allies (the UK and Commonwealth, France 1939–40, the USSR and the USA from 1941, and China).
1945–49	Germany was divided, within its 1937 frontiers, into British, US, French, and Soviet occupation zones.
1949	Germany was partitioned into the communist **German Democratic Republic** and the capitalist **German Federal Republic** under the 'Basic Law' Constitution with Konrad Adenauer as chancellor; establishment of the German Democratic Republic as an independent state.
1953	Uprising in East Berlin suppressed by Soviet troops.
1954	Grant of full sovereignty to both West Germany and East Germany.
1957	West Germany was a founder-member of the European Economic Community; recovery of Saarland from France.
1961	Construction of Berlin Wall.
1963	Retirement of Chancellor Adenauer.
1964	Treaty of Friendship and Mutual Assistance signed between East Germany and USSR.
1969	Willy Brandt became chancellor of West Germany.
1971	Erich Honecker elected SED leader in East Germany.
1972	Basic Treaty between West Germany and East Germany; treaty ratified 1973, normalizing relations between the two.
1974	Resignation of Brandt; Helmut Schmidt became chancellor.
1975	East German friendship treaty with USSR renewed for 25 years.

1982	Helmut Kohl became West German chancellor.
1987	Official visit of Honecker to the Federal Republic.
1988	Death of Franz-Josef Strauss, leader of the West German Bavarian CSU.
1989	West Germany: rising support for far right in local and European elections, declining support for Kohl. East Germany: mass exodus to West Germany began. Honecker replaced by Egon Krenz. National borders opened in Nov, including Berlin Wall. Reformist Hans Modrow appointed prime minister. Krenz replaced.
1990	March: East German multiparty elections won by a coalition led by the right-wing CDU. 3 Oct: official reunification of East and West Germany. 2 Dec: first all-German elections since 1932, resulting in a victory for Kohl.
1991	Kohl's popularity declined after tax increase. The CDU lost its Bundesrat majority to the SPD. Racism continued with violent attacks on foreigners.
1992	Neo-Nazi riots against immigrants continued.
1993	Unemployment exceeded 7%; severe recession. Outbreaks of racist violence. Restrictions on refugee admission introduced.
1994	Kohl's nominee, Roman Herzog, elected president.

INDIA

2500–1500 BC	Harappan civilization of planned, defended cities in the Indus valley.
1500–1200	Aryan peoples invaded from the Iranian plateau and began settlement of the Ganges valley. Brahmanism (an early stage of Hinduism) developed, as did Sanskrit language. Caste system emerged. Iron used in agriculture. Start of India's 'second urbanization.'
c. 600	Rise of Magadha kingdom.
527	Death of Vardhamana Mahavira, founder of the Jain religion.
483	First council of Buddhists held to establish the teachings of Gautama Buddha.
362–321	Nandu dynasty.
327–325	Expedition of Alexander the Great into India.
325–185	First Hindu empire in N India under Chandragupta, who founded the Mauryan dynasty.

268–231	Reign of Asoka, with two-thirds of India under his control. Capital established at Pataliputra.
185	Empire began to break down into smaller kingdoms.
c. AD 78	Accession of Kanishka, Kusana king of the northwest.
c. 240	Kusanas overthrown by Sassanians.
320–480	Gupta dynasty reunited N India.
c. 500	Huns secured control over NW India.
600–42	Establishment of Pallava and Chalukya power in S India.
606–47	Harsha-vardhana ruled as king of Kanauj.
c. 700	Buddhism driven out of India by Hinduism.
712	Arab Muslim invasions of Indus valley began.
740	Chalukyas defeated the Pallavas.
c. 750	Pala dynasty founded in E India by Gopala.
c. 840	Pratiharas rose under King Bhoja.
c. 907	Chola power established in S India.
997–1030	Mahmud the Great of Ghazni mounted campaigns against India and annexed Punjab.
1110	Visnuvardharna and Hoysalas rose in Deccan.
1162–1206	Muhammad Ghuri destroyed the Ghaznavid empire and defeated Prithviraj Chauhan at Battle of Tarain (1192).
1206	Sultanate of Delhi established.
1221	Genghis Khan advanced as far as the Indus.
1296–1316	Alauddin Khalji finally defeated the Rajput princes and repelled Mongol incursions.
1325–51	Sultanate extended by Muhammad ibn Tughluq.
1336	Kingdom of Vijayanagara founded in S India.
1347	Bahmani kingdom founded in Deccan.
1398–99	Tamerlane invaded, annexing Punjab and limiting the power of the sultanate.
1414–50	Rule of the Sayyids at Delhi.
1451	Accession of Bahlol Lodi at Delhi.
1505	First Portuguese trading contacts.
1526	Last Muslim invasion of India culminated in Battle of Panipat, where Babur defeated the sultan of Delhi and established the Mogul empire.
1539	Death of Guru Nanak, founder of Sikhism.
1556–1605	Reign of Emperor Akbar, who pacified N India. Edicts on religious toleration and rights for the Hindu population.
1600	(British) East India company formed to establish trade with the subcontinent.
1609	Dutch expelled the Portuguese from Sri Lanka.

1628–58	Shah Jahan extended the Mogul empire into the Deccan.
1658–1707	Reign of Aurangzeb. Great extension of the Mogul empire, but internal dissent caused by persecution and taxation of Hindus.
1674	Maratha (Mahratta) kingdom established by Sivaji.
1725	A Nizamat, largely independent of Moguls, was established at Hyderabad.
1739	Persian king Nadir Shah invaded India and plundered Delhi. With Mogul authority waning, Bengal and Oudh effectively broke away.
1746	Increasing struggle between British and French for influence in India. French success, under Dupleix, was followed by resistance organized by Robert Clive.
1757	British victory over N Indian forces at Battle of Plassey established Clive as governor of Bengal.
1761	Marathas defeated by Afghans at Battle of Panipat. Haidar Ail assumed power in Mysore.
1764	Mogul imperial coalition defeated at Buxar by the East India Company, which secured the dewani (state ruled by a prince) of Bengal 1765.
1774–85	East India Company became an administrative agency. Governor General Warren Hastings reorganized the legal and administrative system and defeated the main anti-British coalition of Indian princes.
1799	Ranjit Singh became ruler of a Sikh state in the Punjab. Tipu, sultan of Mysore, killed by British troops.
1803–04	British defeated Maratha coalition in N India.
1813	East India Company's trading monopoly abolished.
1814–16	Gurkha War led to British annexation of Nepal.
1817–18	Third Maratha War. Maratha and Rajput states sub-jugated.
1824–26	First Burmese War. British annexed Tenasserim, Arakan, and Assam.
1839–42	First Afghan War. British evacuated Punjab.
1849	British annexed Punjab.
1852	Second Burmese War. Lower Myanmar annexed by British.
1856	British annexation of Oudh (Awadh).
1857	Anti-British feeling erupted into mutiny of Indian troops in N India and wider civil rebellion (Indian Mutiny). Mogul Bahadur Shah II proclaimed emperor of India in Delhi.
1858	Mutiny suppressed, but reforms took place. East India Company dissolved and India became a viceroyalty under the British crown.

1861	Central provincial legislative councils formed in Bombay and Madras under the Indian Councils Act.
1876–78	Famine killed five million people.
1885	Indian National Congress founded in Bombay as a focus for nationalism.
1896–1900	Series of famines claimed another seven million lives.
1905	Partition of the province of Bengal provoked the Swadeshi movement, an Indian boycott on buying British goods.
1906	All-India Muslim League founded at Dhaka.
1909	Indian Councils Act (Morley-Minto reforms) introduced the elective principle to the central legislative council and provided for separate electorates for Muslims on all councils.
1911	At his coronation durbar (court), George V announced the reunification of Bengal and the transfer of the capital of British India from Calcutta to Delhi.
1915	M K Gandhi returned to India from South Africa.
1918	Influenza pandemic killed 17 million Indians.
1919	Rowlatt Act, enabling the government to try political cases without juries, provoked riots. Amritsar massacre saw 379 killed. Government of India Act (Montagu-Chelmsford reforms) provided for diarchy, with Indians being given a separate legislature, a share in provincial government, and control over certain 'transferred' ministries, including education and health.
1920–22	Gandhi won control of Congress, which became committed to *swaraj* (self-rule), and launched non-cooperation campaign. M A Jinnah, leader of the Muslim League, left Congress.
1922–24	Gandhi imprisoned.
1930	Gandhi arrested after undertaking civil disobedience salt march directed against the Salt Tax.
1935	Government of India Act provided for Indian control of the federal legislature, with defence and external affairs remaining the viceroy's responsibility, and for provincial parliamentary self-government.
1940	Lahore session of Muslim League demanded that India be partitioned along religious lines.
1942	Much of Congress leadership arrested after it commenced a 'Quit India' campaign.
1943–44	Bengal famine claimed 1.5 million lives.
1945	New Labour government in UK sought 'an early realization of self-government in India'.

1947	British India partitioned into the independent dominions of India (predominantly Hindu), and East and West Pakistan (mainly Muslim). Bloody communal riots broke out in Punjab as Hindu, Sikh, and Muslim refugees fled to the new states.
1947	Independence achieved from Britain.
1950	Federal republic proclaimed.
1962	Border skirmishes with China.
1964	Death of prime minister Nehru. Border war with Pakistan over Kashmir.
1966	Indira Gandhi became prime minister.
1971	War with Pakistan leading to creation of Bangladesh.
1975–77	State of emergency proclaimed.
1977–79	Janata Party government in power.
1980	Indira Gandhi returned in landslide victory.
1984	Indira Gandhi assassinated; Rajiv Gandhi elected with record majority.
1987	Signing of 'Tamil' Colombo peace accord with Sri Lanka; Indian Peacekeeping Force (IPKF) sent there. Public revelation of Bofors corruption scandal.
1988	New opposition party, Janata Dal, established by former finance minister V P Singh. Voting age lowered from 21 to 18.
1989	Congress (I) lost majority in general election, after Gandhi associates implicated in financial misconduct; Janata Dal minority government formed, with V P Singh prime minister.
1990	Central rule imposed in Jammu and Kashmir. V P Singh resigned; new minority Janata Dal government formed by Chandra Shekhar. Interethnic and religious violence in Punjab and elsewhere.
1991	Central rule imposed in Tamil Nadu. Shekhar resigned; elections called for May. May: Rajiv Gandhi assassinated. June: elections resumed, resulting in a Congress (I) minority government led by P V Narasimha Rao. Separatist violence continued.
1992	Congress (I) won control of state assembly and a majority in parliament in Punjab state elections. Split in Janata Dal opposition resulted in creation of National Front coalition party (including rump of Janata Dal party). Widespread communal violence killed over 1,200 people, mainly Muslims, following destruction of a mosque in Ayodhya, N India, by Hindu extremists.
1993	Sectarian violence in Bombay left 500 dead. Rao narrowly survived confidence vote in parliament.

INDUSTRIAL REVOLUTION

1709	Abraham Darby introduced coke smelting to his ironworks at Coalbrookdale in Shropshire.
1712	The first workable steam powered engine was developed by Thomas Newcomen.
1730	The seed drill was invented by Jethro Tull. This was a critical point of the agricultural revolution which freed labour from the fields and lowered crop prices.
1740	Crucible steelmaking was discovered by accident by Benjamin Huntsman, a clockmaker of Doncaster.
1759	The first Canal Act was passed by the British parliament; this led to the construction of a national network of inland waterways for transport and industrial supplies. By 1830 there were 4,000 miles of canals in Britain.
1763	The spinning jenny, which greatly accelerated cotton spinning, was invented by James Hargreaves in Blackburn.
1764	Pierre Trosanquet, a French engineer, developed a new method of road building. Similar techniques were used by Thomas Telford in Britain to build modern roads from 1803.
1765	James Watt produced a more reliable and efficient version of the Newcomen engine.
1779	The spinning mule, which made the production of fine yarns by machine possible, was developed in Bolton by Samuel Crompton.
1785	The power loom marked the start of the mechanized textile industry.
1785–99	Techniques of mass production of interchangeable parts were developed by the arms industry in the United States, led by Eli Whitney.
1793	The problem of supplying cotton fast enough for the textile industry was solved by Eli Whitney's cotton gin.
1797	The first true industrial lathe was invented, virtually simultaneously, by Henry Maudslay in England and David Wilkinson in the USA.
1802	The first electric battery capable of mass production was designed by William Cruickshank in England.
1811–16	Textile workers, known as 'Luddites' staged widespread protests against low pay and unemployment in Nottinghamshire, which involved destroying new machines.

c. 1812	The population of Manchester passed 100,000.
c. 1813	Industrial employment overtook agricultural employment in England for the first time.
1825	The first regular railway services started between Stockton and Darlington in north east England.
1826	The Journeymen Steam Engine Fitters, the first substantial industrial trade union, was established in Manchester.
1829	The 'Rainhill trials' showed the power of steam engines, especially Stephenson's 'Rocket'.
1831–52	British industrial production doubled.
1832	Hippolyte Pixii of France produced a prototype electricity generator using magnets.
1832	The Reform Act concerning elections to the British parliament gave representation to the industrial cities.
1833	The first effective Factory Act was passed in Britain regulating child labour in cotton mills.
c. 1840	The USA became the world leader for railroads, with over 3,000 miles laid. By 1860 this would rise to 30,000.
1840s	Vanderbilt and Astor became the most prominent millionaires of the industrial age.
1842	Cotton industry workers in England staged a widespread strike.
1846	Repeal of the Corn Law in Britain reduced agricultural prices, thereby helping industry.
1851	Britain celebrated its industrial achievements in the Great Exhibition.
1852–80	British industrial production doubled again.
1858	The 'great stink' of London dramatized the increasing pollution in the cities.
c. 1860	New York City became the first US city with over a million inhabitants.

IRELAND

432	St Patrick's mission to Ireland.
563	St Columba founded the monastery at Iona.
590	St Columbanus sailed to France.
795	First Viking raided on Ireland.
841	Vikings found Dublin.

1002	Brian Boru acknowledged High King of Ireland.
1014	Brian Boru killed as he defeats Norsemen at Battle of Clontarf.
1169	Norman invasion of Ireland began.
1171	Henry II landed at Waterford.
1175	Treaty of Windsor.
1315	Edward Bruce invaded Ireland.
1318	Edward Bruce killed at Battle of Faughart.
1366	Statutes of Kilkenny.
1394	First visit of Richard II to Ireland.
1399	Second visit of Richard II to Ireland.
1494	Poyning's parliament.
1513	Rule of Garret More, Earl of Kildare.
1534	Rebellion of 'Silken Thomas'.
1541	Irish parliament confirmed Henry VIII as king of Ireland.
1569	First Desmond rebellion.
1579	Second Desmond rebellion.
1586	Plantation of Munster.
1594	Rebellion of Hugh O'Neill, Earl of Tyrone.
1598	Battle of the Yellow Ford.
1601	Battle of Kinsale; O'Neill defeated.
1603	Treaty of Mellifont.
1607	Flight of the Earls.
1609	Plantation of Ulster.
1633	Sir Thomas Wentworth became Lord Deputy of Ireland.
1641	Ulster rising began.
1642	Confederation of Kilkenny formed.
1646	Owen Roe O'Neill defeated Robert Monro at Battle of Benburb.
1649	Oliver Cromwell captured Drogheda and Wexford.
1652	Land confiscation began.
1681	Oliver Plunkett executed in London.
1689	Siege of Londonderry.
1690	William III won Battle of the Boyne.
1691	Treaty of Limerick, followed by land confiscation.
1695	Penal laws introduced against Catholics.
1720	Act declaring British parliament's right to legislate for Ireland passed.
1779	Volunteers paraded in Dublin; trade restrictions repealed.
1782	Convention of Volunteers at Dungannon; Irish parliamentary independence conceded.
1791	Society of United Irishmen formed.
1792	Catholic Relief Acts eased penal laws against Catholics.

1795	Orange Order founded in Co Armagh.
1798	United Irishmen's rising failed; Wolfe Tone committed suicide.
1800	Act of Union established United Kingdom of Great Britain and Ireland. Effective 1801.
1823	Catholic Association founded by Daniel O'Connell to campaign for Catholic political rights.
1828	O'Connell elected for County Clare; forced granting of rights for Catholics to sit in Parliament.
1829	Catholic Emancipation Act.
1838	Tithe Act (abolishing payment) removed a major source of discontent.
1840	Franchise in Ireland reformed. 'Young Ireland' formed.
1846–51	Potato famine resulted in widespread death and emigration. Population reduced by 20%.
1850	Irish Franchise Act extended voters from 61,000 to 165,000.
1858	Fenian Brotherhood formed.
1867	Fenian insurrection failed.
1869	Church of Ireland disestablished.
1870	Land Act provided greater security for tenants but failed to halt agrarian disorders. Protestant Isaac Butt formed Home Government Association (Home Rule League).
1874	Home Rule League won 59 Parliamentary seats and adopted a policy of obstruction.
1880	Charles Stuart Parnell became leader of Home Rulers, dominated by Catholic groups. 'Boycotts' against landlords unwilling to agree to fair rents.
1881	Land Act greeted with hostility. Parnell imprisoned. 'No Rent' movement began.
1882	'Kilmainham Treaty' between government and Parnell agreed conciliation. Chief Secretary Cavendish and Under Secretary Burke murdered in Phoenix Park, Dublin.
1885	Franchise Reform gave Home Rulers 85 seats in new parliament and balance between Liberals and Tories. Home Rule Bill rejected.
1886	Home Rule Bill rejected again.
1890	Parnell cited in divorce case, which split Home Rule movement.
1893	Second Home Rule Bill defeated in House of Lords; Gaelic League founded.
1900	Irish Nationalists reunited under Redmond. 82 MPs elected.
1902	Sinn Féin founded by Arthur Griffith.

1906	Bill for devolution of power to Ireland rejected by Nationalists.
1910	Sir Edward Carson led Unionist opposition to Home Rule.
1912	Home Rule Bill for whole of Ireland introduced. (Protestant) Ulster Volunteers formed to resist.
1913	Home Rule Bill defeated in House of Lords but overridden. (Catholic) Irish Volunteers founded in the South.
1914	Nationalists persuaded to exclude Ulster from Bill for six years but Carson rejected it. Curragh 'mutiny' cast doubt on reliability of British troops against Protestants. Extensive gun-running by both sides. World War I deferred implementation.
1916	Easter Rising: nationalists against British rule seized the Dublin general post office and proclaimed a republic; the revolt was suppressed by the British army and most of the leaders were executed.
1918–21	Guerrilla warfare against British army led to split in rebel forces.
1921	Anglo-Irish Treaty resulted in creation of the Irish Free State (Southern Ireland).
1937	Independence achieved from Britain.

Republic of Ireland

1949	Eire left the Commonwealth and became the Republic of Ireland.
1973	Fianna Fáil defeated after 40 years in office; Liam Cosgrave formed a coalition government.
1977	Fianna Fáil returned to power, with Jack Lynch as prime minister.
1979	Lynch resigned, succeeded by Charles Haughey.
1981	Garret Fitzgerald formed a coalition.
1983	New Ireland Forum formed, but rejected by the British government.
1985	Anglo-Irish Agreement signed.
1986	Protests by Ulster Unionists against the agreement.
1987	General election won by Charles Haughey.
1988	Relations with UK at low ebb because of disagreement over extradition decisions.
1989	Haughey failed to win majority in general election. Progressive Democrats given cabinet positions in coalition government.
1990	Mary Robinson elected president; John Bruton became Fine Gael leader.
1992	Jan: Haughey resigned after losing parliamentary majority.

Feb: Albert Reynolds became Fianna Fáil leader and prime minister. June: National referendum approved ratification of Maastricht Treaty. Nov: Reynolds lost confidence vote; election result inconclusive.

1993   Fianna Fáil–Labour coalition formed; Reynolds re-elected prime minister. May: Irish president, Mary Robinson, meets Queen Elizabeth in London. Dec: Major and Reynolds issue joint Anglo-Irish peace proposal for Northern Ireland, the Downing Street Declaration. Six-year national development plan announced.

IRELAND, NORTHERN: RECENT HISTORY

1967   Northern Ireland Civil Rights Association set up to press for equal treatment for Catholics in the provinces.

1968   Series of civil rights marches sparked off rioting and violence, especially in Londonderry.

1969   Election results weakened Terence O'Neil's Unionist government. Further rioting led to call-up of (Protestant-based) B-Specials to Royal Ulster Constabulary. Chichester-Clark replaced O'Neil. Irish Republican Army (IRA) split into 'official' and more radical 'provisional' wings. Resumption of IRA activities: urban guerrilla warfare in N and kidnap and murder in S. RUC disarmed and B-Specials replaced by nonsectarian Ulster Defence Regiment (UDR). British Army deployed in Belfast and Londonderry.

1971   First British soldier killed. Brian Faulkner replaced Chichester-Clark. IRA stepped up bombing campaign. Internment of people suspected of IRA membership introduced.

1972   'Bloody Sunday' in Londonderry when British troops fired on demonstrators: 13 killed. Direct rule from Westminster introduced. Constitution suspended. IRA extended bombing campaign to mainland England. Seven soldiers killed in bomb attack in Aldershot.

1973   Sunningdale Agreement, to establish Council of Ireland with representatives from N and S.

1974   'Power sharing' between Protestant and Catholic groups tried but failed. Bombs in Guildford and Birmingham caused a substantial number of fatalities.

1976	British Ambassador in Dublin, Christopher Ewart Biggs, assassinated. Ulster Peace Movement founded by Betty Williams and Mairead Corrigan, later awarded Nobel Prize for Peace.
1979	British MP Airey Neave assassinated by Irish National Liberation Army (INLA) at the House of Commons.
1980	Meeting of British Prime Minister Margaret Thatcher and Irish premier Charles Haughey on a peaceful settlement to the Irish question. Hunger strikes and 'dirty protests' started by Republican prisoners in pursuit of political status.
1981	Hunger strikes by detainees of Maze Prison led to deaths of Bobby Sands and nine other hunger strikers; Anglo-Irish Intergovernmental Council formed.
1982	Northern Ireland Assembly created to devolve legislative and executive powers back to the province. Social Democratic Labour Party (19%) and Sinn Féin (10%) boycotted the assembly.
1984	Series of reports from various groups on the future of the province. IRA bomb at Conservative Party conference in Brighton killed five people. Second Anglo-Irish Intergovernmental Council summit meeting agreed to oppose violence and cooperate on security; Britain rejected ideas of confederation or joint sovereignty.
1985	Meeting of Margaret Thatcher and Irish premier Garrett Fitzgerald at Hillsborough produced Anglo-Irish agreement on the future of Ulster; regarded as a sell-out by Unionists.
1986	Unionist opposition to Anglo-Irish agreement included protests and strikes. Loyalist violence against police and Unionist MPs boycotted Westminster.
1987	IRA bombed British Army base in West Germany. Unionist boycott of Westminster ended. Extradition clauses of Anglo-Irish Agreement approved in Eire. IRA bombed Remembrance Day service at Enniskillen, killing 11 people – later admitted it to be a 'mistake'.
1988	Three IRA bombers killed by security forces on Gibraltar.
1989	After serving fourteen years in prison, the 'Guildford Four' were released when their convictions were ruled unsound by the Court of Appeal.
1990	Anglo-Irish Agreement threatened when Eire refused extraditions. Convictions of 'Birmingham Six' also called into question and sent to the Court of Appeal.

1991   IRA renewed bombing campaign on British mainland, targeting a meeting of the cabinet in Downing Street and mainline railway stations. Formal talks on political future of Northern Ireland initiated by Peter Brooke, Secretary of State for Northern Ireland.

1992   Jan: government sent 100 extra troops following further acts of terrorism. June: leaders of four main political parties as well as British and Irish government ministers held round-table talks for first time in 70 years; and agenda for further talks on the future of the province agreed. Aug: UDA officially proscribed as an illegal organization. Nov: round-table talks of future of province ended without agreement.

1993   May: Northern Ireland Secretary, Sir Patrick Mayhew, denied secret talks with IRA, but it emerged that there had been clandestine contact between the government and Sinn Fein/IRA representatives on possible end to conflict. June: Irish president Mary Robinson met Sinn Fein leader Gerry Adams during visit to Belfast. Aug: talks began between John Hulme, leader of SDLP, and Gerry Adams, president of Sinn Fein. Dec: John Major and the Irish prime minister Albert Reynolds issued joint Anglo-Irish peace proposal for Northern Ireland, the Downing Street Declaration. Gerry Adams called for 'direct and unconditional talks' between Britain and Ireland and Sinn Fein/IRA.

NORTH AMERICA: EARLY HISTORY

---

c. 35,000   American Indians entered North America from Asia.
BC

c. 9000   Marmes man, earliest human remains.

300   Earliest Moundbuilder sites.

c. 1000   Leif Ericsson reached North America.
AD

12th–   Height of the Moundbuilder and Pueblo cultures.
14th C

1492   Columbus first sighted land in the Caribbean 12 Oct.

1497   Giovanni Caboto reached Canada.

1565   First Spanish settlements in Florida.

1585   First attempted English settlement in North Carolina.

1607   First permanent English settlement, Jamestown, Virginia.

RUSSIA AND THE SOVIET UNION

9th–10th C	Viking chieftains established their own rule in Novgorod, Kiev, and other cities.
10th–12 C	Kiev temporarily united the Russian peoples into an empire. Christianity was introduced from Constantinople 988.
13th C	The Mongols (the Golden Horde) overran the southern steppes 1223, compelling the Russian princes to pay tribute.
14th C	Byelorussia and Ukraine came under Polish rule.
1462–1505	Ivan the Great, Grand Duke of Muscovy, threw off the Mongol yoke and united the northwest.
1547–84	Ivan the Terrible assumed the title of tsar and conquered Kazan and Astrakhan. During his reign the colonization of Siberia began.
1613	The first Romanov tsar, Michael, was elected after a period of chaos.
1667	Following a Cossack revolt, E Ukraine was reunited with Russia.
1682–1725	Peter the Great modernized the bureaucracy and army. He founded a navy and a new capital, St Petersburg; introduced Western education; and wrested the Baltic seaboard from Sweden. By 1700 the colonization of Siberia had reached the Pacific.
1762–96	Catherine the Great annexed the Crimea and part of Poland and recovered W Ukraine and White Russia.
1798–1814	Russia intervened in the Revolutionary and Napoleonic Wars (1798–1801, 1805–07) and after repelling Napoleon's invasion, took part in his overthrow (1812–14).
1827–29	War with Turkey resulted from Russian attempts to dominate the Balkans.
1853–56	The Crimean War.
1858–60	The treaties of Aigun 1858 and Peking 1860 were imposed on China, annexing territories north of the Amur and east of the Ussuri rivers.
1861	Serfdom was abolished (on terms unfavourable to the peasants). A rapid growth of industry followed, a working-class movement developed, and revolutionary ideas spread, culminating in the assassination of Alexander II 1881.
1877–78	Balkan war with Turkey.
1898	The Social Democratic Party was founded.

1904–05	The occupation of Manchuria resulted in war with Japan.
1905	A revolution, although suppressed, compelled the tsar to accept a parliament (the Duma) with limited powers.
1914	Russo-German rivalries in the Balkans, which had brought Russia into an alliance with France 1895 and Britain 1907, were one of the causes of the outbreak of World War I.
1917	During World War I, the Russian Revolution began. Provisional democratic government established by Mensheviks. Communist takeover by Bolsheviks under Lenin.
1922	Soviet Union established.
1924	Death of Lenin.
1928	Stalin emerged as absolute ruler after ousting Trotsky.
1930s	Purges of Stalin's opponents took place.
1939	Nonaggression pact signed with Germany.
1941–45	Great Patriotic War against Germany.
1949	Comecon created.
1953	Stalin died. Beria removed. 'Collective leadership' in power.
1955	Warsaw Pact created.
1956	Khrushchev made February 'secret speech'. Hungarian uprising.
1957–58	Ousting of 'antiparty' group and Bulganin.
1960	Sino-Soviet rift.
1962	Cuban missile crisis.
1964	Khrushchev ousted by new 'collective leadership'.
1968	Czechoslovakia invaded.
1969	Sino-Soviet border war.
1972	Salt I arms-limitation agreed with USA.
1977	Brezhnev elected president.
1979	Salt II. Soviet invasion of Afghanistan.
1980	Kosygin replaced as prime minister by Tikhonov.
1980–81	Polish crisis.
1982	Deaths of Suslov and Brezhnev. Andropov became Communist Party leader.
1984	Chernenko succeeded Andropov.
1985	Gorbachev succeeded Chernenko and introduced wide-ranging reforms. Gromyko appointed president.
1986	Gorbachev's power consolidated at 27th Party Congress. Chernobyl nuclear disaster.
1987	USSR and USA agreed to scrap intermediate-range nuclear missiles. Boris Yeltsin, Moscow party chief, dismissed for criticizing slow pace of reform.

1988   Nationalists challenged in Kazakhstan, Baltic republics,
        Armenia, and Azerbaijan. Earthquake killed thousands in
        Armenia. Constitution radically overhauled; private sector
        encouraged at Special All-Union Party Conference.
        Gorbachev replaced Gromyko as head of state.

1989   Troops withdrew from Afghanistan. General election held,
        with candidate choice for new Congress of the USSR People's
        Deputies (CUPD). Nationalist riots in Georgia. 74 members of
        (25%) CPSU Central Committee removed. Gorbachev elected
        state president; conservative communist regimes in Eastern
        Europe overthrown. Relations with Chinese normalized.
        Lithuania allowed multiparty elections. Gorbachev
        renounced 'Brezhnev doctrine'; Soviet Union admitted inva-
        sion of Afghanistan and intervention in Czechoslovakia to
        have been mistakes; Gorbachev opposed calls to modify
        Soviet constitution; Lithuanian Communist Party declared
        independence from Moscow.

1990   Troops sent to Azerbaijan during civil war with Armenia.
        CPSU Central Committee agreed to end one-party rule.
        Increased powers voted to state president by CUPD.
        Gorbachev opposed independence of Baltic republics; sanc-
        tions imposed on Lithuania; elections showed strength of
        liberal Communists. Boris Yeltsin elected president of
        Russian republic by RSFSR parliament and left the
        Communist Party.

1991   Plan to preserve USSR as 'renewed federation of equal sover-
        eign republics' approved in unionwide referendum, though
        boycotted by six republics. June: Yeltsin elected president of
        Russian Republic in direct, popular election and issued
        decree banning Communist Party cells in the RSFSR.
        Shevardnadze left CPSU and, with other liberal reformers,
        formed Democratic Reform Movement. New Union treaty
        approved by nine republics. Aug: coup by hardline commu-
        nists, led by Yanayev and Pavlov, removed Gorbachev from
        power; Gorbachev restored but position greatly undermined
        by Yeltsin who initiated a rapid dissolution of communist
        rule, the KGB, and all existing communist structures. In wake
        of failed coup several republics declared independence. Sept:
        independence of the republics of Latvia, Lithuania, and Estonia
        formally and internationally acknowledged. Nov: Efforts to
        form a new 'Union of Sovereign States' failed. Dec: Gorbachev

resigned; new federated arrangement emerged, the Commonwealth of Independent States (CIS); Soviet parliament voted USSR out of existence.

1991 Russian Soviet Federal Socialist Republic (RSFSR) took the name of Russian Federation.

1992 Jan: admitted into Conference on Security and Cooperation in Europe; assumed former USSR's permanent seat on UN Security Council; prices freed. Feb: demonstrations in Moscow and other cities as living standards plummeted. June: Yeltsin–Bush summit meeting. March: 18 out of 20 republics signed treaty agreeing to remain within loose Russian Federation; Tatarstan and Checheno-Ingush refused to sign. Dec: Victor Chernomyrdin elected prime minister; new constitution agreed in referendum. START II arms-reduction agreement signed with USA.

1993 March: power struggle between Yeltsin and Congress of People's Deputies. Referendum gave vote of confidence in Yeltsin's presidency but did not support constitutional change. Sept: Yeltsin dissolved parliament. Sept–Oct: attempted coup, led by conservative opponents, foiled by troops loyal to Yeltsin. Dec: new parliament elected, with surprising successes for extremist Liberal Democratic Party. New constitution approved in plebiscite.

1994 Jan: prominent reformers quit cabinet.

SCOTLAND

3,000 BC Neolithic settlements include Beaker People and Skara Brae on Orkney.

1st miln Picts reached Scotland from mainland Europe.

AD 1st C More than 400 brochs, thick-walled circular towers, built in far N regions.

79–84 Roman invasion by Julius Agricola; defeat of Caledonians at Mons Graupius, E Scotland.

122–128 Hadrian's Wall built to keep the northern tribes out of England.

c. 142 Antonine Wall from Forth to the Clyde, a stone and turf wall, built by Roman general Lollius Urbicus as a forward defence.

c. 185 Antonine Wall abandoned.

297 First reference to Picts in Latin documents.

c. 500	The Scots, Gaelic-speaking Irish immigrants, led by Fergus, son of Erc, settled in Kingdom of Dalriada (modern Argyll), with capital at Dunadd.
563	St Columba founded the monastery on Iona and began conversion of Picts to Christianity.
9th C	Norsemen conquered Orkney, Shetland, Western Isles, and much of Highlands.
c. 843	Unification of Picts, Scots, Britons, and Angles under Kenneth I MacAlpin.
1018	At Battle of Carham Malcolm II defeated Northumbrian army, bringing Lothian under Scottish rule.
1034	Duncan became king of United Scotland.
1040	Duncan murdered by Macbeth.
1069	Malcolm III (Ceann Mor) married English Princess Margaret, who introduced several reforms to the Scottish church.
1263	Battle of Largs: defeat of Scots by Norwegian king Haakon.
1295	First treaty between Scotland and France (the 'Auld Alliance').
1296	Edward I of England invaded and declared himself King of Scotland.
1297	William Wallace and Andrew Moray defeated English at Battle of Stirling Bridge.
1314	Robert the Bruce defeated English under Edward II at Battle of Bannockburn.
1326	Parliament at Cambuskenneth the first to be attended by nobles, clergy, and burghs.
1328	Scottish independence under Robert the Bruce recognized by England.
1371	Robert II, first Stuart king, crowned.
1513	Scots defeated by English (and King James IV killed) at Battle of Flodden.
1542	Mary, Queen of Scots succeeded to throne when less than a week old.
1544	Henry VII laid waste to Edinburgh and the Borders (the 'Rough Wooing').
1557	The First Covenant signed, pledging break with Rome.
1559	John Knox returned permanently to Scotland, to participate in shift of Scottish church to Protestantism.
1567	Mary forced to abdicate and the following year fled to England.
1603	Crowns of England and Scotland united under James VI who became James I of England.
1638	National Covenant condemned Charles I's changes in church ritual; Scottish rebellion.

1643	Solemn League and Covenant: Scottish Covenanters ally with English Parliament against Charles I.
1651	Cromwell invaded Scotland and defeated Scots at Dunbar and Inverkeithing.
1689	At Killiecrankie, Jacobite forces under Graham of Claverhouse, Viscount Dundee, defeated William of Orange's army, but Dundee mortally wounded.
1692	Massacre of Glencoe: William of Orange ordered MacDonalds of Glencoe murdered in their sleep.
1707	Act of Union united Scottish and English parliaments.
1715	The 'Fifteen': Jacobite rebellion in support of James Edward Stuart, 'James VII'.
1745	The 'Fortyfive': Charles Edward Stuart landed in Scotland and marched as far south as Derby before turning back.
1746	Jacobites defeated at Battle of Culloden by English forces under Duke of Cumberland.
1767	Creation of Edinburgh New Town, planned by James Craig (1749–1795).
1843	The Disruption: 400 ministers left the Church of Scotland to form the Free Church of Scotland.
1886	Crofters Act provided security of tenure for crofters.
1888	James Keir Hardie founded Scottish Labour Party.
1926	Secretary for Scotland became British cabinet post.
1928	National Party of Scotland formed (became Scottish National Party 1934).
1970s	Aberdeen the centre of North Sea oil development.
1975	Scottish counties replaced by nine regions and three island areas.
1979	Referendum rejected proposal for directly elected Scottish assembly.
1989	Local rates replaced by 'poll tax' despite wide opposition.
1990	350,000 warrants issued by March for nonpayment of poll tax.

SOUTH AMERICA

20,000 BC	Humans began to populate the continent.
c. 1000–300	Chavín civilization flourished in Peru.
AD 1494	Treaty of Tordesillas assigned what is now Brazil to Portugal, the rest of South America to Spain.
15th C	The Inca civilization developed in Peru.

16th C	Spain and Portugal invaded and conquered South America, killing and enslaving the people.
1513	The Spanish explorer Balboa discovered the Pacific Ocean.
1532–35	Francisco Pizarro conquered Peru and the Incas for Spain.
1780	Peruvian Túpac Amaru (José Condorcanqui), who claimed descent from Inca chieftains, led a revolt against Spanish rule and was executed.
19th C	Simon Bolívar and José de San Martín liberated South America's Spanish colonies. Brazil gained independence without struggle. Massive European immigration.
1818	Chile declared independence.
1822	Bolívar and San Martín met but failed to agree on plans for South American independence.
1865–70	President F S Lopez involved Paraguay in a war with Brazil, Argentina, and Uruguay. Paraguay was defeated and over half its population killed, including Lopez.
1879–83	Pacific War, between Chile and the forces of Bolivia and Peru, ended with Chile's acquisition of all of Bolivia's coastal territory and part of Peru's southern coast. Bolivia still seeks access to the coast.
1889	Brazilian monarchy overthrown and republic established.
1932–35	Chaco war, between Paraguay and Bolivia; the territorial dispute which caused it was settled by arbitration 1938.
1930s	US Marines intervened in Nicaragua.
1952	Bolivian revolution, with nationalization of the tin mines.
1970–73	CIA-backed military coup ended the rule of Salvador Allende's elected socialist government in Chile.
1977	Panama and the USA signed a treaty to give Panama control of the Panama Canal in 1999.
20th C	Rapid industrialization and population growth.
1980s	Widespread inability to meet interest payments on loans incurred from economically powerful countries to finance rapid industrialization and capture export markets.
1982	Argentina's invasion of the Falkland Islands triggered war with the UK; the UK regained the Islands.
1992	The first Earth Summit convened in Rio de Janeiro, Brazil, in an effort to cooperate in solving global environmental problems. Celebration in the USA of Columbus' first voyage to the New World; Native American representatives protested.

UNITED KINGDOM

1707	Act of Union between England and Scotland under Queen Anne.
1721	Robert Walpole unofficially first prime minister, under George I.
1783	Loss of North American colonies that form USA; Canada retained.
1801	Act of Ireland united Britain and Ireland.
1819	Peterloo massacre: cavalry charged a meeting of supporters of parliamentary reform.
1832	Great Reform Bill became law, shifting political power from upper to middle class.
1838	Chartist working-class movement formed.
1846	Corn Laws repealed by Robert Peel.
1851	Great Exhibition in London.
1867	Second Reform Bill, extending the franchise, introduced by Disraeli and passed.
1906	Liberal victory; programme of social reform.
1911	Powers of House of Lords curbed.
1914	Irish Home Rule Bill introduced.
1914–18	World War I.
1916	Lloyd George became prime minister.
1920	Home Rule Act incorporated NE of Ireland (Ulster) into the United Kingdom of Great Britain and Northern Ireland.
1921	Ireland, except for Ulster, became a dominion (Irish Free State, later Eire, 1937).
1924	First Labour government led by Ramsay MacDonald.
1926	General Strike.
1931	Coalition government; unemployment reached 3 million.
1939	World War II began.
1940	Winston Churchill became head of coalition government.
1945	Labour government under Clement Attlee; welfare state established.
1951	Conservatives under Winston Churchill defeated Labour.
1956	Suez Crisis.
1964	Labour victory under Harold Wilson.
1970	Conservatives under Edward Heath defeated Labour.
1972	Parliament prorogued in Northern Ireland; direct rule from Westminster began.
1973	UK joined European Economic Community.

1974	Three-day week, coal strike; Wilson replaced Heath.
1976	James Callaghan replaced Wilson as prime minister.
1977	Liberal–Labour pact.
1979	Victory for Conservatives under Margaret Thatcher.
1981	Formation of Social Democratic Party (SDP). Riots occurred in inner cities.
1982	Unemployment over 3 million. Falklands War.
1983	Thatcher re-elected.
1984–85	Coal strike, the longest in British history.
1986	Abolition of metropolitan counties.
1987	Thatcher re-elected for third term.
1988	Liberals and most of SDP merged into the Social and Liberal Democrats, leaving a splinter SDP. Inflation and interest rates rose.
1989	The Green Party polled 2 million votes in the European elections.
1990	Riots as poll tax introduced in England. Troops sent to the Persian Gulf following Iraq's invasion of Kuwait. British hostages held in Iraq, later released. Britain joined European exchange rate mechanism (ERM). Thatcher replaced by John Major as Conservative leader and prime minister.
1991	British troops took part in US-led war against Iraq under United Nations umbrella. Severe economic recession and rising unemployment.
1992	Recession continued. April: Conservative Party won fourth consecutive general election, but with reduced majority. John Smith replaced Neil Kinnock as Labour leader. Sept: sterling devalued and UK withdrawn from ERM. Oct: drastic coal mine closure programme encountered massive public opposition; later reviewed. Major's popularity at unprecedentedly low rating. Nov: government motion in favour of ratification of Maastricht Treaty narrowly passed. Revelations of past arms sales to Iraq implicated senior government figures, including the prime minister.
1993	Recession continued. Conservatives defeated in two by- elections; chancellor of the Exchequer replaced. July: Maastricht Treaty ratified by parliament. Dec: peace proposal for Northern Ireland, the Downing Street Declaration, issued jointly with Irish government.

1994   Series of scandals implicating Conservative MPs rocked public
         confidence in the government. UK intransigence on European
         Union issues angered European partners while failing to
         assuage Euro-sceptics at home. Major under increasing pres-
         sure to step down or 'go to the country'. May: Liberal
         Democrats made substantial gains in local elections.

UNITED STATES OF AMERICA

1776   Declaration of Independence.
1787   US constitution drawn up.
1789   Washington elected as first president.
1803   Louisiana Purchase.
1812–14 War with England, arising from commercial disputes caused
         by Britain's struggle with Napoleon.
1819   Florida purchased from Spain.
1836   The battle of the Alamo, Texas, won by Mexico.
1841   First wagon train left Missouri for California.
1846   Mormons, under Brigham Young, founded Salt Lake City,
         Utah.
1846-48 Mexican War resulted in cession to USA of Arizona,
         California, part of Colorado and Wyoming, Nevada, New
         Mexico, Texas, and Utah.
1848–49 California gold rush.
1860   Lincoln elected president.
1861–65 Civil War between North and South.
1865   Slavery abolished. Lincoln assassinated.
1867   Alaska bought from Russia.
1890   Battle of Wounded Knee, the last major battle between
         American Indians and US troops.
1898   War with Spain ended with the Spanish cession of
         Philippines, Puerto Rico, and Guam; it was agreed that Cuba
         be independent. Hawaii annexed.
1917–18 USA entered World War I.
1919–21 Wilson's 14 Points became base for League of Nations.
1920   Women achieved the vote.
1924   American Indians made citizens by Congress.
1929   Wall Street stock-market crash.
1933   F D Roosevelt's New Deal to alleviate the Depression put into
         force.

1941–45	The Japanese attack on Pearl Harbor Dec 1941 precipitated US entry into World War II.
1945	USA ended war in the Pacific by dropping atom bombs on Hiroshima and Nagasaki, Japan.
1950–53	US involvement in Korean War. McCarthy anticommunist investigations (HUAC) became a 'witch hunt'.
1954	Civil Rights legislation began with segregation ended in public schools.
1957	Civil Rights bill on voting.
1958	First US satellite in orbit.
1961	Abortive CIA-backed invasion of Cuba at the Bay of Pigs.
1963	President Kennedy assassinated; L B Johnson assumed the presidency.
1964–68	'Great Society' civil-rights and welfare measures in the Omnibus Civil Rights bill.
1964–75	US involvement in Vietnam War.
1965	US intervention in Dominican Republic.
1969	US astronaut Neil Armstrong was the first human on the Moon.
1973	OPEC oil embargo almost crippled US industry and consumers. Inflation began.
1973–74	Watergate scandal began in effort to re-elect Richard Nixon and ended just before impeachment; Nixon resigned as president; replaced by Gerald Ford, who 'pardoned' Nixon.
1975	Final US withdrawal from Vietnam.
1979	US–Chinese diplomatic relations normalized.
1979–80	Iranian hostage crisis; relieved by Reagan concessions and released on his inauguration day Jan 1981.
1981	Space shuttle mission was successful.
1983	US invasion of Grenada.
1986	'Irangate' scandal over secret US government arms sales to Iran, with proceeds to antigovernment Contra guerrillas in Nicaragua.
1987	Reagan and Gorbachev (for USSR) signed intermediate-range nuclear forces treaty. Wall Street stock-market crash caused by programme trading.
1988	USA became world's largest debtor nation, owing $532 billion. George Bush elected president.
1989	Bush met Gorbachev at Malta, end to Cold War declared; large cuts announced for US military; USA invaded Panama; Noriega taken into custody.
1990	Bush and Gorbachev met again. Nelson Mandela freed in

South Africa, toured USA. US troops sent to Middle East following Iraq's invasion of Kuwait.

1991 Jan–Feb: US-led assault drove Iraq from Kuwait in Gulf War. US support was given to the USSR during the dissolution of communism and the recognition of independence of the Baltic republics. July: Strategic Arms Reduction Treaty (START) signed at US–Soviet summit in Moscow.

1992 Bush's popularity slumped as economic recession continued. Widespread riots in Los Angeles. Nov: Bill Clinton won presidential elections for the Democrats; independent candidate Ross Perot won nearly 20% of votes. Dec: 'Operation Restore Hope' in Somalia launched, involving dispatch of 28,000 US troops to lead international relief effort.

1993 Jan: Clinton inaugurated. US-led air strikes on Baghdad, Iraq. July: US missile attack on Baghdad claimed as 'self defence'. Aug: medium-term economic plan passed by Congress to cut federal budget deficit. Oct: health-care reform proposals unveiled, recommending comprehensive coverage for all. Nov: North American Free Trade Agreement (NAFTA) between USA, Canada, and Mexico ratified; wide-ranging anti-crime bill passed.

1994 Jan: Signs of economic recovery. Clintons implicated in dubious financial dealings during the 1980s (the Whitewater affair); special inquiry launched. March: majority of US troops withdrawn from Somalia.

WALES

c. 400 BC Wales occupied by Celts from central Europe.

AD 50–60 Wales became part of the Roman Empire.

c. 200 Christianity adopted.

c. 450– Wales became the chief Celtic stronghold in the west since the
600 Saxons invaded and settled in S Britain. The Celtic tribes united against England.

8th C Frontier pushed back to Offa's Dyke.

9th– Vikings raided the coasts. At this time Wales was divided into
11th C small states organized on a clan basis, although princes such as Rhodri (844–878), Howel the Good (c. 904–949), and Griffith ap Llewelyn (1039–1063) temporarily united the country.

11th– Continual pressure on Wales from the Normans across the
12th C English border was resisted, notably by Llewelyn I and II.

1277	Edward I of England accepted as overlord by the Welsh.
1284	Edward I completed the conquest of Wales that had been begun by the Normans.
1294	Revolt against English rule put down by Edward I.
1350–1500	Welsh nationalist uprisings against the English; the most notable was that led by Owen Glendower.
1485	Henry Tudor, a Welshman, became Henry VII of England.
1536–43	Acts of Union united England and Wales after conquest under Henry VIII. Wales sent representatives to the English Parliament; English law was established in Wales; English became the official language.
18th C	Evangelical revival made Nonconformism a powerful factor in Welsh life. A strong coal and iron industry developed in the south.
19th C	The miners and ironworkers were militant supporters of Chartism, and Wales became a stronghold of trade unionism and socialism.
1893	University of Wales founded.
1920s–30s	Wales suffered from industrial depression; unemployment reached 21% 1937, and a considerable exodus of population took place.
post-1945	Growing nationalist movement and a revival of the language, earlier suppressed or discouraged.
1966	Plaid Cymru, the Welsh National Party, returned its first member to Westminster.
1979	Referendum rejected a proposal for limited home rule.
1988	Bombing campaign against estate agents selling Welsh properties to English buyers.

WORLD WAR I

1914 June	Assassination of Archduke Franz Ferdinand of Austria 28 June.
July	German government issued 'blank cheque' to Austria, offering support in war against Serbia. Austrian ultimatum to Serbia. Serbs accepted all but two points. Austria refused to accept compromise and declared war. Russia began mobilization to defend Serbian ally. Germany demanded Russian demobilization.
Aug	Germany declared war on Russia. France mobilized to assist Russian ally. Germans occupied Luxembourg and demanded

access to Belgian territory, which was refused. Germany declared war on France and invaded Belgium. Britain declared war on Germany, then on Austria. Dominions within the Empire, including Australia, automatically involved. Battle of Tannenburg between Central Powers and Russians. Russian army encircled.

Sept British and French troops halted German advance just short of Paris, and drove them back. First Battle of the Marne, and of the Aisne. Beginning of trench warfare.

Oct–Nov First Battle of Ypres. Britain declared war on Turkey.

1915 Apr– May Gallipoli offensive launched by British and dominion troops against Turkish forces. Second Battle of Ypres. First use of poison gas by Germans. Italy joined war against Austria. German submarine sank ocean liner *Lusitania* 7 May, later helping to bring USA into the war.

Aug– Sept Warsaw evacuated by the Russians. Battle of Tarnopol. Vilna taken by the Germans. Tsar Nicholas II took supreme control of Russian forces.

1916 Jan Final evacuation of British and dominion troops from Gallipoli.

Feb German offensive against Verdun began, with huge losses for little territorial gain.

May Naval battle of Jutland between British and German imperial fleets ended inconclusively, but put a stop to further German naval participation in the war.

June Russian (Brusilov) offensive against the Ukraine began.

July– Nov First Battle of the Somme, a sustained Anglo-French offensive which won little territory and lost a huge number of lives.

Aug Hindenburg and Ludendorff took command of the German armed forces. Romania entered the war against Austria but was rapidly overrun.

Sept Early tanks used by British on Western Front.

Nov Nivelle replaced Joffre as commander of French forces. Battle of the Ancre on the Western Front.

Dec French completed recapture of Verdun fortifications. Austrians occupied Bucharest.

1917 Feb Germany declared unrestricted submarine warfare. Russian Revolution began and tsarist rule overthrown.

March British seizure of Baghdad and occupation of Persia.

March– April Germans retreated to Siegfried Line (Arras-Soissons) on Western Front.

April–May	USA entered the war against Germany. Unsuccessful British and French offensives. Mutinies among French troops. Nivelle replaced by Pétain.
July–Nov	Third Ypres offensive including Battle of Passchendaele.
Sept	Germans occupied Riga.
Oct–Nov	Battle of Caporetto saw Italian troops defeated by Austrians.
Dec	Jerusalem taken by British forces under Allenby.
1918 Jan	US President Woodrow Wilson proclaimed 'Fourteen Points' as a basis for peace settlement.
March	Treaty of Brest-Litovsk with Central Powers ended Russian participation in the war, with substantial concessions of territory and reparations. Second Battle of the Somme began with German spring offensive.
July–Aug	Allied counter-offensive, including tank attack at Amiens, drove Germans back to the Siegfried Line.
Sept	Hindenburg and Ludendorff called for an armistice.
Oct	Armistice offered on the basis of the 'Fourteen Points'. German naval and military mutinies at Kiel and Wilhelmshaven.
Nov	Austria-Hungary signed armistice with Allies. Kaiser Wilhelm II of Germany went into exile. Provisional government under social democrat Friedrich Ebert formed. Germany agreed armistice. Fighting on Western Front stopped.
1919 Jan	Peace conference opened at Versailles.
May	Demands presented to Germany.
June	Germany signed peace treaty at Versailles, followed by other Central Powers: Austria (Treaty of St Germain-en-Laye, Sept), Bulgaria (Neuilly, Nov), Hungary (Trianon, June 1920), and Turkey (Sèvres, Aug 1920).

WORLD WAR II

1939 Sept	German invasion of Poland; Britain and France declared war on Germany; the USSR invaded Poland; fall of Warsaw (Poland divided between Germany and USSR).
Nov	The USSR invaded Finland.
1940 March	Soviet peace treaty with Finland.

April	Germany occupied Denmark, Norway, the Netherlands, Belgium, and Luxembourg. In Britain, a coalition government was formed under Churchill.
May	Germany outflanked the defensive French Maginot Line.
May–June	Evacuation of 337,131 Allied troops from Dunkirk, France, across the Channel to England.
June	Italy declared war on Britain and France; the Germans entered Paris; the French prime minister Pétain signed an armistice with Germany and moved the seat of government to Vichy.
July–Oct	Battle of Britain between British and German air forces.
Sept	Japanese invasion of French Indochina.
Oct	Abortive Italian invasion of Greece.
1941 April	Germany occupied Greece and Yugoslavia.
June	Germany invaded the USSR; Finland declared war on the USSR.
July	The Germans entered Smolensk, USSR.
Dec	The Germans came within 40 km/25 mi of Moscow, with Leningrad (now St Petersburg) under siege. First Soviet counteroffensive. Japan bombed Pearl Harbor, Hawaii, and declared war on the USA and Britain. Germany and Italy declared war on the USA.
1942 Jan	Japanese conquest of the Philippines.
June	Naval battle of Midway, the turning point of the Pacific War.
Aug	German attack on Stalingrad (now Volgograd), USSR.
Oct–Nov	Battle of El Alamein in N Africa, turn of the tide for the Western Allies.
Nov	Soviet counteroffensive on Stalingrad.
1943 Jan	The Casablanca Conference issued the Allied demand of unconditional surrender; the Germans retreated from Stalingrad.
March	The USSR drove the Germans back to the river Donetz.
May	End of Axis resistance in N Africa.
July	A coup by King Victor Emmanuel and Marshal Badoglio forced Mussolini to resign.
Aug	Beginning of the campaign against the Japanese in Burma (now Myanmar); US Marines landed on Guadalcanal, Solomon Islands.
Sept	Italy surrendered to the Allies; Mussolini was rescued by the Germans who set up a Republican Fascist government in N Italy; Allied landings at Salerno; the USSR retook Smolensk.

Oct	Italy declared war on Germany.
Nov	The US Navy defeated the Japanese in the Battle of Guadalcanal.
Nov–Dec	The Allied leaders met at the Tehran Conference.
1944 Jan	Allied landing in Nazi-occupied Italy: Battle of Anzio.
March	End of the German U-boat campaign in the Atlantic.
May	Fall of Monte Cassino, S Italy.
6 June	D-day: Allied landings in Nazi-occupied and heavily defended Normandy.
July	The bomb plot by German generals against Hitler failed.
Aug	Romania joined the Allies.
Sept	Battle of Arnhem on the Rhine; Soviet armistice with Finland.
Oct	The Yugoslav guerrilla leader Tito and Soviets entered Belgrade.
Dec	German counteroffensive, Battle of the Bulge.
1945 Feb	The Soviets reached the German border; Yalta conference; Allied bombing campaign over Germany (Dresden destroyed); the US reconquest of the Philippines was completed; the Americans landed on Iwo Jima, S of Japan.
April	Hitler committed suicide; Mussolini was captured by Italian partisans and shot.
May	German surrender to the Allies.
June	US troops completed the conquest of Okinawa (one of the Japanese Ryukyu Islands).
July	The Potsdam Conference issued an Allied ultimatum to Japan.
Aug	Atom bombs were dropped by the USA on Hiroshima and Nagasaki; Japan surrendered.

Science and Technology

ASTRONOMY

2300 BC	Chinese astronomers made their earliest observations.
2000	Babylonian priests made their first observational records.
1900	Stonehenge was constructed: first phase.
365	The Chinese observed Jupiter's satellites with the naked eye.
3rd C	Aristarchus argued that the Sun is the centre of the Solar System.
2nd C AD	Ptolemy's complicated Earth-centred system was promulgated, which dominated the astronomy of the Middle Ages.
1543	Copernicus revived the ideas of Aristarchus in *De Revolutionibus*.
1608	Hans Lippershey invented the telescope, which was first used by Galileo 1609.
1609	Johannes Kepler's first two laws of planetary motion were published (the third appeared 1619).
1632	The world's first official observatory was established in Leiden in the Netherlands.
1633	Galileo's theories were condemned by the Inquisition.
1675	The Royal Greenwich Observatory was founded in England.
1687	Isaac Newton's *Principia* was published, including his 'law of universal gravitation'.
1705	Edmond Halley correctly predicted that the comet that had passed the Earth in 1682 would return in 1758; the comet was later to be known by his name.
1781	William Herschel discovered Uranus and recognized stellar systems beyond our Galaxy.
1796	Pierre Laplace elaborated his theory of the origin of the solar system.
1801	Giuseppe Piazzi discovered the first asteroid, Ceres.
1814	Joseph von Fraunhofer first studied absorption lines in the solar spectrum.
1846	Neptune was identified by Johann Galle, following predictions by John Adams and Urbain Leverrier.
1859	Gustav Kirchhoff explained dark lines in the Sun's spectrum.
1887	The earliest photographic star charts were produced.
1889	Edward Barnard took the first photographs of the Milky Way.

1920	Arthur Eddington began the study of interstellar matter.
1923	Edwin Hubble proved that the galaxies are systems independent of the Milky Way, and by 1930 had confirmed the concept of an expanding universe.
1930	The planet Pluto was discovered by Clyde Tombaugh.
1931	Karl Jansky founded radio astronomy.
1945	Radar contact with the Moon was established by Z Bay of Hungary and the US Army Signal Corps Laboratory.
1948	The 5 m/200 in Hale reflector telescope was installed at Mount Palomar, California, USA.
1957	The Jodrell Bank telescope dish in England was completed.
1957	The first Sputnik satellite (USSR) opened the age of space observation.
1962	The first X-ray source was discovered in Scorpius.
1963	The first quasar was discovered.
1967	The first pulsar was discovered by Jocelyn Bell and Antony Hewish.
1969	The first crewed Moon landing was made by US astronauts.
1976	A 6 m/240 in reflector telescope was installed at Mount Semirodniki, USSR.
1977	Uranus was discovered to have rings.
1977	The spacecrafts *Voyager 1* and *2* were launched, passing Jupiter and Saturn 1979–1981.
1978	The spacecrafts *Pioneer Venus 1* and *2* reached Venus.
1978	A satellite of Pluto, Charon, was discovered by James Christy of the US Naval Observatory.
1986	Halley's comet returned. *Voyager 2* flew past Uranus and discovered six new moons.
1987	Supernova SN1987A flared up, becoming the first supernova to be visible to the naked eye since 1604.
1988	The most distant individual star was recorded – a supernova, 5 billion light years away, in the AC118 cluster of galaxies.
1989	*Voyager 2* flew by Neptune and discovered eight moons and three rings.
1990	Hubble Space Telescope was launched into orbit by the US space shuttle.
1991	The space probe *Galileo* flew past the asteroid Gaspra, approaching it to within 26,000 km/16,200 mi.
1992	COBE satellite detected ripples from the Big Bang that mark the first stage in the formation of galaxies.

BIOCHEMISTRY

c. 1830	Johannes Müller discovered proteins.
1833	Anselme Payen and J F Persoz first isolated an enzyme.
1862	Haemoglobin was first crystallized.
1869	The genetic material DNA (deoxyribonucleic acid) was discovered by Friedrich Mieschler.
1899	Emil Fischer postulated the 'lock-and-key' hypothesis to explain the specificity of enzyme action.
1913	Leonor Michaelis and M L Menten developed a mathematical equation describing the rate of enzyme-catalysed reactions.
1915	Thyroxine was first isolated from thyroid-gland tissue.
1920	The chromosome theory of heredity was postulated by Thomas H Morgan; growth hormone was discovered by Herbert McLean Evans and J A Long.
1921	Insulin was first isolated from the pancreas by Frederick Banting and Charles Best.
1926	Insulin was obtained in pure crystalline form.
1927	Thyroxine was first synthesized.
1928	Alexander Fleming discovered penicillin.
1931	Paul Karrer deduced the structure of retinol (vitamin A); vitamin D compounds were obtained in crystalline form by Adolf Windaus and Askew, independently of each other.
1932	Charles Glen King isolated ascorbic acid (vitamin C).
1933	Tadeus Reichstein synthesized ascorbic acid.
1935	Richard Kuhn and Karrer established the structure of riboflavin (vitamin B2).
1936	Robert Williams established the structure of thiamine (vitamin B1); biotin was isolated by Kogl and Tonnis.
1937	Niacin was identified by Conrad Arnold Elvehjem.
1938	Pyridoxine (vitamin B6) was isolated in pure crystalline form.
1940	Hans Krebs proposed the citric acid (Krebs) cycle; Hickman isolated retinol in pure crystalline form; Williams established the structure of pantothenic acid; biotin was identified by Albert Szent-Györgyi, Vincent Du Vigneaud, and co-workers.
1941	Penicillin was isolated and characterized by Howard Florey and Ernst Chain.
1943	The role of DNA in genetic inheritance was first demonstrated by Oswald Avery, Colin MacLeod, and Maclyn McCarty.
1950	The basic components of DNA were established by Erwin Chargaff; the alpha-helical structure of proteins was established by Linus Pauling and R B Corey.

1953	James Watson and Francis Crick determined the molecular structure of DNA.
1956	Mahlon Hoagland and Paul Zamecnick discovered transfer RNA (ribonucleic acid); mechanisms for the biosynthesis of RNA and DNA were discovered by Arthur Kornberg and Severo Ochoa.
1958	The structure of RNA was determined.
1960	Messenger RNA was discovered by Sydney Brenner and François Jacob.
1961	Marshall Nirenberg and Ochoa determined the chemical nature of the genetic code.
1965	Insulin was first synthesized.
1966	The immobilization of enzymes was achieved by Chibata.
1968	Brain hormones were discovered by Roger Guillemin and Andrew Schally.
1975	J Hughes and Hans Kosterlitz discovered encephalins.
1976	Guillemin discovered endorphins.
1977	J Baxter determined the genetic code for human growth hormone.
1978	Human insulin was first produced by genetic engineering.
1979	The biosynthetic production of human growth hormone was announced by Howard Goodman and J Baxter of the University of California, and by D V Goeddel and Seeburg of Genentech.
1982	Louis Chedid and Michael Sela developed the first synthesized vaccine.
1983	The first commercially available product of genetic engineering (Humulin) was launched.
1985	Alec Jeffreys devised genetic fingerprinting.
1993	UK researchers introduced a healthy version of the gene for cystic fibrosis into the lungs of mice with induced cystic fibrosis, restoring normal function.

BIOLOGY

c. 500 BC	First studies of the structure and behaviour of animals, by the Greek Alcmaeon of Croton.
c. 450	Hippocrates of Kos undertook the first detailed studies of human anatomy.
c. 350	Aristotle laid down the basic philosophy of the biological sciences and outlined a theory of evolution.

c. 300	Theophrastus carried out the first detailed studies of plants.
c. AD 175	Galen established the basic principles of anatomy and physiology.
c. 1500	Leonardo da Vinci studied human anatomy to improve his drawing ability and produced detailed anatomical drawings.
1628	William Harvey described the circulation of the blood and the function of the heart as a pump.
1665	Robert Hooke used a microscope to describe the cellular structure of plants.
1672	Marcelle Malphigi undertook the first studies in embryology by describing the development of a chicken egg.
1677	Anthony van Leeuwenhoek greatly improved the microscope and used it to describe spermatozoa as well as many microorganisms.
1736	Carolus (Carl) Linnaeus published his systematic classification of plants, so establishing taxonomy.
1768–79	James Cook's voyages of discovery in the Pacific revealed an undreamed-of diversity of living species, prompting the development of theories to explain their origin.
1796	Edward Jenner established the practice of vaccination against smallpox.
1809	Jean-Baptiste Lamarck advocated a theory of evolution through inheritance of acquired characters.
1839	Theodor Schwann proposed that all living matter is made up of cells.
1857	Louis Pasteur established that microorganisms are responsible for fermentation, creating the discipline of microbiology.
1859	Charles Darwin published *On the Origin of Species*.
1866	Gregor Mendel pioneered the study of inheritance with his experiments on peas, but achieved little recognition.
1900	Mendel's work was rediscovered and the science of genetics founded.
1935	Konrad Lorenz published the first of many major studies of animal behaviour, which founded the discipline of ethology.
1953	James Watson and Francis Crick described the molecular structure of the genetic material, DNA.
1964	William Hamilton recognized the importance of inclusive fitness, so paving the way for the development of sociobiology.
1975	Discovery of endogenous opiates (the brain's own painkillers) opened up a new phase in the study of brain chemistry.
1976	Har Gobind Khorana and his colleagues constructed the first

artificial gene to function naturally when inserted into a bacterial cell, a major step in genetic engineering.

1982	Gene databases were established at Heidelberg, Germany, and at Los Alamos, USA.
1985	The first human cancer gene, retinoblastoma, was isolated by researchers at the Massachusetts Eye and Ear Infirmary and the Whitehead Institute, Massachusetts.
1988	The Human Genome Organization (HUGO) was established in Washington DC with the aim of mapping the complete sequence of DNA.
1991	Biosphere 2, an experiment attempting to reproduce the world's biosphere in miniature within a sealed glass dome, was launched in Arizona, USA.
1992	Researchers at the University of California, USA, stimulated the multiplication of isolated brain cells of mice, overturning the axiom that mammalian brains cannot produce replacement cells once birth has taken place.
1994	Scientists from Pakistan and the USA unearthed a 50-million-year-old fossil whale with hind legs that would have enabled it to walk on land.

CAR

1769	Nicholas-Joseph Cugnot built a steam tractor in France.
1801	Richard Trevithick built a steam coach.
1860	Jean Etienne Lenoir built a gas-fuelled internal-combustion engine.
1865	The British government passed the Red Flag Act, requiring a person to precede a 'horseless carriage' with a red flag.
1876	Nikolaus August Otto improved the gas engine, making it a practical power source.
1885	Gottlieb Daimler developed a successful lightweight petrol engine and fitted it to a bicycle to create the prototype of the present-day motorcycle; Karl Benz fitted his lightweight petrol engine to a three-wheeled carriage to pioneer the motorcar.
1886	Gottlieb Daimler fitted his engine to a four-wheeled carriage to produce a four-wheeled motorcar.
1891	René Panhard and Emile Levassor established the present design of cars by putting the engine in front.
1896	Frederick Lanchester introduced epicyclic gearing, which foreshadowed automatic transmission.

1899	Caamille Jenatzy broke the 100 kph barrier in an electric car *La Jamais Contente* at Achères, France, reaching 105.85 kph/65.60 mph.
1901	The first Mercedes took to the roads; it was the direct ancestor of the present car. Ransome Olds in the USA introduced mass production on an assembly line.
1904	Louis Rigolly broke the 100 mph barrier, reaching 166.61 kph/103.55 mph in a Gobron-Brillé at Nice, France.
1906	Rolls-Royce introduced the Silver Ghost, which established the company's reputation for superlatively engineered cars.
1908	Henry Ford also used assembly-line production to manufacture his celebrated Model T, nicknamed the Tin Lizzie because it used lightweight steel sheet for the body, which looked tinny.
1911	Cadillac introduced the electric starter and dynamo lighting.
1913	Ford introduced the moving conveyor belt to the assembly line, further accelerating production of the Model T.
1920	Duesenberg began fitting four-wheel hydraulic brakes.
1922	The Lancia Lambda featured unitary (all-in-one) construction and independent front suspension.
1927	Henry Segrave broke the 200 mph barrier in a Sunbeam, reaching 327.89 kph/203.79 mph.
1928	Cadillac introduced the synchromesh gearbox, greatly facilitating gear changing.
1934	Citroën pioneered front-wheel drive in their 7CV model.
1936	Fiat introduced their baby car, the Topolino, 500 cc.
1938	Germany produced its 'people's car', the Volkswagen Beetle.
1948	Jaguar launched the XK120 sports car; Michelin introduced the radial-ply tyre; Goodrich produced the tubeless tyre.
1950	Dunlop announced the disc brake.
1951	Buick and Chrysler introduced power steering.
1952	Rover's gas-turbine car set a speed record of 243 kph/152 mph.
1954	Carl Bosch introduced fuel injection for cars.
1955	Citroën produced the advanced DS-19 'shark-front' car with hydropneumatic suspension.
1957	Felix Wankel built his first rotary petrol engine.
1959	BMC (now Rover) introduced the Issigonis-designed Mini, with front-wheel drive, transverse engine, and independent rubber suspension.
1965	US car manufacturers were forced to add safety features after the publication of Ralph Nader's *Unsafe at Any Speed*.

1966	California introduced legislation on air pollution by cars.

1966 California introduced legislation on air pollution by cars.

1970 American Gary Gabelich drove a rocket-powered car, *Blue Flame*, to a new record speed of 1,001.473 kph/622.287 mph.

1972 Dunlop introduced safety tyres, which seal themselves after a puncture.

1979 American Sam Barrett exceeded the speed of sound in the rocket-engined *Budweiser Rocket*, reaching 1,190.377 kph/739.666 mph, a speed not officially recognized as a record because of timing difficulties.

1980 The first mass-produced car with four-wheel drive, the Audi Quattro, was introduced; Japanese car production overtook that of the USA.

1981 BMW introduced the on-board computer, which monitored engine performance and indicated to the driver when a service was required.

1983 British driver Richard Noble set an official speed record in the jet-engined *Thrust 2* of 1,019.4 kph/633.5 mph; Austin Rover introduced the Maestro, the first car with a 'talking dashboard' that alerted the driver to problems.

1987 The solar-powered *Sunraycer* travelled 3,000 km/1,864 mi from Darwin to Adelaide, Australia, in six days.

1988 California introduced stringent controls on car emissions.

1989 The first mass-produced car with four-wheel steering, the Mitsubishi Galant, was launched.

1990 Fiat of Italy and Peugeot of France launched electric passenger cars on the market.

1991 Satellite-based car navigation systems were launched in Japan. European Parliament voted to adopt stringent control of car emissions.

1992 Mazda and NEC of Japan developed an image-processing system for cars, which views the road ahead through a video camera, identifies road signs and markings, and helps the driver to avoid obstacles.

1993 A Japanese electric car, the *IZA*, built by the Tokyo Electric Power Company, reached a speed of 176 kph/109 mph (10 kph/6 mph faster than the previous record for an electric car). The *Honda Dream* won the Darwin-to-Adelaide race for solar-powered cars in record time, achieving an average speed of 85 kph/53 mph and a top speed of 125 kph/77 mph.

CHANNEL TUNNEL

1751	French farmer Nicolas Desmaret suggested a fixed link across the English Channel.
1802	French mining engineer Albert Mathieu-Favier proposed to Napoleon I a Channel tunnel through which horse-drawn carriages might travel. Discussions with British politicians ceased 1803 when war broke out between the two countries.
1834	Aim de Gamond of France suggested the construction of a submerged tube across the Channel.
1842	De la Haye of Liverpool designed an underwater tube, the sections of which would be bolted together underwater by workers without diving apparatus.
1851	Hector Horeau proposed a tunnel that would slope down towards the middle of the Channel and up thereafter, so that the carriages would be propelled downhill by their own weight and for a short distance uphill, after which compressed air would take over as the motive power.
1857	A joint committee of British and French scientists approved the aim of constructing a Channel tunnel.
1875	Channel-tunnel bills were passed by the British and French parliaments.
1876	An Anglo-French protocol was signed laying down the basis of a treaty governing construction of a tunnel.
1878	Borings began from the French and British sides of the Channel.
1882	British government abandoned the project after public opinion, fearing invasion by the French, turned against the tunnel.
1904	Signing of the Entente Cordiale between France and the UK enabled plans to be reconsidered.
1907	A new Channel-tunnel bill was defeated in the British parliament.
1930	A Channel-tunnel bill narrowly failed in British parliament.
1930–40	British prime minister Winston Churchill and the French government supported the digging of a tunnel.
1955	Defence objections to a tunnel were lifted in the UK by prime minister Harold Macmillan.
1957	Channel Tunnel Study Group established.
1961	Study Group plans for a double-bore tunnel presented to British government.
1964	Ernest Marples, Minister of Transport, and his French counterpart gave go-ahead for construction.

1967	British government invited tunnel-building proposals from private interests.
1973	Anglo-French treaty on trial borings signed.
1974	New tunnel bill introduced in British parliament but was not passed before election called by Harold Wilson.
1975	British government cancelled project due to escalating costs.
1981	Anglo-French summit agreed to investigation of possible tunnel.
1982	Intergovernmental study group on tunnel established.
1984	Construction of tunnel agreed in principle at Anglo-French summit.
1986	Anglo-French treaty signed; design submitted by a consortium called the Channel Tunnel Group accepted.
1987	Legislation completed, Anglo-French treaty ratified; construction started in Nov.
1990	First breakthrough of service tunnel took place Dec.
1991	Breakthrough of first rail tunnel in May; the second rail tunnel was completed in June.
1994	Tunnel officially opened.

CHEMISTRY

c. 3000 BC	Egyptians were producing bronze – an alloy of copper and tin.
c. 450	Greek philosopher Empedocles proposed that all substances are made up of a combination of four elements – Earth, air, fire, and water – an idea that was developed by Plato and Aristotle and persisted for over 2,000 years.
c. 400	Greek philosopher Democritus theorized that matter consists ultimately of tiny, indivisible particles, *atomos*.
AD 1	Gold, silver, copper, lead, iron, tin, and mercury were known.
200	The techniques of solution, filtration, and distillation were known.
7th–17th C	Chemistry was dominated by alchemy, the attempt to transform nonprecious metals such as lead and copper into gold. Though misguided, it led to the discovery of many new chemicals and techniques, such as sublimation and distillation.
12th C	Alcohol was first distilled in Europe.
1242	Gunpowder introduced to Europe from the Far East.
1620	Scientific method of reasoning expounded by Francis Bacon in his *Novum Organum*.

1650	Leyden University in the Netherlands set up the first chemistry laboratory.
1661	Robert Boyle defined an element as any substance that cannot be broken down into still simpler substances and asserted that matter is composed of 'corpuscles' (atoms) of various sorts and sizes, capable of arranging themselves into groups, each of which constitutes a chemical substance.
1662	Boyle described the inverse relationship between the volume and pressure of a fixed mass of gas (Boyle's law).
1697	Georg Stahl proposed the erroneous theory that substances burn because they are rich in a certain substance, called phlogiston.
1755	Joseph Black discovered carbon dioxide.
1774	Joseph Priestley discovered oxygen, which he called 'dephlogisticated air'. Antoine Lavoisier demonstrated his law of conservation of mass.
1777	Lavoisier showed air to be made up of a mixture of gases, and showed that one of these – oxygen – is the substance necessary for combustion (burning) and rusting to take place.
1781	Henry Cavendish showed water to be a compound.
1792	Alessandra Volta demonstrated the electrochemical series.
1807	Humphry Davy passed electric current through molten compounds (the process of electrolysis) in order to isolate elements, such as potassium, that had never been separated by chemical means. Jöns Berzelius proposed that chemicals produced by living creatures should be termed 'organic'.
1808	John Dalton published his atomic theory, which states that every element consists of similar indivisible particles – called atoms – which differ from the atoms of other elements in their mass; he also drew up a list of relative atomic masses.
1811	Publication of Amedeo Avogadro's hypothesis on the relation between the volume and number of molecules of a gas, and its temperature and pressure.
1813–14	Berzelius devised the chemical symbols and formulae still used to represent elements and compounds.
1828	Franz Wöhler converted ammonium cyanate into urea – the first synthesis of an organic compound from an inorganic substance.
1832–33	Michael Faraday expounded the laws of electrolysis, and adopted the term 'ion' for the particles believed to be responsible for carrying current.
1846	Thomas Graham expounded his law of diffusion.
1853	Robert Bunsen invented the Bunsen burner.

1858	Stanislao Cannizzaro differentiated between atomic and molecular weights (masses).

1858   Stanislao Cannizzaro differentiated between atomic and molecular weights (masses).

1861   Organic chemistry was defined by German chemist Friedrich Kekulé as the chemistry of carbon compounds.

1864   John Newlands devised the first periodic table of the elements.

1869   Dmitri Mendeleyev expounded his periodic table of the elements (based on atomic mass), leaving gaps for elements that had not yet been discovered.

1874   Jacobus van't Hoff suggested that the four bonds of carbon are arranged tetrahedrally, and that carbon compounds can therefore be three-dimensional and asymmetric.

1884   Swedish chemist Svante Arrhenius suggested that electrolytes (solutions or molten compounds that conduct electricity) dissociate into ions, atoms or groups of atoms that carry a positive or negative charge.

1894   William Ramsey and Lord Rayleigh discovered the first inert gases, argon.

1897   The electron was discovered by J J Thomson.

1901   Mikhail Tsvet invented paper chromatography as a means of separating pigments.

1909   Sören Sörensen devised the pH scale of acidity.

1912   Max von Laue showed crystals to be composed of regular, repeating arrays of atoms by studying the patterns in which they diffract X-rays.

1913–14   Henry Moseley equated the atomic number of an element with the positive charge on its nuclei, and drew up the periodic table, based on atomic number, that is used today.

1916   Gilbert Newton Lewis explained covalent bonding between atoms as a sharing of electrons.

1927   Nevil Sidgwick published his theory of valency, based on the numbers of electrons in the outer shells of the reacting atoms.

1930   Electrophoresis, which separates particles in suspension in an electric field, was invented by Arne Tiselius.

1932   Deuterium (heavy hydrogen), an isotope of hydrogen, was discovered by Harold Urey.

1940   Edwin McMillan and Philip Abelson showed that new elements with a higher atomic number than uranium can be formed by bombarding uranium with neutrons, and synthesized the first transuranic element, neptunium.

1942   Plutonium was first synthesized by Glenn T Seaborg and Edwin McMillan.

1950   Derek Barton deduced that some properties of organic compounds are affected by the orientation of their functional groups.

1954	Einsteinium and fermium were synthesized.
1955	Ilya Prigogine described the thermodynamics of irreversible processes (the transformations of energy that take place in, for example, many reactions within living cells).
1962	Neil Bartlett prepared the first compound of an inert gas, xenon hexafluoroplatinate; it was previously believed that inert gases could not take part in a chemical reaction.
1965	Robert B Woodward synthesized complex organic compounds.
1981	Quantum mechanics applied to predict course of chemical reactions by US chemist Roald Hoffmann and Kenichi Fukui of Japan.
1982	Element 109, unnilennium, synthesized.
1985	Fullerenes, a new class of carbon solids made up of closed cages of carbon atoms, were discovered by Harold Kroto and David Walton at the University of Sussex, England.
1987	US chemists Donald Cram and Charles Pederson, and Jean-Marie Lehn of France created artificial molecules that mimic the vital chemical reactions of life processes.
1990	Jean-Marie Lehn, Ulrich Koert, and Margaret Harding reported the synthesis of a new class of compounds, called nucleohelicates, that mimic the double helical structure of DNA, turned inside out.
1993	US chemists at the University of California and the Scripps Institute synthesized rapamycin, one of a group of complex, naturally occurring antibiotics and immunosuppressants that are being tested as anticancer agents.

COMPUTING

1614	John Napier invented logarithms.
1615	William Oughtred invented the slide rule.
1623	Wilhelm Schickard (1592–1635) invented the mechanical calculating machine.
1645	Blaise Pascal produced a calculator.
1672–74	Gottfried Leibniz built his first calculator, the Stepped Reckoner.
1801	Joseph-Marie Jacquard developed an automatic loom controlled by punch cards.
1820	The first mass-produced calculator, the Arithometer, was developed by Charles Thomas de Colmar (1785–1870).

1822	Charles Babbage completed his first model for the difference engine.
1830s	Babbage created the first design for the analytical engine.
1890	Herman Hollerith developed the punched-card ruler for the US census.
1936	Alan Turing published the mathematical theory of computing.
1938	Konrad Zuse constructed the first binary calculator, using Boolean algebra.
1939	US mathematician and physicist J V Atanasoff (1903–) became the first to use electronic means for mechanizing arithmetical operations.
1943	The Colossus electronic code-breaker was developed at Bletchley Park, England. The Harvard University Mark I or Automatic Sequence Controlled Calculator (partly financed by IBM) became the first program-controlled calculator.
1946	ENIAC (electronic numerator, integrator, analyser, and computer), the first, fully electronic digital computer, was completed at the University of Pennsylvania, USA.
1948	Manchester University (England) Mark I, the first stored-program computer, was completed. William Shockley of Bell Laboratories invented the transistor.
1951	Launch of Ferranti Mark I, the first commercially produced computer. Whirlwind, the first real-time computer, was built for the US air-defence system. Grace Murray Hopper of Remington Rand invented the compiler computer program.
1952	EDVAC (electronic discrete variable computer) was completed at the Institute for Advanced Study, Princeton, USA (by John Von Neumann and others).
1953	Magnetic core memory was developed.
1958	The first integrated circuit was constructed.
1963	The first minicomputer was built by Digital Equipment (DEC). The first electronic calculator was built by Bell Punch Company.
1964	Launch of IBM System/360, the first compatible family of computers. John Kemeny and Thomas Kurtz of Dartmouth College invented BASIC (Beginner's All-purpose Symbolic Instruction Code), a computer language similar to FORTRAN.
1965	The first supercomputer, the Control Data CD6600, was developed.
1971	The first microprocessor, the Intel 4004, was announced.
1974	CLIP–4, the first computer with a parallel architecture, was developed by John Backus at IBM.

1975	Altair 8800, the first personal computer (PC), or microcomputer, was launched.
1981	The Xerox Star system, the first WIMP system (windows, icons, menus, and pointing devices), was developed. IBM launched the IBM PC.
1984	Apple launched the Macintosh computer.
1985	The Inmos T414 transputer, the first 'off-the- shelf' microprocessor for building parallel computers, was announced.
1988	The first optical microprocessor, which uses light instead of electricity, was developed.
1989	Wafer-scale silicon memory chips, able to store 200 million characters, were launched.
1990	Microsoft released Windows 3, a popular windowing environment for PCs.
1992	Philips launched the CD-I (Compact-Disc Interactive) player, based on CD audio technology, to provide interactive multimedia programs for the home user.
1993	Intel launched the Pentium chip containing 3.1 million transistors and capable of 100 MIPs (millions of instructions per second). The Personal Digital Assistant (PDA), which recognizes users' handwriting, went on sale.

EARTH SCIENCE

1735	English lawyer George Hadley described the circulation of the atmosphere as large-scale convection currents centred on the equator.
1746	A French expedition to Lapland proved the Earth to be flattened at the poles.
1743	Christopher Packe produced the first geological map, of S England.
1744	The first map produced on modern surveying principles was produced by Cæsar-François Cassini in France.
1745	In Russia, Mikhail Vasilievich Lomonosov published a catalogue of over 3,000 minerals.
1760	Lomonosov explained the formation of icebergs. John Mitchell proposed that earthquakes are produced when one layer of rock rubs against another.
1766	The fossilized bones of a huge animal (later called *Mosasaurus*) were found in a quarry near the river Meuse, the Netherlands.

1776	James Keir suggested that some rocks, such as those making up the Giant's Causeway in Ireland, may have formed as molten material that cooled and then crystallized.
1779	French naturalist Comte George de Buffon speculated that the Earth may be much older than the 6,000 years suggested by the Bible.
1785	Scottish geologist James Hutton proposed the theory of uniformitarianism: all geological features are the result of processes that are at work today, acting over long periods of time.
1786	German-Swiss Johann von Carpentier described the European ice age.
1793	Jean Baptiste Lamarck argued that fossils are the remains of once-living animals and plants.
1794	William Smith produced the first large-scale geological maps of England.
1795	In France, Georges Cuvier identified the fossil bones discovered in the Netherlands in 1766 as being those of a reptile, now extinct.
1804	French physicists Jean Biot and Joseph Gay-Lussac studied the atmosphere from a hot-air balloon.
1809	The first geological survey of the eastern USA was produced by William Maclure.
1815	In England, William Smith showed how rock strata (layers) can be identified on the basis of the fossils found in them.
1822	Mary Ann Mantell discovered on the English coast the first fossil to be recognized as that of a dinosaur (an iguanodon). In Germany, Friedrich Mohs introduced a scale for specifying mineral hardness.
1825	Cuvier proposed his theory of catastrophes as the cause of the extinction of large groups of animals.
1830	Scottish geologist Charles Lyell published the first volume of *The Principles of Geology*, which described the Earth as being several hundred million years old.
1839	In the USA, Louis Agassiz described the motion and laying down of glaciers, confirming the reality of the ice ages.
1842	English palaeontologist Richard Owen coined the name 'dinosaur' for the reptiles, now extinct, that lived about 175 million years ago.
1846	Irish physicist William Thomson (Lord Kelvin) estimated, using the temperature of the Earth, that the Earth is 100 million years old.

1850	US naval officer Matthew Fontaine Maury mapped the Atlantic Ocean, noting that it is deeper near its edges than at the centre.
1853	James Coffin described the three major wind bands that girdle each hemisphere.
1854	English astronomer George Airy calculated the mass of the Earth by measuring gravity at the top and bottom of a coal mine.
1859	Edwin Drake drilled the world's first oil well at Titusville, Pennsylvania, USA.
1872	The beginning of the world's first major oceanographic expedition, the four-year voyage of the *Challenger*.
1882	Scottish physicist Balfour Stewart postulated the existence of the ionosphere (the ionized layer of the outer atmosphere) to account for differences in the Earth's magnetic field.
1884	German meteorologist Vladimir Köppen introduced a classification of the world's temperature zones.
1895	In the USA, Jeanette Picard launched the first balloon to be used for stratospheric research.
1896	Swedish chemist Svante Arrhenius discovered a link between the amount of carbon dioxide in the atmosphere and the global temperature.
1897	Norwegian-US meteorologist Jacob Bjerknes and his father Vilhelm developed the mathematical theory of weather forecasting.
1902	British physicist Oliver Heaviside and US engineer Arthur Edwin Kennelly predicted the existence of an electrified layer in the atmosphere that reflects radio waves. In France, Léon Teisserenc discovered layers of different temperatures in the atmosphere, which he called the troposphere and stratosphere.
1906	Richard Dixon Oldham proved the Earth to have a molten core by studying seismic waves.
1909	Yugoslav physicist Andrija Mohorovičić discovered a discontinuity in the Earth's crust, about 30 km/18 mi below the surface, that forms the boundary between the crust and the mantle.
1912	In Germany, Alfred Wegener proposed the theory of continental drift and the existence of a supercontinent, Pangaea, in the distant past.
1913	French physicist Charles Fabry discovered the ozone layer in the upper atmosphere.
1914	German-US geologist Beno Gutenberg discovered the discontinuity that marks the boundary between the Earth's mantle and the outer core.

1915	English geologist Arthur Holmes used radioactivity to date rocks, establishing the Earth to be 4.6 billion years old.
1922	British meteorologist Lewis Fry Richardson developed a method of numerical weather forecasting.
1925	A German expedition discovered the Mid-Atlantic ridge by means of sonar. Edward Appleton discovered a layer of the atmosphere that reflects radio waves; it was later named after him.
1929	By studying the magnetism of rocks, Japanese geologist Motonori Matuyama showed that the Earth's magnetic field reverses direction from time to time.
1935	US seismologist Charles Francis Richter established a scale for measuring the magnitude of earthquakes.
1936	Danish seismologist Inge Lehmann postulated the existence of a solid inner core of the Earth from the study of seismic waves.
1939	In Germany, Walter Maurice Elsasser proposed that eddy currents in the molten iron core cause the Earth's magnetism.
1950	Hungarian-US mathematician John Von Neumann made the first 24-hour weather forecast by computer.
1956	US geologists Bruce Charles Heezen and Maurice Ewing discovered a global network of oceanic ridges and rifts that divide the Earth's surface into plates.
1958	Using rockets, US physicist James Van Allen discovered a belt of radiation (later named after him) around the Earth.
1960	The world's first weather satellite, *TIROS 1*, was launched. US geologist Harry Hammond Hess showed that the sea floor spreads out from ocean ridges and descends back into the mantle at deep-sea trenches.
1963	British geophysicists Fred Vine and Drummond Matthews analysed the magnetism of rocks in the Atlantic Ocean floor and found conclusive proof of seafloor spreading.
1985	A British expedition to the Antarctic discovered a hole in the ozone layer above the South Pole.
1991	A borehole in the Kola Peninsula in Arctic Russia, begun in the 1970s, reached a depth of 12,261 m/40,240 ft (where the temperature was found to be 210°C/410°F). It is expected to reach a depth of 15,000 m/49,000 ft by 1995.

ELECTRONICS

| 1897 | The electron was discovered by English physicist John Joseph Thomson. |

1904	English physicist Ambrose Fleming invented the diode valve, which allows flow of electricity in one direction only.
1906	The triode electron valve, the first device to control an electric current, was invented by US physicist Lee De Forest.
1947	John Bardeen, William Shockley, and Walter Brattain invented the junction germanium transistor at the Bell Laboratories, New Jersey, USA.
1952	British physicist G W A Dunner proposed the integrated circuit.
1953	Jay Forrester of the Massachusetts Institute of Technology, USA, built a magnetic memory smaller than existing vacuum-tube memories.
1954	The silicon transistor was developed by Gordon Teal of Texas Instruments, USA.
1958	The first integrated circuit, containing five components, was built by US electrical physicist Jack Kilby.
1959	The planar transistor, which is built up in layers, or planes, was designed by Robert Noyce of Fairchild Semiconductor Corporation, USA.
1961	Steven Hofstein designed the field-effect transistor used in integrated circuits.
1971	The first microprocessor, the Intel 4004, was designed by Ted Hoff in the USA; it contained 2,250 components and could add two four-bit numbers in 11–millionths of a second.
1974	The Intel 8080 microprocessor was launched; it contained 4,500 components and could add two eight-bit numbers in 2.5–millionths of a second.
1979	The Motorola 68000 microprocessor was introduced; it contained 70,000 components and could multiply two 16-bit numbers in 3.2–millionths of a second.
1981	The Hewlett-Packard Superchip was introduced; it contained 450,000 components and could multiply two 32–bit numbers in 1.8–millionths of a second.
1985	The Inmos T414 transputer, the first microprocessor designed for use in parallel computers, was launched.
1988	The first optical microprocessor, which uses light instead of electricity, was developed.
1989	Wafer-scale silicon memory chips were introduced: the size of a beer mat, they are able to store 200 million characters.
1990	Memory chips capable of holding 4 million bits of information began to be mass-produced in Japan. The chips can store the equivalent of 520,000 characters, or the contents of a 16-page

newspaper. Each chip contains 9 million components packed on a piece of silicon less than 15 mm long by 5 mm wide.

1992 Transistors made from high-temperature superconducting ceramics rather than semiconductors produced in Japan by Sanyo Electric. The new transistors are 10 times faster than semiconductor transistors.

1993 US firm Intel launched the Pentium 64-bit microprocessor, with two separate integer processing units that can run in parallel, promising to be 10 times faster than earlier processors.

FLIGHT

1783 First human flight, by Jean F Pilâtre de Rozier and the Marquis d'Arlandes, in Paris, using a hot-air balloon made by Joseph and Etienne Montgolfier; first ascent in a hydrogen-filled balloon by Jacques Charles and M N Robert in Paris.

1785 Jean-Pierre Blanchard and John J Jeffries made the first balloon crossing of the English Channel.

1852 Henri Giffard flew the first steam-powered airship over Paris.

1853 George Cayley flew the first true aeroplane, a model glider 1.5 m/5 ft long.

1891–96 Otto Lilienthal piloted a glider in flight.

1903 First powered and controlled flight of a heavier-than-air craft (aeroplane) by Orville Wright, at Kitty Hawk, North Carolina, USA.

1908 First powered flight in the UK by Samuel Cody.

1909 Louis Blériot flew across the English Channel in 36 minutes.

1914–18 World War I stimulated improvements in speed and power.

1919 First E–W flight across the Atlantic by Albert C Read, using a flying boat; first nonstop flight across the Atlantic E–W by John William Alcock and Arthur Whitten Brown in 16 hours 27 minutes; first complete flight from Britain to Australia by Ross Smith and Keith Smith.

1923 Juan de la Cieva flew the first autogiro with a rotating wing.

1927 Charles Lindbergh made the first W–E solo nonstop flight across the Atlantic.

1928 First transpacific flight, from San Francisco to Brisbane, by Charles Kinsford Smith and C T P Ulm.

1930 Frank Whittle patented the jet engine; Amy Johnson became the first woman to fly solo from England to Australia.

1937 The first fully pressurized aircraft, the Lockheed XC-35, came into service.

1939	Erich Warsitz flew the first Heinkel jet plane, in Germany; Igor Sikorsky designed the first helicopter, with a large main rotor and a smaller tail rotor.
1939–45	World War II – developments included the Hawker Hurricane and Supermarine Spitfire Fighters, and Avro Lancaster and Boeing Flying Fortress bombers.
1947	A rocket-powered plane, the Bell X-1, was the first aircraft to fly faster than the speed of sound.
1949	The de Havilland Comet, the first jet airliner, entered service; James Gallagher made the first nonstop round-the-world flight, in a Boeing Superfortress.
1953	The first vertical takeoff aircraft, the Rolls-Royce 'Flying Bedstead', was tested.
1968	The world's first supersonic airliner, the Russian TU-144, flew for the first time.
1970	The Boeing 747 jumbo jet entered service, carrying 500 passengers.
1976	Anglo-French Concorde, making a transatlantic crossing in under three hours, came into commercial service. A Lockheed SR-17A, piloted by Eldon W Joersz and George T Morgan, set the world air-speed record of 3,529.56 kmh/2,193.167 mph over Beale Air Force Base, California, USA.
1978	A US team made the first transatlantic crossing by balloon, in the helium-filled *Double Eagle II*.
1979	First crossing of the English Channel by a human-powered aircraft, *Gossamer Albatross*, piloted by Bryan Allen.
1981	The solar-powered *Solar Challenger* flew across the English Channel, from Paris to Kent, taking 5 hours for the 262 km/162.8 mi journey.
1986	Dick Rutan and Jeana Yeager made the first nonstop flight around the world without refuelling, piloting *Voyager*, which completed the flight in 9 days 3 minutes 44 seconds.
1987	Richard Branson and Per Lindstrand made the first transatlantic crossing by hot-air balloon, in *Virgin Atlantic Challenger*.
1988	*Daedelus*, a human-powered craft piloted by Kanellos Kanellopoulos, flew 118 km/74 mi across the Aegean Sea.
1991	Richard Branson and Per Lindstrand crossed the Pacific Ocean in the hot-air balloon *Virgin Otsouka Pacific Flyer* from the southern tip of Japan to NW Canada in 46 hours 15 minutes.
1992	US engineers demonstrated a model radio-controlled ornithopter, the first aircraft to be successfully propelled and manoeuvred by flapping wings.

1993   The US Federal Aviation Authority made the use of an auto-
           matic on-board collision avoidance system (TCAS-2)
           mandatory in US airspace.

MATHEMATICS

c. 2500   The people of Mesopotamia (now Iraq) developed a posi-
BC   tional numbering (place-value) system, in which the value of
           a digit depends in its position in a number.
c. 2000   Mesopotamian mathematicians solved quadratic equations
           (algebraic equations in which the highest power of a variable
           is 2).
876   A symbol for zero was used for the first time, in India.
c. 550   Greek mathematician Pythagoras formulated a theorem relat-
           ing the lengths of the sides of a right-angled triangle. The
           theorem was already known by earlier mathematicians in
           China, Mesopotamia, and Egypt.
c. 450   Hipparcos of Metapontum discovered that some numbers are
           irrational (cannot be expressed as the ratio of two
           integers).
300   Euclid laid out the laws of geometry in his book *Elements*,
           which was to remain a standard text for 2,000 years.
c. 230   Eratosthenes developed a method for finding all prime num-
           bers.
c. 100   Chinese mathematicians began using negative numbers.
c. 190   Chinese mathematicians used powers of 10 to express magni-
           tudes.
c. AD 210 Diophantus of Alexandria wrote the first book on algebra.
c. 600   A decimal number system was developed in India.
829   Persian mathematician Muhammad ibn-Mūsā al-Khwārizmî
           published a work on algebra that made use of the decimal
           number system.
1202   Italian mathematician Leonardo Fibonacci studied the
           sequence of numbers (1, 1, 2, 3, 5, 8, 13, 21, ...) in which each
           number is the sum of the two preceding ones.
1550   In Germany, Rheticus published trigonometrical tables that
           simplified calculations involving triangles.
1614   Scottish mathematician John Napier invented logarithms,
           which enable lengthy calculations involving multiplication
           and division to be carried out by addition and subtraction.

1623	Wilhelm Schickard invented the mechanical calculating machine.
1637	French mathematician and philosopher René Descartes introduced coordinate geometry.
1654	In France, Blaise Pascal and Pierre de Fermat developed probability theory.
1666	Isaac Newton developed differential calculus, a method of calculating rates of change.
1675	German mathematician Gottfried Wilhelm Leibniz introduced the modern notation for integral calculus, a method of calculating volumes.
1679	Leibniz introduced binary arithmetic, in which only two symbols are used to represent all numbers.
1684	Leibniz published the first account of differential calculus.
1718	Jakob Bernoulli in Switzerland published his work on the calculus of variations (the study of functions that are close to their minimum or maximum values).
1746	In France, Jean le Rond d'Alembert developed the theory of complex numbers.
1747	D'Alembert used partial differential equations in mathematical physics.
1798	Norwegian mathematician Caspar Wessel introduced the vector representation of complex numbers.
1799	Karl Friedrich Gauss of Germany proved the fundamental theorem of algebra: the number of solutions of an algebraic equation is the same as the exponent of the highest term.
1810	In France, Jean Baptiste Joseph Fourier published his method of representing functions by a series of trigonometric functions.
1812	French mathematician Pierre Simon Laplace published the first complete account of probability theory.
1822	In the UK, Charles Babbage began construction of the first mechanical computer, the difference machine, a device for calculating logarithms and trigonometric functions.
1827	Gauss introduced differential geometry, in which small features of curves are described by analytical methods.
1829	In Russia, Nikolai Ivanonvich Lobachevsky developed hyperbolic geometry, in which a plane is regarded as part of a hyperbolic surface, shaped like a saddle. In France, Evariste Galois introduced the theory of groups (collections whose members obey certain simple rules of addition and multiplication).

1844	French mathematician Joseph Liouville found the first transcendental number, which cannot be expressed as an algebraic equation with rational coefficients. In Germany, Hermann Grassmann studied vectors with more than three dimensions.
1854	George Boole in the UK published his system of symbolic logic, now called Boolean algebra.
1858	English mathematician Arthur Cayley developed calculations using ordered tables called matrices.
1865	August Ferdinand Möbius in Germany described how a strip of paper can have only one side and one edge.
1892	German mathematician Georg Cantor showed that there are different kinds of infinity and studied transfinite numbers.
1895	Jules Henri Poincaré published the first paper on topology, often called 'the geometry of rubber sheets'.
1931	In the USA, Austrian-born mathematician Kurt Gödel proved that any formal system strong enough to include the laws of arithmetic is either incomplete or inconsistent.
1937	English mathematician Alan Turing published the mathematical theory of computing.
1944	John Von Neumann and Oscar Morgenstern developed game theory in the USA.
1945	The first general purpose, fully electronic digital computer, ENIAC (electronic numerator, integrator, analyser, and computer), was built at the University of Pennsylvania, USA.
1961	Meteorologist Edward Lorenz at the Massachusetts Institute of Technology, USA, discovered a mathematical system with chaotic behaviour, leading to a new branch of mathematics chaos theory.
1962	Benoit Mandelbrot in the USA invented fractal images, using a computer that repeats the same mathematical pattern over and over again.
1975	US mathematician Mitchell Feigenbaum discovered a new fundamental constant (approximately 4.669201609103), which plays an important role in chaos theory.
1980	Mathematicians worldwide completed the classification of all finite and simple groups, a task that took over a hundred mathematicians more than 35 years to complete and whose results took up more than 14,000 pages in mathematical journals.
1989	A team of US computer mathematicians at Amdahl Corporation, California, discovered the highest known prime number (it contains 65,087 digits).

1993   US mathematician Andrew Wiles published a 1,000– page proof of Fermat's last theorem, one of the most baffling challenges in pure mathematics.

MEDICINE, WESTERN

c. 400 BC Hippocrates recognized that disease had natural causes.

c. AD 200 Galen consolidated the work of the Alexandrian doctors.

1543   Andreas Vesalius gave the first accurate account of the human body.

1628   William Harvey discovered the circulation of the blood.

1768   John Hunter began the foundation of experimental and surgical pathology.

1785   Digitalis was used to treat heart disease; the active ingredient was isolated 1904.

1798   Edward Jenner published his work on vaccination.

1877   Patrick Manson studied animal carriers of infectious diseases.

1882   Robert Koch isolated the bacillus responsible for tuberculosis.

1884   Edwin Klebs isolated the diphtheria bacillus.

1885   Louis Pasteur produced a vaccine against rabies.

1890   Joseph Lister demonstrated antiseptic surgery.

1895   Wilhelm Röntgen discovered X-rays.

1897   Martinus Beijerinck discovered viruses.

1899   Felix Hoffman developed aspirin; Sigmund Freud founded psychiatry.

1900   Karl Landsteiner identified the first three blood groups, later designated A, B, and O.

1910   Paul Ehrlich developed the first specific antibacterial agent, Salvarsan, a cure for syphilis.

1922   Insulin was first used to treat diabetes.

1928   Alexander Fleming discovered penicillin.

1932   Gerhard Domagk discovered the first antibacterial sulphonamide drug, Prontosil.

1937   Electro-convulsive therapy (ECT) was developed.

1940s   Lithium treatment for manic-depressive illness was developed.

1950s   Antidepressant drugs and beta-blockers for heart disease were developed. Manipulation of the molecules of synthetic chemicals became the main source of new drugs. Peter Medawar studied the body's tolerance of transplanted organs and skin grafts.

1950	Proof of a link between cigarette smoking and lung cancer was established.
1953	Francis Crick and James Watson announced the structure of DNA. Jonas Salk developed a vaccine against polio.
1958	Ian Donald pioneered diagnostic ultrasound.
1960s	A new generation of minor tranquillizers called benzodiazepines was developed.
1967	Christiaan Barnard performed the first human heart-transplant operation.
1971	Viroids, disease-causing organisms even smaller than viruses, were isolated outside the living body.
1972	The CAT scan, pioneered by Godfrey Hounsfield, was first used to image the human brain.
1975	César Milstein developed monoclonal antibodies.
1978	World's first 'test-tube baby' was born in the UK.
1980s	AIDS (acquired immune-deficiency syndrome) was first recognized in the USA. Barbara McClintock's discovery of the transposable gene was recognized.
1980	The World Health Organization reported the eradication of smallpox.
1983	The virus responsible for AIDS, now known as human immunodeficiency virus (HIV), was identified by Luc Montagnier at the Institut Pasteur, Paris; Robert Gallo at the National Cancer Institute, Maryland, USA discovered the virus independently 1984.
1984	The first vaccine against leprosy was developed.
1987	The world's longest-surviving heart-transplant patient died in France, 18 years after his operation.
1989	Grafts of fetal brain tissue were first used to treat Parkinson's disease.
1990	Gene for maleness discovered by UK researchers.
1991	First successful use of gene therapy (to treat severe combined immune deficiency) was reported in the USA.
1993	First trials of gene therapy against cystic fibrosis took place in the USA.

NUCLEAR ENERGY

1896	French physicist Henri Becquerel discovered radioactivity.
1905	In Switzerland, Albert Einstein showed that mass can be converted into energy.

1911	New Zealand physicist Ernest Rutherford proposed the nuclear model of the atom.
1919	Rutherford split the atom, by bombarding a nitrogen nucleus with alpha particles.
1939	Otto Hahn, Fritz Strassman, and Lise Meitner announced the discovery of nuclear fission.
1942	Enrico Fermi built the first nuclear reactor, in a squash court at the University of Chicago, USA.
1946	The first fast reactor, called Clementine, was built at Los Alamos, New Mexico.
1951	The Experimental Breeder Reactor, Idaho, USA, produced the first electricity to be generated by nuclear energy.
1954	The first reactor for generating electricity was built in the USSR, at Obninsk.
1956	The world's first commercial nuclear power station, Calder Hall, came into operation in the UK.
1957	The release of radiation from Windscale (now Sellafield) nuclear power station, Cumbria, England, caused 39 deaths to 1977. In Kyshym, USSR, the venting of plutonium waste caused high but undisclosed casualties (30 small communities were deleted from maps produced in 1958).
1959	Experimental fast reactor built in Dounreay, N Scotland.
1979	Nuclear reactor accident at Three Mile Island, Pennsylvania, USA.
1986	An explosive leak from a reactor at Chernobyl, the Ukraine, resulted in clouds of radioactive material spreading as far as Sweden; 31 people were killed and thousands of square kilometres were contaminated.
1991	The first controlled and substantial production of nuclear-fusion energy (a two-second pulse of 1.7 MW) was achieved at JET, the Joint European Torus, at Culham, Oxfordshire, England.
1993	The Tokamak Fusion Test Reactor at Princeton University, USA, generated 6.2 MW of power for four seconds – the most energy ever generated by controlled nuclear fusion.

PHYSICS

c. 400 BC	The first 'atomic' theory was put forward by Democritus.
c. 250	Archimedes' principle of buoyancy was established.
AD 1600	Magnetism was described by William Gilbert.

1608	Hans Lippershey invented the refracting telescope.
c. 1610	The principle of falling bodies descending to earth at the same speed was established by Galileo.
1642	The principles of hydraulics were put forward by Blaise Pascal.
1643	The mercury barometer was invented by Evangelista Torricelli.
1656	The pendulum clock was invented by Christiaan Huygens.
1662	Boyle's law concerning the behaviour of gases was established by Robert Boyle.
c. 1665	Isaac Newton put forward the law of gravity, stating that the Earth exerts a constant force on falling bodies.
1690	The wave theory of light was propounded by Christiaan Huygens.
1704	The corpuscular theory of light was put forward by Isaac Newton.
1714	The mercury thermometer was invented by Daniel Fahrenheit.
1764	Specific and latent heats were described by Joseph Black.
1771	The link between nerve action and electricity was discovered by Luigi Galvani.
c. 1787	Charles's law relating the pressure, volume, and temperature of a gas was established by Jacques Charles.
1795	The metric system was adopted in France.
1798	The link between heat and friction was discovered by Benjamin Rumford.
1800	Alessandro Volta invented the Voltaic cell.
1801	Interference of light was discovered by Thomas Young.
1808	The 'modern' atomic theory was propounded by John Dalton.
1811	Avogadro's hypothesis relating volumes and numbers of molecules of gases was proposed by Amedeo Avogadro.
1814	Fraunhofer lines in the solar spectrum were mapped by Joseph von Fraunhofer.
1815	Refraction of light was explained by Augustin Fresnel.
1819	The discovery of electromagnetism was made by Hans Oersted.
1821	The dynamo principle was described by Michael Faraday; the thermocouple was discovered by Thomas Seebeck.
1822	The laws of electrodynamics were established by André Ampère.
1824	Thermodynamics as a branch of physics was proposed by Sadi Carnot.

1827	Ohm's law of electrical resistance was established by Georg Ohm; Brownian movement resulting from molecular vibrations was observed by Robert Brown.
1829	The law of gaseous diffusion was established by Thomas Graham.
1831	Electromagnetic induction was discovered by Faraday.
1834	Faraday discovered self-induction.
1842	The principle of conservation of energy was observed by Julius von Mayer.
c. 1847	The mechanical equivalent of heat was described by James Joule.
1849	A measurement of speed of light was put forward by French physicist Armand Fizeau (1819–1896).
1851	The rotation of the Earth was demonstrated by Jean Foucault.
1858	The mirror galvanometer, an instrument for measuring small electric currents, was invented by William Thomson (Lord Kelvin).
1859	Spectrographic analysis was made by Robert Bunsen and Gustav Kirchhoff.
1861	Osmosis was discovered.
1873	Light was conceived as electromagnetic radiation by James Maxwell.
1877	A theory of sound as vibrations in an elastic medium was propounded by John Rayleigh.
1880	Piezoelectricity was discovered by Pierre Curie.
1887	The existence of radio waves was predicted by Heinrich Hertz.
1895	X-rays were discovered by Wilhelm Röntgen.
1896	The discovery of radioactivity was made by Antoine Becquerel.
1897	Joseph Thomson discovered the electron.
1899	Ernest Rutherford discovered alpha and beta rays.
1900	Quantum theory was propounded by Max Planck; the discovery of gamma rays was made by French physicist Paul-Ulrich Villard (1860–1934).
1902	Oliver Heaviside discovered the ionosphere.
1904	The theory of radioactivity was put forward by Rutherford and Frederick Soddy.
1905	Albert Einstein propounded his special theory of relativity.
1908	The Geiger counter was invented by Hans Geiger and Rutherford.
1911	The discovery of the atomic nucleus was made by Rutherford.
1913	The orbiting electron atomic theory was propounded by

	Danish physicist Niels Bohr.
1915	X-ray crystallography was discovered by William and Lawrence Bragg.
1916	Einstein put forward his general theory of relativity; mass spectrography was discovered by William Aston.
1924	Edward Appleton made his study of the Heaviside layer.
1926	Wave mechanics was introduced by Erwin Schrödinger.
1927	The uncertainty principle of atomic physics was established by Werner Heisenberg.
1931	The cyclotron was developed by Ernest Lawrence.
1932	The discovery of the neutron was made by James Chadwick; the electron microscope was developed by Vladimir Zworykin.
1933	The positron, the antiparticle of the electron, was discovered by Carl Anderson.
1934	Artificial radioactivity was developed by Frédéric and Irène Joliot-Curie.
1939	The discovery of nuclear fission was made by Otto Hahn and Fritz Strassmann.
1942	The first controlled nuclear chain reaction was achieved by Enrico Fermi.
1956	The neutrino, an elementary particle, was discovered by Clyde Cowan and Fred Reines.
1960	The Mössbauer effect of atom emissions was discovered by Rudolf Mössbauer; the first maser was developed by US physicist Theodore Maiman (1927–).
1963	Maiman developed the first laser.
1964	Murray Gell-Mann and George Zweig discovered the quark.
1967	Jocelyn Bell (now Burnell) and Antony Hewish discovered pulsars (rapidly rotating neutron stars that emit pulses of energy).
1971	The theory of superconductivity was announced, where electrical resistance in some metals vanishes above absolute zero.
1979	The discovery of the asymmetry of elementary particles was made by US physicists James W Cronin and Val L Fitch.
1982	The discovery of processes involved in the evolution of stars was made by Subrahmanyan Chandrasekhar and William Fowler.
1983	Evidence of the existence of weakons (W and Z particles) was confirmed at CERN, validating the link between the weak nuclear force and the electromagnetic force.
1986	The first high-temperature superconductor was discovered,

able to conduct electricity without resistance at a temperature of –238°C/–396°F.

1989 CERN's Large Electron Positron Collider (LEP), a particle accelerator with a circumference of 27 km/16.8 mi, came into operation.

1991 LEP experiments demonstrated the existence of three generations of elementary particles, each with two quarks and two leptons.

1992 Japanese researchers developed a material that becomes superconducting at –103°C/–153°F (about 45°C/80°F warmer than the previous record).

1993 Top quark discovered at Fermilab, the US particle-physics laboratory, near Chicago, USA.

RAILWAYS

1500s Tramways – wooden tracks along which trolleys ran – were in use in mines.

1789 Flanged wheels running on cast-iron rails were first introduced; cars were still horse-drawn.

1804 Richard Trevithick built the first steam locomotive, and ran it on the track at the Pen-y-darren ironworks in South Wales.

1825 George Stephenson in England built the first public railway to carry steam trains – the Stockton and Darlington line – using his engine *Locomotion*.

1829 Stephenson designed his locomotive *Rocket*.

1830 Stephenson completed the Liverpool and Manchester Railway, the first steam passenger line. The first US-built locomotive, *Best Friend of Charleston*, went into service on the South Carolina Railroad.

1835 Germany pioneered steam railways in Europe, using *Der Adler*, a locomotive built by Stephenson.

1863 Robert Fairlie, a Scot, patented a locomotive with pivoting driving bogies, allowing tight curves in the track (this was later applied in the Garratt locomotives). London opened the world's first underground railway, powered by steam.

1869 The first US transcontinental railway was completed at Promontory, Utah, when the Union Pacific and the Central Pacific railroads met. George Westinghouse of the USA invented the compressed-air brake.

1879 Werner von Siemens demonstrated an electric train in

Germany. Volk's Electric Railway along the Brighton seafront in England was the world's first public electric railway.

1883　　Charles Lartique built the first monorail, in Ireland.

1885　　The trans-Canada continental railway was completed, from Montréal in the east to Port Moody, British Columbia, in the west.

1890　　The first electric underground railway opened in London.

1901　　The world's longest-established monorail, the Wuppertal Schwebebahn, went into service in Germany.

1912　　The first diesel locomotive took to the rails in Germany.

1938　　The British steam locomotive *Mallard* set a steam-rail speed record of 203 kph/126 mph.

1941　　Swiss Federal Railways introduced a gas-turbine locomotive.

1964　　Japan National Railways inaugurated the 515 km/320 mi New Tokaido line between Osaka and Tokyo, on which the 210 kph/130 mph 'bullet' trains run.

1973　　British Rail's High Speed Train (HST) set a diesel-rail speed record of 229 kph/142 mph.

1979　　Japan National Railways' maglev test vehicle ML-500 attained a speed of 517 kph/321 mph.

1981　　France's Train à Grande Vitesse (TGV) superfast trains began operation between Paris and Lyons, regularly attaining a peak speed of 270 kph/168 mph.

1987　　British Rail set a new diesel-traction speed record of 238.9 kph/148.5 mph, on a test run between Darlington and York; France and the UK began work on the Channel Tunnel, a railway link connecting the two countries, running beneath the English Channel.

1988　　The West German Intercity Experimental train reached 405 kph/252 mph on a test run between Würzburg and Fulda.

1990　　A new rail-speed record of 515 kph/320 mph was established by a French TGV train, on a stretch of line between Tours and Paris.

1991　　The British and French twin tunnels met 23 km/14 mi out to sea to form the Channel Tunnel.

1993　　British Rail privatization plans announced; government investment further reduced.

SHIPS

8000–7000 BC	Reed boats were developed in Mesopotamia and Egypt; dugout canoes were used in NW Europe.
4000–3000	The Egyptians used single-masted square-rigged ships on the Nile.
1200	The Phoenicians built keeled boats with hulls of wooden planks.
1st C BC	The Chinese invented the rudder.
AD 200	The Chinese built ships with several masts.
200–300	The Arabs and Romans developed fore-and-aft rigging that allowed boats to sail across the direction of wind.
800–900	Square-rigged Viking longboats crossed the North Sea to Britain, the Faroe Islands, and Iceland.
1090	The Chinese invented the magnetic compass.
1400–1500	Three-masted ships were developed in W Europe, stimulating voyages of exploration.
1620	Dutch engineer Cornelius Drebbel invented the submarine.
1776	US engineer David Bushnell built a hand-powered submarine, *Turtle*, with buoyancy tanks.
1777	The first boat with an iron hull was built in Yorkshire, England.
1783	Frenchman Jouffroy d'Abbans built the first paddle-driven steamboat.
1802	Scottish engineer William Symington launched the first stern paddle-wheel steamer, the *Charlotte Dundas*.
1807	The first successful steamboat, the *Clermont*, designed by US engineer and inventor Robert Fulton, sailed between New York and Albany.
1836	The screw propeller was patented, by Francis Pettit Smith in the UK.
1838	British engineer Isambard Kingdom Brunel's *Great Western*, the first steamship built for crossing the Atlantic, sailed from Bristol to New York in 15 days.
1845	*Great Britain*, also built by Isambard Kingdom Brunel, became the first propeller-driven iron ship to cross the Atlantic.
1845	The first clipper ship, *Rainbow*, was launched in the USA.
1863	*Plongeur*, the first submarine powered by an air-driven engine, was launched in France.
1866	The British clippers *Taeping* and *Ariel* sailed, laden with tea, from China to London in 99 days.

1886	German engineer Gottlieb Daimler built the first boat powered by an internal-combustion engine.
1897	English engineer Charles Parson fitted a steam turbine to *Turbinia*, making it the fastest boat of the time.
1900	Irish-American John Philip Holland designed the first modern submarine *Holland VI*, fitted with an electric motor for underwater sailing and an internal-combustion engine for surface travel; E Forlanini of Italy built the first hydrofoil.
1902	The French ship *Petit-Pierre* became the first boat to be powered by a diesel engine.
1955	The first nuclear-powered submarine, *Nautilus*, was built in the USA; the hovercraft was patented by British inventor Christopher Cockerell.
1959	The first nuclear-powered surface ship, the Soviet ice-breaker *Lenin*, was commissioned; the US *Savannah* became the first nuclear-powered merchant (passenger and cargo) ship.
1980	Launch of the first wind-assisted commercial ship for half a century, the Japanese tanker *Shin-Aitoku-Maru*.
1983	German engineer Ortwin Fries invented a hinged ship designed to bend into a V-shape in order to scoop up oil spillages in its jaws.
1989	*Gentry Eagle* set a record for the fastest crossing of the Atlantic in a power vessel, taking 2 days, 14 hours, and 7 minutes.
1990	*Hoverspeed Great Britain*, a wave-piercing catamaran, crossed the Atlantic in 3 days, 7 hours, and 52 minutes, setting a record for the fastest crossing by a passenger vessel. The world's largest car and passenger ferry, the *Silja Serenade*, entered service between Stockholm and Helsinki, carrying 2,500 passengers and 450 cars.
1992	Japanese propellerless ship *Yamato* driven by magnetohydrodynamics completes its sea trials. The ship uses magnetic forces to suck in and eject sea water like a jet engine.

SPACE FLIGHT

1903	Russian scientist Konstantin Tsiolkovsky published the first practical paper on aeronautics.
1926	US engineer Robert Goddard launched the first liquid-fuel rocket.
1937–45	In Germany, Wernher von Braun developed the V2 rocket.

1957	4 Oct: The first space satellite, *Sputnik 1* (USSR, Russian 'fellow-traveller'), orbited the Earth at a height of 229–898 km/142–558 mi in 96.2 min.
	3 Nov: *Sputnik 2* was launched carrying a dog, 'Laika'; it died on board seven days later.
1958	31 Jan: *Explorer 1*, the first US satellite, discovered the Van Allen radiation belts.
1961	12 April: the first crewed spaceship, *Vostok 1* (USSR), with Yuri Gagarin on board, was recovered after a single orbit of 89.1 min at a height of 142–175 km/88–109 mi.
1962	20 Feb: John Glenn in *Friendship 7* (USA) became the first American to orbit the Earth. *Telstar* (USA), a communications satellite, sent the first live television transmission between the USA and Europe.
1963	16–19 June: Valentina Tereshkova in *Vostok 1* (USSR) became the first woman in space.
1967	24 April: Vladimir Komarov was the first person to be killed in space research, when his ship, *Soyuz 1* (USSR), crash-landed on the Earth.
1969	20 July: Neil Armstrong of *Apollo 11* (USA) was the first person to walk on the Moon.
1970	10 Nov: *Luna 17* (USSR) was launched; its space probe, *Lunokhod*, took photographs and made soil analyses of the Moon's surface.
1971	19 April: *Salyut 1* (USSR), the first orbital space station, was established; it was later visited by the *Soyuz 11* crewed spacecraft.
1973	*Skylab 2*, the first US orbital space station, was established.
1975	15–24 July: *Apollo 18* (USA) and *Soyuz 19* (USSR) made a joint flight and linked up in space.
1979	The European Space Agency's satellite launcher, *Ariane 1*, was launched.
1981	12 April: The first reusable crewed spacecraft, the space shuttle *Columbia* (USA), was launched.
1986	Space shuttle *Challenger* (USA) exploded shortly after take-off, killing all seven crew members.
1988	US shuttle programme resumed with launch of *Discovery*. Soviet shuttle *Buran* was launched from the rocket *Energiya*. Soviet cosmonauts Musa Manarov and Vladimir Titov in space station *Mir* spent a record 365 days 59 min in space.
1990	April: Hubble Space Telescope (USA) was launched from Cape Canaveral.

1 June: X-ray and ultraviolet astronomy satellite *ROSAT* (USA/Germany/UK) was launched from Cape Canaveral.

2 Dec: *Astro-1* ultraviolet observatory and the Broad Band X-ray Telescope were launched from the space shuttle *Columbia*. Japanese television journalist Toyohiro Akiyama was launched with Viktor Afanasyev and Musa Manarov to the space station *Mir*.

1991 5 April: The Gamma Ray Observatory was launched from the space shuttle *Atlantis* to survey the sky at gamma-ray wavelengths.

18 May: Astronaut Helen Sharman, the first Briton in space, was launched with Anatoli Artsebarsky and Sergei Krikalek to *Mir* space station, returning to Earth 26 May in *Soyuz TM-11* with Viktor Afanasyev and Musa Manarov. Manarov set a record for the longest time spent in space, 541 days, having also spent a year aboard *Mir* 1988.

1992 European satellite *Hipparcos*, launched 1989 to measure the position of 120,000 stars, failed to reach geostationary orbit and went into a highly elliptical orbit, swooping to within 500 km/308 mi of the Earth every ten hours. The mission was later retrieved.

16 May: Space shuttle *Endeavour* returned to Earth after its maiden voyage. During its mission, it circled the Earth 141 times and travelled 4 million km/2.5 million mi.

23 Oct: *LAGEOS II* (Laser Geodynamics Satellite) was released from the space shuttle *Columbia* into an orbit so stable that it will still be circling the Earth in billions of years.

Dec: Space shuttle *Endeavour* successfully carried out mission to replace the Hubble Space Telescope's solar panels and repair its mirror.

1994 4 Feb: Japan's heavy-lifting *H-2* rocket was launched successfully, carrying an uncrewed shuttle craft.

SPACE PROBES

1959	13 Sept: *Luna 2* (USSR) hit the Moon, the first craft to do so.
	10 Oct: *Luna 3* photographed the far side of the Moon.
1962	14 Dec: *Mariner 2* (USA) flew past Venus; launch date 26 Aug 1962.
1964	31 July: *Ranger 7* (USA) hit the Moon, having sent back 4,316 pictures before impact.
1965	14 July: *Mariner 4* flew past Mars; launch date 28 Nov 1964.

1966	3 Feb: *Luna 9* achieved the first soft landing on the Moon, having transmitted 27 close up panoramic photographs; launch date 31 Jan 1966.
	2 June: *Surveyor 1* (USA) landed softly on the Moon and returned 11,150 pictures; launch date 30 May 1965.
1971	13 Nov: *Mariner 9* entered orbit of Mars; launch date 30 May 1971.
1973	3 Dec: *Pioneer 10* (USA) flew past Jupiter; launch date 3 March 1972.
1974	29 March: *Mariner 10* flew past Mercury; launch date 3 Nov 1973.
1975	22 Oct: *Venera 9* (USSR) landed softly on Venus and returned its first pictures; launch date 8 June 1975.
1976	20 July: *Viking 1* (USA) first landed on Mars; launch date 20 Aug 1975.
	3 Sept: *Viking 2* transmitted data from the surface of Mars.
1977	20 Aug: *Voyager 2* (USA) launched. 5 Sept: *Voyager 1* launched.
1978	4 Dec: *Pioneer-Venus 1* (USA) orbited Venus; launch date 20 May 1978.
1979	5 March and 9 July: *Voyager 1* and *Voyager 2* encountered Jupiter, respectively.
1980	12 Nov: *Voyager 1* reached Saturn.
1981	25 Aug: *Voyager 2* flew past Saturn.
1982	1 March: *Venera 13* transmitted its first colour pictures of the surface of Venus; launch date 30 Oct 1981.
1983	10 Oct: *Venera 15* mapped the surface of Venus from orbit; launch date 2 June 1983.
1985	2 July: *Giotto* (European Space Agency) launched to Halley's comet.
1986	24 Jan: *Voyager 2* encountered Uranus.
	13–14 March: *Giotto* met Halley's comet, closest approach 596 km/370 mi, at a speed 50 times faster than that of a bullet.
1989	4 May: *Magellan* (USA) launched from space shuttle *Atlantis* on a 15–month cruise to Venus across 15 million km/9 million mi of space.
	25 Aug: *Voyager 2* reached Neptune (4,400 million km/2,700 million mi from Earth), approaching it to within 4,850 km/3,010 mi.
	18 Oct: *Galileo* (USA) launched from space shuttle *Atlantis* for six-year journey to Jupiter.

1990	10 Aug: *Magellan* arrived at Venus and transmitted its first pictures 16 Aug 1990.
	6 Oct: *Ulysses* (European Space Agency) launched from space shuttle *Discovery*, to study the Sun.
1991	29 Oct: *Galileo* made the closest-ever approach to an asteroid, Gaspra, flying within 1,600 km/990 mi.
1992	8 Feb: *Ulysses* flew past Jupiter at a distance of 380,000 km/236,000 mi from the surface, just inside the orbit of Io and closer than 11 of Jupiter's 16 moons.
	10 July: *Giotto* (USA) flew at a speed of 14 kms/8.5 mps to within 200 km/124 mi of comet Grigg-Skellerup, 12 light years (240 million km/150 mi) away from Earth.
	25 Sept: *Mars Observer* (USA) launched from Cape Canaveral, the first US mission to Mars for 17 years.
	10 Oct: *Pioneer-Venus 1* burned up in the atmosphere of Venus.
1993	21 Aug: *Mars Observer* disappeared three days before it was due to drop into orbit around Mars.
	28 Aug: *Galileo* flew past the asteroid Ida.

TELECOMMUNICATIONS

1794	Claude Chappe in France built a long-distance signalling system using semaphore.
1839	Charles Wheatstone and William Cooke devised an electric telegraph in England.
1843	Samuel Morse transmitted the first message along a telegraph line in the USA, using his Morse code of signals – short (dots) and long (dashes).
1858	The first transatlantic telegraph cable was laid.
1876	Alexander Graham Bell invented the telephone.
1877	Thomas Edison invented the carbon transmitter for the telephone.
1878	The first telephone exchange was opened at New Haven, Connecticut.
1884	The first long-distance telephone line was installed, between Boston and New York.
1891	A telephone cable was laid between England and France.
1892	The first automatic telephone exchange was opened, at La Porte, Indiana.

1894	Guglielmo Marconi pioneered wireless telegraphy in Italy, later moving to England.
1900	Reginald Fessenden in the USA first broadcast voice by radio.
1901	Marconi transmitted the first radio signals across the Atlantic.
1904	John Ambrose Fleming invented the thermionic valve.
1907	Charles Krumm introduced the forerunner of the teleprinter.
1920	Stations in Detroit and Pittsburgh began regular radio broadcasts.
1922	The BBC began its first radio transmissions, for the London station 2LO.
1932	The Post Office introduced the Telex in Britain.
1956	The first transatlantic telephone cable was laid.
1962	Telstar pioneered transatlantic satellite communications, transmitting live TV pictures.
1966	Charles Kao in England advanced the idea of using optical fibres for telecommunications transmissions.
1969	Live TV pictures were sent from astronauts on the Moon back to Earth.
1975	The Post Office announced Prestel, the world's first viewdata system, using the telephone lines to link a computer data bank with the TV screen.
1977	The first optical fibre cable was installed in California.
1984	First commercial cellphone service started in Chicago, USA.
1988	International Services Digital Network (ISDN), an international system for sending signals in digital format along optical fibres and coaxial cable, launched in Japan.
1989	The first transoceanic optical fibre cable, capable of carrying 40,000 simultaneous telephone conversations, was laid between Europe and the USA.
1991	ISDN introduced in the UK.
1992	Videophones, made possible by advances in image compression and the development of ISDN, introduced in the UK.
1993	Electronic version of the *Guardian* newspaper, for those with impaired vision, launched in the UK. The newspaper is transmitted to the user's home and printed out in braille or spoken by a speech synthesizer.

TELEVISION

1878	William Crookes in England invented the Crookes tube, which produced cathode rays.

1884	Paul Nipkow in Germany built a mechanical scanning device, the Nipkow disc, a rotating disc with a spiral pattern of holes in it.
1897	Karl Ferdinand Braun, also in Germany, modified the Crookes tube to produce the ancestor of the TV receiver picture tube.
1906	Boris Rosing in Russia began experimenting with the Nipkow disc and cathode-ray tube, eventually succeeding in transmitting some crude TV pictures.
1923	Vladimir Zworykin in the USA invented the first electronic camera tube, the iconoscope.
1926	John Logie Baird demonstrated a workable TV system, using mechanical scanning by Nipkow disc.
1928	Baird demonstrated colour TV.
1929	The BBC began broadcasting experimental TV programmes, using Baird's system.
1936	The BBC began regular broadcasting, using Baird's system, from Alexandra Palace, London.
1940	Experimental colour TV transmission began in the USA, using the present-day system of colour reproduction.
1953	Successful colour TV transmissions began in the USA.
1956	The first videotape recorder was produced in California by the Ampex Corporation.
1962	TV signals were transmitted across the Atlantic via the Telstar satellite.
1970	The first videodisc system was announced by Decca in Britain and AEG-Telefunken in Germany, but it was not perfected until the 1980s, when laser scanning was used for playback.
1973	The BBC and Independent Television in the UK introduced the world's first teletext systems, Ceefax and Oracle, respectively.
1975	Sony introduced their videocassette tape-recorder system, Betamax, for domestic viewers, six years after their professional U-Matic system. The UK Post Office (now British Telecom) announced their Prestel viewdata system.
1979	Matsushita in Japan developed a pocket-sized, flat-screen TV set, using a liquid-crystal display.
1986	Data broadcasting using digital techniques was developed; an enhancement of teletext was produced.
1989	The Japanese began broadcasting high-definition television; satellite television was introduced in the UK.
1990	The BBC introduced a digital stereo sound system (NICAM); MAC, a European system allowing greater picture definition, more data, and sound tracks, was introduced.

| 1992 | All-digital high-definition television demonstrated in the USA. |
| 1993 | A worldwide standard for digital television agreed at meeting of manufacturers and broadcasters in Sydney, Australia. |

WEAPONS

13th C	Gunpowder brought to the West from China (where it was long in use but only for fireworks).
c. 1300	Guns invented by the Arabs, with bamboo muzzles reinforced with iron.
1346	Battle of Crécy in which gunpowder was probably used in battle for the first time.
1376	Explosive shells used in Venice.
17th C	Widespread use of guns and cannon in the Thirty Years' War and English Civil War.
1800	Henry Shrapnel invented shrapnel for the British army.
1862	Machine gun invented by Richard Gatling used against American Indians in the USA.
1863	TNT discovered by German chemist J Wilbrand.
1867	Dynamite patented by Alfred Nobel.
1915	Poison gas (chlorine) used for the first time by the Germans in World War I.
1916	Tanks used for the first time by the British at Cambrai.
1945	First test explosion and military use of atom bomb by the USA against Japan.
1954–73	Vietnam War, use of chemical warfare (defoliants and other substances) by the USA.
1983	Star Wars or Strategic Defense Initiative research announced by the USA to develop space laser and particle-beam weapons as a possible future weapons system in space.
1991	'Smart' weapons used by the USA and allied powers in the Gulf War; equipped with computers (using techniques such as digitized terrain maps) and laser guidance, they reached their targets with precision accuracy (for example a 'smart' bomb destroyed the Ministry of Air Defence in Baghdad by flying into an air shaft).

The Arts

CINEMA

1826-34	Various machines invented to show moving images: the stroboscope, zoetrope, and thaumatrope.
1872	Eadweard Muybridge demonstrated movement of horses' legs by using 24 cameras.
1877	Invention of Praxinoscope; developed as a projector of successive images on screen 1879 in France.
1878–95	Marey, a French physiologist, developed various types of camera for recording human and animal movements.
1887	Augustin le Prince produced the first series of images on a perforated film; Thomas A Edison, having developed the phonograph, took the first steps in developing a motion-picture recording and reproducing device to accompany recorded sound.
1888	William Friese-Greene (1855–1921) showed the first celluloid film and patented a movie camera.
1889	Edison invented 35–mm film.
1890–94	Edison, using perforated film, developed his Kinetograph camera and Kinetoscope individual viewer; developed commercially in New York, London, and Paris.
1895	The Lumière brothers projected, to a paying audience, a film of an oncoming train arriving at a station. Some of the audience fled in terror.
1896	Charles Pathé introduced the Berliner gramophone, using discs in synchronization with film. Lack of amplification, however, made the performances ineffective.
1899	Edison tried to improve amplification by using banks of phonographs.
1900	Attempts to synchronize film and disc were made by Leon Gaumont (1863–1946) in France and Goldschmidt in Germany, leading later to the Vitaphone system of the USA.
1902	Georges Méliès made *Le Voyage dans la lune/A Trip to the Moon*.
1903	The first Western was made in the USA: *The Great Train Robbery* by Edwin Porter.
1906	The earliest colour film (Kinemacolor) was patented in Britain by George Albert Smith (1864–1959).

1907–11	The first films shot in the Los Angeles area called Hollywood. In France, Emile Cohl (1857–1938) experimented with film animation.
1910	With the influence of US studios and fan magazines, film actors and actresses began to be recognized as international stars.
1911	The first Hollywood studio, Horsley's Centaur Film Company, was established, followed in 1915 by Carl Laemmle's Universal City and Thomas Ince's studio.
1912	In Britain, Eugene Lauste designed experimental 'sound on film' systems.
1914–18	Full newsreel coverage of World War I.
1915	*The Birth of a Nation*, D W Griffith's epic on the American Civil War, was released in the USA.
1917	35 mm was officially adopted as the standard format for motion picture film by the Society of Motion Picture Engineers of America.
1918–19	A sound system called Tri-Ergon was developed in Germany, which led to sound being recorded on film photographically. Photography with sound was also developed in the USA by Lee De Forest in his Phonofilm system.
1923	First sound film (as Phonofilm) demonstrated.
1926	*Don Juan*, a silent film with a synchronized music score, was released.
1927	Release of the first major sound film, *The Jazz Singer*, consisting of some songs and a few moments of dialogue, by Warner Brothers, New York City. The first Academy Awards (Oscars) were presented.
1928	Walt Disney released his first Mickey Mouse cartoon, *Steamboat Willie*. The first all-talking film, *Lights of New York*, was released.
1930	*The Big Trail*, a Western filmed and shown in 70 mm rather than the standard 35 mm format, was released. 70 mm is still used, mainly for big-budget epics such as *Lawrence of Arabia*.
1932	Technicolor (three-colour) process introduced and used for a Walt Disney cartoon film.
1935	*Becky Sharp*, the first film in three-colour Technicolor was released.
1937	Walt Disney released the first feature-length (82 minutes) cartoon, *Snow White and the Seven Dwarfs*.
1939	*Gone with the Wind*, regarded as one of Hollywood's greatest achievements, was released.
1952	Cinerama, a wide-screen presentation using three cameras and three projectors, was introduced in New York.

1953	Commercial 3–D (three-dimensional) cinema and wide-screen CinemaScope were launched in the USA. CinemaScope used a single camera and projector to produce a wide-screen effect with an anamorphic lens. The 3–D cameras were clumsy and the audiences disliked wearing the obligatory glasses. The new wide-screen cinema was accompanied by the introduction of Stereographic sound, which eventually became standard.
1959	The first film in Smell-O-Vision, *The Scent of Mystery*, was released. The process did not catch on.
1980	Most major films were released in Dolby stereo.
1981	Designated 'the Year of Color Film' by director Martin Scorsese in a campaign to draw attention to, and arrest, the deterioration of colour film shot since 1950.
1982	One of the first and most effective attempts at feature-length, computer-generated animation was *Tron*, Walt Disney's $20–million bid to break into the booming fantasy market. 3–D made a brief comeback; some of the films released that used the process, such as *Jaws 3–D* and *Friday the 13th Part 3*, were commercial successes, but the revival was short-lived.
1987	US House Judiciary Committee petitioned by leading Hollywood filmmakers to protect their work from electronic 'colorization', the new process by which black-and-white films were tinted for television transmission.
1988	Robert Zemeckis' (1952–) *Who Framed Roger Rabbit* set new technical standards in combining live action with cartoon animation.

DANCE

1000 BC	King David danced 'with all his might' before the ark of the Covenant in Jerusalem – one of the earliest known instances of ritual dance.
405	*Bacchants* by Euripides was staged in Athens. The play demanded a considerable amount of dancing.
142	Consul Scipio Aemilianus Africanus closed the burgeoning dance schools of Rome in a drive against hedonism.
AD 774	Pope Zacharias forbade dancing.
1050	The *Ruodlieb*, a poem written by a monk at Tegernsee, Bavaria, contained the first European reference to dancing in couples.
1313	Rabbi Hacén ben Salomo of Zaragoza, in Aragon, like many other Jews in medieval times, was the local dancing master.

1489	A rudimentary allegorical ballet was performed in honour of the marriage of the Duke of Milan, at Tortona, Italy.
1581	In Paris, the first modern-style unified ballet, the *Ballet comique de la reine*, was staged at the court of Catherine de'Medici.
1588	Dance and ballet's first basic text, *L'Orchésographie*, by the priest Jehan Tabouret, was printed in Langres, near Dijon.
1651	In London, John Playford published *The English Dancing Master*. The 18th edition (1728) described 900 country dances.
1661	Louis XIV founded L'Académie Royale de Danse in Paris.
1670	The first classic ballet, *Le Bourgeois Gentilhomme*, was produced in Chambord, France.
1681	La Fontaine, the first professional female ballet dancer, made her debut in *Le Triomphe de L'amour* at the Paris Opéra.
1734	The dancer Marie Sallé adopted the gauze tunic, precursor to the Romantic tutu, and Marie Camargo shortened her skirts.
1738	The Kirov Ballet was established in St Petersburg, Russia.
1760	The great dancer and choreographer Jean-Georges Noverre published in Lyons *Lettres sur la danse et sur les ballets*, one of the most influential of all ballet books.
1776	The Bolshoi Ballet was established in Moscow.
1778	Noverre and Mozart collaborated on *Les Petits Riens* in Paris. The cast included the celebrated Auguste Vestris.
late 1700s	The waltz originated in Austria and Germany from a popular folk dance, the *Ländler*.
1820	Carlo Blasis, teacher and choreographer, published his *Traité élémentaire théoretique and pratique de l'arte de la danse* in Milan which, together with his later works of dance theory, codified techniques for future generations of dancers.
1821	The first known picture of a ballerina *sur les pointes*, the French Fanny Bias by F Waldeck, dates from this year.
1832	The first performance of *La Sylphide* at the Paris Opéra opened the Romantic era of ballet and established the central significance of the ballerina. Marie Taglioni, the producer's daughter, who created the title role, wore the new-style Romantic tutu.
1841	Ballet's Romantic masterpiece *Giselle* with Carlotta Grisi in the leading role, was produced in Paris.
1845	Four great rival ballerinas of the Romantic era – Taglioni, Grisi, Fanny Cerrito, and Lucile Grahn – appeared together in Perrot's *Pas de Quatre* in London.

1866	*The Black Crook*, the ballet extravaganza from which US vaudeville and musical comedy developed, began its run of 474 performances in New York.
1870	*Coppélia*, 19th-century ballet's comic masterpiece, was presented in Paris.
1877	*La Bayadère* and *Swan Lake* were premiered in Moscow, but the latter failed through poor production and choreography. The Petipa-Ivanov version, in which Pierina Legnani performed 32 *fouettés*, established the work 1895.
1897	Anna Pavlova made her debut in St Petersburg with the Imperial Russian Ballet.
1905	Isadora Duncan appeared in Russia, making an immense impression with her 'antiballet' innovations derived from Greek dance.
1906	Vaslav Nijinsky made his debut in St Petersburg.
1909	The first Paris season given by Diaghilev's troupe of Russian dancers, later to become known as the Ballets Russes, marked the beginning of one of the most exciting periods in Western ballet.
1913	The premiere of Nijinsky's *Le Sacre du printemps/The Rite of Spring* provoked a scandal in Paris.
1914	The foxtrot developed from the two-step in the USA.
1915	The Denishawn School of Modern Dance was founded in Los Angeles.
1926	Martha Graham, one of the most innovative figures in modern dance, gave her first recital in New York. In England, students from the Rambert School of Ballet, opened by Marie Rambert 1920, gave their first public performance in *A Tragedy of Fashion*, the first ballet to be choreographed by Frederick Ashton.
1928	The first performance of George Balanchine's *Apollo* in Paris, by the Ballets Russes, marked the birth of Neo-Classicism in ballet.
1931	Ninette de Valois' Vic-Wells Ballet gave its first performance in London. In 1956 the company became the Royal Ballet.
1933	The Hollywood musical achieved artistic independence through Busby Berkeley's kaleidoscopic choreography in *42nd Street* and Dave Gould's airborne finale in *Flying Down to Rio*, in which Fred Astaire and Ginger Rogers appeared together for the first time.
1939	The American Ballet Theater was founded in New York.
1940	The Dance Notation Bureau was established in New York for recording ballets and dances.

1948	The New York City Ballet was founded with George Balanchine as artistic director and principal choreographer. The film *The Red Shoes* appeared, choreographed by Massine and Robert Helpmann, starring Moira Shearer.
1950	The Festival Ballet, later to become the London Festival Ballet, was created by Alicia Markova and Anton Dolin, who had first danced together with the Ballets Russes de Monte Carlo 1929.
1952	Gene Kelly starred and danced in the film *Singin' in the Rain*.
1953	The US experimental choreographer Merce Cunningham, who often worked with the composer John Cage, formed his own troupe.
1956	The Bolshoi Ballet opened its first season in the West at Covent Garden in London, with Galina Ulanova dancing in *Romeo and Juliet*.
1957	Jerome Robbins conceived and choreographed the musical *West Side Story*, demonstrating his outstanding ability to work in both popular and classical forms.
1960	The progressive French choreographer Maurice Béjart became director of the Brussels-based Ballet du XXième Siècle company.
1961	Rudolf Nureyev defected from the USSR while dancing with the Kirov Ballet in Paris. He was to have a profound influence on male dancing in the West. The South African choreographer John Cranko became director and chief choreographer of the Stuttgart Ballet, transforming it into a major company.
1962	Glen Tetley's ballet *Pierrot lunaire*, in which he was one of the three dancers, was premiered in New York. In the same year he joined the Nederlands Dans Theater.
1965	US choreographer Twyla Tharp produced her first works.
1966–67	The London School of Contemporary Dance was founded from which entrepreneur Robin Howard and the choreographer Robert Cohan created the London Contemporary Dance Theatre, later to become an internationally renowned company.
1968	Arthur Mitchell, the first black principal dancer to join the New York City Ballet, founded the Dance Theatre of Harlem.
1974	Mikhail Baryshnikov defected from the USSR while dancing with the Kirov Ballet in Toronto, and made his US debut with the American Ballet Theater.
1977	The release of Robert Stigwood's film *Saturday Night Fever* popularized disco dancing worldwide.

1980	Natalia Makarova, who had defected from the USSR 1979, staged the first full-length revival of Petipa's *La Bayadère* in the West with the American Ballet Theater in New York.
1981	Wayne Sleep, previously principal dancer with the Royal Ballet, starred as lead dancer in Andrew Lloyd-Webber's musical *Cats*, choreographed by Gillian Lynne.
1983	Peter Martins, principal dancer with the New York City Ballet, became choreographer and co-director with Jerome Robbins on the death of Balanchine. Break dancing became widely popular in Western inner cities.
1984	The avant-garde group Michael Clark and Company made its debut in London.
1988	Avant-garde choreographer Mark Morris and his company replaced Maurice Béjart's at the Théâtre de la Monnaie, Brussels.
1990	*Maple Leaf Rag*, Martha Graham's final work, was premiered in New York City. Classical dancer Peter Schaufuss became artistic director of the Berlin Ballet.
1991	The Royal Ballet moved to Birmingham, England, adopting the new name of the Birmingham Royal Ballet.

LITERATURE IN ENGLISH

871–99	The Anglo-Saxon king Alfred the Great initiated translations from Latin into English, such as the Venerable Bede's *Ecclesiastical History of the English People*.
10th C	The epic poem *Beowulf* was written down. The earliest surviving poem in Old English, it was composed orally about 200 years before and is based on Germanic legend.
c. 1375	The anonymous *Sir Gawayne and the Greene Knight* was written in Middle English. This epic poem still used the alliterative style of Old English verse rather than the rhyming technique of later poetry.
c. 1382	The first complete English translation of the Bible appeared, the 'Wyclif' Bible.
c. 1387	Geoffrey Chaucer's *Canterbury Tales* was the first major work written in modern English.
1476	William Caxton set up his printing press in London, which encouraged the development of English prose writing.
1485	Caxton printed the first great English prose work, Sir Thomas Malory's *Morte D'Arthur*, our main source for the Arthurian legends.

1557	Thomas Wyatt's *Songes and Sonnettes* published (posthumously), introducing the sonnet form to England. They include translations and imitations of the Italian poet Petrarch's work.
1603	John Florio's translations from French of Montaigne's *Essais*. Montaigne was the originator of the modern essay.
1608	The English explorer John Smith's description of the American colonies in *A True Relation of such occurrences and accidents of noate as hath hapnd in Virginia* considered as the beginning of American literature.
1611	The Authorized Version (King James Version) of the Bible published.
1622	The first English newspaper, the *Weekly Newes*, began publication.
1623	The first collected edition of William Shakespeare's plays, known as the *First Folio*, published seven years after his death.
1633	Posthumous publication of the collected poems of John Donne, the most prominent of the Metaphysical poets.
1667	John Milton's epic poem *Paradise Lost* used elaborate Latinate language and many classical and biblical references to create a grand style.
1668	John Dryden's essay *Of Dramatick Poesie* and others made him the first English literary critic (often in defence of his own poetry and plays). He advocated using classical Greek and Roman poetry and drama as models.
1702	The first British daily newspaper, *The Daily Courant*, began publication, followed during the next decade by the journals *the Tatler* and *Spectator*.
1712–14	Alexander Pope's epic poem *The Rape of the Lock* used rhyming couplets in a classical, elevated style to describe the theft of a lock of hair. The wit and satire that it employed flourished in the Age of Reason.
1719	*The Life and Strange and Surprising Adventures of Robinson Crusoe* by Daniel Defoe, sometimes considered the first English novel, was published. Other 18th-century novelists include Samuel Richardson (*Pamela* 1740), Henry Fielding (*Tom Jones* 1749) and Laurence Sterne (*Tristram Shandy* 1759–67).
1726	Jonathan Swift's satire *Gulliver's Travels* was published.
1755	Samuel Johnson published his *Dictionary of the English Language*, which remained the standard dictionary for over a century.

1798	*The Lyrical Ballads,* a selection of poems by William Wordsworth and Samuel Taylor Coleridge, introduced Romanticism in England. The Romantics reacted against the restrictions of rational classicism by emphasizing passion, intuition and the imagination.
1811	With *Sense and Sensibility* Jane Austen became the first major woman novelist.
1824	Lord Byron died while fighting for Greek independence. Having left Britain as the result of a scandal, he was seen throughout Europe as the Romantic poet-hero par excellence.
1837	Nathaniel Hawthorne's *Twice Told Tales* established the American short story as an art form that was to attract many major writers, from Poe and Melville in the 19th century to Mansfield, James and Hemingway in the twentieth.
1837–8	Charles Dickens' novel *Oliver Twist* showed his social concern, seen also in the work of other 19th-century novelists such as the Russian Fyodor Dostoevsky and the Frenchman Emile Zola, about poverty and other social evils.
1841	Edgar Allan Poe's *The Murders in the Rue Morgue* initiates the genre of the detective story, continued by Arthur Conan Doyle later in the century.
1851	The first free public library in Britain opened in Winchester; the first in the USA opened in Boston in 1854.
1865	*Alice's Adventures in Wonderland* by Lewis Carroll (Charles Dodgson) was one of several late 19th-century children's works which are now classics. Other writers included Beatrix Potter, J M Barrie and Louise May Alcott.
1869	With *The Innocents Abroad,* Mark Twain (Samuel Langhorne) established himself as a humourist.
1871–2	George Eliot (Mary Ann Evans) published her novel *Middlemarch;* she was already considered the greatest English novelist of her day.
1881	Henry James' novel *The Portrait of a Lady* explores with a new psychological subtlety the theme of young American culture meeting European cultural tradition.
1891	Thomas Hardy shocked the reading public with *Tess of the d'Urbervilles,* his novel about a girl who has had an illegitimate baby.
1893	The poet William Butler Yeats published his collection of stories *The Celtic Twilight.* Based on Irish mysticism and fairy tales, they show his commitment to reviving Irish national culture.

1895	H G Wells' novel *The Time Machine* was published, a seminal work in the genre of science fiction.
1898	George Bernard Shaw's *Plays Pleasant and Unpleasant* demonstrated his socialist vision.
20th C	The novel became the dominant literary form, developing in a wide variety of directions and genres.
1913	D H Lawrence expressed in *Sons and Lovers* his idea of the vital and creative force of sexuality; *Lady Chatterley's Lover* (1928) was banned in Britain as obscene until 1960.
1919	Ezra Pound published the first three of his influential *Cantos*. Using subjects and verse forms taken from many cultures and ages, they attempt to evaluate social and individual morality.
1922	James Joyce's novel *Ulysses* broke with traditional narrative and exposition, employing a stream-of-consciousness technique. T S Eliot's bleak view of modern life in his collection of poetry *The Waste Land* was greeted by many as outrageous.
1938	Jean-Paul Sartre published his novel *La Nausée/Nausea*, expressing the philosophy of existentialism, which has influenced many modern writers.
1945	George Orwell's (Eric Blair's) political satire *Animal Farm* was published.
1961	The experience of World War II and its absurdity expressed by the black humour of Joseph Heller's novel *Catch-22*.
1983	Alice Walker's novel *The Color Purple* published. Other writers concerned with feminism and minority consciousness include Maya Angelou and Toni Morrison.
1986	The Nigerian Wole Soyinka became the first African author to receive the Nobel Prize for Literature.

MUSIC, WESTERN

AD 590	St Gregory the Great was elected pope. Under his rule, music attained new heights, initiating Gregorian chant.
1026	The Italian monk Guido d'Arezzo completed his treatise *Micrologus*. He founded modern notation and tonic sol-fa.
1207	Minnesingers (poet-musicians) Walther von der Vogelweide, Tannhauser, and Wolfram von Eschenbach competed in a song contest at Wartburg Castle, later celebrated in Wagner's opera *Die Meistersinger von Nürnberg*.
1240	The earliest known canon, *Sumer is Icumen In*, was composed around this year.

1280   *Carmina Burana*, a collection of students' songs, was compiled in Benediktbuern, Bavaria; Carl Orff was later inspired by their subject matter.

1288   France's greatest troubadour, Adam de la Halle, died in Naples.

1320   *Ars nova*, a tract by Philippe de Vitry, gave its name to a new, more graceful era in music.

1364   Music's first large-scale masterpiece, the *Notre Dame Mass* of Guillaume de Machaut, was performed in Reims to celebrate the coronation of Charles V of France.

1453   John Dunstable, England's first composer of significance, died in London.

1473   The earliest known printed music, the *Collectorium super Magnificat* by Johannes Gerson, was published in Esslingen, near Stuttgart.

1521   Josquin Desprez, the leading musician of his time, died in Condé-sur-Escaut, Burgundy.

1550s   Production of violins began at the workshop of Andrea Amati in Cremona.

1575   Thomas Tallis and William Byrd jointly published their *Cantiones sacrae*, a collection of 34 motets.

1576   Hans Sachs, the most famous of the Meistersinger (mastersinger) poets and composers, died in Nuremberg.

1597   The first opera, *La Dafne* by Jacopo Peri, was staged privately at the Corsi Palazzo in Florence.

1610   Monteverdi's *Vespers* was published in Venice.

1637   The world's first opera house opened in Venice.

1644   Antonio Stradivari was born. More than 600 of his violins, made in Cremona, survived into the 20th century.

1672   The violinist John Banister inaugurated the first season of public concerts in London.

1709   Bartolemmeo Cristofori unveiled the first fortepiano in Florence.

1721   Bach completed his six *Brandenburg Concertos* for Baroque orchestra.

1722   Jean-Philippe Rameau's book *Traité de l'harmonie* was published, founding modern harmonic theory.

1725   Vivaldi's orchestral suite *The Four Seasons* was published in Amsterdam.

1732   Covent Garden Theatre opened in London.

1742   Handel's *Messiah* received its world premiere in Dublin.

1757	Johann Stamitz died in Mannheim, where he had made important contributions to the development of the symphony and raised the status of the orchestra.
1761	Haydn took up liveried service as vice kapellmeister with the aristocratic Esterházy family, to whom he was connected until his death 1809.
1788	Mozart completed his last three symphonies, numbers 39–41, in six weeks.
1798	The *Allgemeine Musikalische Zeitung*, a journal of music criticism, was first published in Leipzig.
1805	Beethoven's 'Eroica' Symphony was first performed; it vastly expanded the horizons of orchestral music.
1814	Maelzel invented the metronome.
1815	Schubert's output for this year included two symphonies, two masses, 20 waltzes, and 145 songs.
1821	Weber's *Der Freischütz/The Marksman* introduced heroic German Romanticism to opera.
1828	The limits of instrumental virtuosity were redefined by violinist Paganini's Vienna debut.
1830	Berlioz's dazzlingly avant-garde and programmatic *Symphonie fantastique* startled Paris concertgoers.
1831	Grand opera was inaugurated with *Robert le diable* by Giacomo Meyerbeer.
1851	Jenny Lind, a singer managed by P T Barnum, earned $176,675 from nine months' concerts in the USA.
1842	The Vienna Philharmonic Orchestra gave its first concerts.
1854	In Weimar, Liszt conducted the premieres of his first symphonic poems.
1855	Like most orchestras around this date, the New York Philharmonic for the first time sat down while playing (cellists were already seated).
1865	Wagner's opera *Tristan and Isolde* scaled new heights of expressiveness using unprecedented chromaticism. Schubert's *Unfinished Symphony* (1822) was premiered in Vienna.
1875	The first of a series of collaborations between Arthur Sullivan and the librettist W S Gilbert, *Trial by Jury*, was given its premiere.
1876	Wagner's *The Ring of the Nibelung* was produced in Bayreuth. Brahms' *First Symphony* was performed in Karlsruhe.
1877	Edison invented the cylindrical tin-foil phonograph.
1883	The Metropolitan Opera House opened in New York with a

production of Gounod's *Faust*.

1885	Liszt composed *Bagatelle without Tonality* (his *Faust Symphony* of 1857 opened with a 12–note row).
1894	Debussy's *Prélude à l'après-midi d'un faune* anticipated 20th-century composition with its use of the whole-tone scale.
1895	Henry Wood conducted the first Promenade Concert at the Queen's Hall in London.
1899	Scott Joplin's *Maple Leaf Rag* was published in Sedalia, Missouri.
1902	Caruso recorded ten arias in a hotel room in Milan, the success of which established the popularity of the phonograph. By the time of his death 1921 he had earned $2 million from sales of his recordings.
1908	Saint-Saëns became the first leading composer to write a film score, for *L'Assassinat du duc de Guise*.
1911	Irving Berlin had his first big success as a songwriter with 'Alexander's Ragtime Band'.
1912	Schoenberg's atonal *Pierrot lunaire*, for reciter and chamber ensemble, foreshadowed many similar small-scale quasi-theatrical works.
1913	Stravinsky's ballet *The Rite of Spring* precipitated a riot at its premiere in Paris.
1919	Schoenberg, who was experimenting with serial technique, set up the Society for Private Musical Performances in Vienna, which lasted until 1921.
1922	Alessandro Moreschi, last of the castrati, died in Rome.
1925	Louis Armstrong made his first records with the Hot Five. Duke Ellington's Washingtonians also started recording.
1927	Jerome Kern's *Show Boat*, with libretto by Oscar Hammerstein II, laid the foundations of the US musical.
1930	The BBC Symphony Orchestra was founded in London under Sir Adrian Boult.
1937	Arturo Toscanini, one of the greatest conductors in the history of music, began his 17–year association with the NBC Symphony Orchestra.
1938	Prokofiev's score for Eisenstein's *Alexander Nevsky* raised film music to new levels. Big-band music became popular.
1939	Elisabeth Lutyens was one of the first English composers to use 12–note composition in her *Chamber Concerto No 1* for nine instruments.
1940	Walt Disney's *Fantasia* introduced classical music, conducted by Leopold Stokowski, to a worldwide audience of filmgoers.

1940s	Bebop jazz was initiated. The jazz greats Charlie Parker and Dizzy Gillespie first recorded together.
1941	The 'Proms' moved to the Royal Albert Hall.
1942	In Chicago, John Cage conducted the premiere of his *Imaginary Landscape No 3*, scored for marimbula, gongs, tin cans, buzzers, plucked coil, electric oscillator, and generator.
1954	Stockhausen's *Electronic Studies* for magnetic tape were broadcast in Cologne. Edgard Varèse's *Déserts*, the first work to combine instruments and prerecorded magnetic tape, was performed in Paris. Elvis Presley made his first rock-and-roll recordings.
1955	Pierre Boulez's *Le Marteau sans maître*, for contralto and chamber ensemble, was performed in Baden-Baden. Its formidable serial technique and exotic orchestration was acclaimed by the avant-garde. The Miles Davis Quintet with John Coltrane united two of the most important innovators in jazz.
1956	The first annual Warsaw Autumn festival of contemporary music was held. This became important for the promotion of Polish composers such as Lutoslåwski and Penderecki.
1957	Leonard Bernstein's *West Side Story* was premiered in New York. A computer, programmed at the University of Illinois by Lejaren Hiller and Leonard Isaacson, composed the *Illiac Suite* for string quartet.
1963	Shostakovich's opera *Lady Macbeth of Mezensk*, earlier banned and condemned in the Soviet newspaper *Pravda* 1936, was produced in a revised version as *Katerina Ismaylova*.
1965	Robert Moog invented a synthesizer that considerably widened the scope of electronic music. The film soundtrack of *The Sound of Music*, with music by Rodgers and lyrics by Hammerstein, was released, and stayed in the sales charts for the next two years. Bob Dylan used electric instrumentation on *Highway 61 Revisited*.
1967	The Beatles' album *Sgt Pepper's Lonely Hearts Club Band*, which took over 500 hours to record, was released. The first Velvet Underground album was released. Psychedelic rock spread from San Francisco, and hard rock developed in the UK and the USA.
1969	Peter Maxwell Davies' theatre piece *Eight Songs for a Mad King*, for vocalist and six instruments, was premiered under his direction in London by the Pierrot Players, later to become the Fires of London ensemble.

1972	Bob Marley's LP *Catch a Fire* began popularization of reggae beyond Jamaica.
1976	Philip Glass' opera *Einstein on the Beach*, using the repetitive techniques of minimalism, was given its first performance in Paris. Punk rock arrived with the Sex Pistols' 'Anarchy in the UK'.
1977	The Institute for Research and Coordination of Acoustics and Music (IRCAM) was founded in Paris under the direction of Pierre Boulez, for visiting composers to make use of advanced electronic equipment.
1981	MTV (Music Television) started broadcasting nonstop pop videos on cable in the USA, growing into a worldwide network in the following decade.
1983	Messiaen's only opera, *Saint François d'Assise*, was given its first performance in Paris. Lutosławski's *Third Symphony* was premiered to worldwide acclaim by the Chicago Symphony Orchestra under Georg Solti. Compact discs were launched in the West.
1986	Paul Simon's *Graceland* album drew on and popularized world music.
1990	Many record chain stores ceased to stock seven-inch singles, accelerating the decline of vinyl records' share of the market.
1991	US rap group NWA declared not obscene by a UK court. Various attempts, especially in the USA, to limit freedom of speech in popular music were generally unsuccessful.
1992	DCC (Digital Compact Cassettes) and MiniDisc (MD), two new audio formats, were launched by Philips and Sony, respectively.

PAINTING, WESTERN

27000–13000 BC	Cave art in south-west Europe expressed the concerns of hunters.
3000–100	Egyptian wall paintings combined front, three-quarter and side views of the human body in a flat 'diagrammatic' style.
2000–1450	The Minoan civilization, based at Knossos in Crete, evolved bright wall paintings.
1000–400	Greek painting by the finest artists survived mainly as vase decorations.
AD 79	Volcanic ash from Vesuvius preserved fine examples of Roman domestic painting and mosaics.

230–450	Early Christian murals painted in catacombs and as mosaics in churches.
330–1453	Byzantine art expressed Orthodox Christian values in formalized mosaics and painted icons.
680–800	Celtic Christian art illuminated religious texts such as the *Lindisfarne Gospel* and the *Book of Kells*.
1290–1337	Italian painting emerged from the Byzantine style with the new depth and realism of Giotto, the first great painter of the Italian Renaissance period .
1315–1425	Italian Gothic and then International Gothic evolved an elegant and decorative style.
1420–1492	Fra Angelico, Piero della Francesca and Botticelli brought a new freshness of vision to Italian painting.
1425–50	A new and vivid realism, owing much to the established use of high quality oil paints, appears in the early Renaissance painters of the North such as Jan van Eyck.
c. 1428	Masaccio incorporated Brunelleschi's laws of perspective in his grand and austere *Holy Trinity*, creating an illusion of depth never seen before in painting.
1470–1569	The Northern Renaissance produced a series of disparate geniuses, including Dürer, Bosch, and Brueghel, who expressed the religious anxieties of the age.
1472–1519	Leonardo da Vinci brought a new sense of mystery and psychological depth to painting.
1500–1564	Michelangelo rediscovered classical grandeur and harnessed it to Christian subjects as in the Sistine Chapel frescoes.
1504–1520	Raphael's short career expressed the Florentine Renaissance ideals with an unsurpassed harmony.
1506–1594	The Venetian Renaissance is manifested in the warm sensuality of Titian, Giorgione, Tintoretto and Veronese.
1520–1600	Mannerists, such as Romano, Pontormo and Parmigianino, applied the discoveries of the High Renaissance in more stylized forms.
1525–1792	The tradition of portrait painting in Britain began with Holbein and continued to Reynolds and Gainsborough.
1560–1609	Caravaggio, a master of dramatic light and shade, led the way towards the Baroque style.
1570–1682	The great age of Spanish painting lasted from the tortured religious idealism of El Greco through to Velazquez.
1577–1640	Rubens was the supreme master of the Baroque grand style.
1620–1670	Dutch genre painting produced masters of portraiture, interiors, landscapes and still life.

1624–82	Poussin and Claude established the idealized classical landscape painting.
1626– 1669	Rembrandt brought an unparalled psychological and emotional depth to the biblical scenes and portraits.
1706– 1806	The elegance of French rococo is captured by Watteau, Boucher and Fragonard.
1780– 1851	The Romantic spirit was expressed in the vision of painters such as Goya, Turner, Constable and Delacroix.
1780– 1867	Ingres and David sustained the classicism of the French revolutionary and post-revolutionary periods.
1840– 1877	Courbet developed a radical realism in his work.
1863	Eschewing half-tones and contemporary pictorial conventions, Manet heralded a new era in art.
1870– 1890	Symbolists and Pre-Raphaelites portrayed visionary ideas through the use of symbols and rich colours.
1874	Monet, Renoir and Degas exhibited at the first Impressionist exhibiton with paintings composed of broken surfaces of light.
1883– 1891	Seurat carried the discoveries of the Impressionists further with his pointillist techniques of dots of colour.
1883– 1903	Gauguin's spiritual and sensual odyssey to Tahiti looked forward to expressionism and fauvism.
1885–90	Van Gogh's personal vision invested ordinary scenes with unparalleled emotion and spirituality through broad strokes of bright colour.
1886– 1906	Cézanne created a new kind of painting with solid forms built with a mosaic of brush strokes. His concentration on geometric forms inspired the Cubist movement.
1892– 1926	Munch and later the Expressionists used colour and form to express their inner emotions.
1905	Matisse and the Fauves showed compositions where form was defined by subjective choice of colour.
1907	Les Demoiselles d'Avignon by Picasso heralded the Cubist movement by rejecting conventional naturalistic representation from only one viewpoint and conventional ideas of beauty.
1910– 1914	Kandinsky developed a purely abstract art.
1913	The Armory Show in New York is often regarded as the beginning of public interest in progressive art in the USA.

1913– 1944	A geometrical abstract art was developed by Malevitch, Tatlin, Rodchenko and Mondrian.
From 1914	Duchamp and Dadaists brought an anarchist element to painting that questioned traditional notions of art.
1914– 1940	Klee's figurative painting was built out of abstract patterns.
From 1924	Surrealist painters, notably Dali, Magritte and Miro, reached for unconscious sources of inspiration.
1940s	Abstract Expressionism, developed in New York by Jackson Pollock and Arshile Gorky, added the element of uninhibited expression to pure abstraction.
From 1956	Pop Art returned to representation, drawing on popular images and commercial techniques.
1944– 1992	Bacon re-asserted figure painting with images of revulsion and horror.
From 1960s	An explosion of new approaches to art, employing a wide variety of new materials or no materials at all, and often undermining the traditional notion of painting itself: Hard Edge, Op art, Superreal, Minimal, Happening, Environmental, Performance, Body, Land, Earth and Conceptual Art.

PHOTOGRAPHY

1515	Leonardo da Vinci described the camera obscura.
1750	The painter Canaletto used a camera obscura as an aid to his painting in Venice.
1790	Thomas Wedgwood in England made photograms – placing objects on leather, sensitized using silver nitrate.
1826	Nicephore Niépce (1765–1833), a French doctor, produced the world's first photograph from nature on pewter plates with a camera obscura and an eight-hour exposure.
1838	Niépce and L J M Daguerre produced the first daguerreotype camera photograph.
1839	Daguerre was awarded an annuity by the French government and his process given to the world.
1840	Invention of the Petzval lens, which reduced exposure time by 90%. Herschel discovered sodium thiosulphate as a fixer for silver halides.
1841	Fox Talbot's calotype process was patented – the first multi-copy method of photography using a negative/positive process, sensitized with silver iodide.

1844–46	Fox Talbot published the first photographic book, *The Pencil of Nature*.
1845	Hill and Adamson began to use calotypes for portraits in Edinburgh.
1851	Fox Talbot used a one-thousandth of a second exposure to demonstrate high-speed photography. Invention of the wet-collodion-on-glass process and the waxed-paper negative. Photographs were displayed at the Great Exhibition in London.
1852	The London Society of Arts exhibited 779 photographs.
1855	Roger Fenton made documentary photographs of the Crimean War from a specially constructed caravan with portable darkroom.
1858	Nadar took the first aerial photographs from a balloon.
1859	Nadar in Paris made photographs underground using battery-powered arc lights.
1860	Queen Victoria was photographed by Mayall. Abraham Lincoln was photographed by Matthew Brady for political campaigning.
1861	The single-lens reflex plate camera was patented by Thomas Sutton. The principles of three-colour photography were demonstrated by Scottish physicist James Clerk Maxwell.
1870	Julia Margaret Cameron used long lenses for her distinctive portraits.
1871	Gelatin-silver bromide was developed.
1878	In the USA Eadweard Muybridge analysed the movements of animals through sequential photographs, using a series of cameras.
1879	The photogravure process was invented.
1880	A silver bromide emulsion was fixed with hypo. Photographs were first reproduced in newspapers in New York using the half-tone engraving process. The first twin-lens reflex camera was produced in London. Gelatin-silver chloride paper was introduced.
1884	George Eastman produced flexible negative film.
1889	The Eastman Company in the USA produced the Kodak No 1 camera and roll film, facilitating universal, hand-held snapshots.
1891	The first telephoto lens. The interference process of colour photography was developed by the French doctor Gabriel Lippmann.
1897	The first issue of Alfred Stieglitz's *Camera Notes* in the USA.

1902	In Germany, Deckel invented a prototype leaf shutter and Zeiss introduced the Tessar lens.
1904	The autochrome colour process was patented by the Lumière brothers.
1905	Alfred Stieglitz opened the gallery '291' in New York promoting photography. Lewis Hine used photography to expose the exploitation of children in American factories, causing protective laws to be passed.
1907	The autochrome process began to be factory-produced.
1914	Oskar Barnack designed a prototype Leica camera for Leitz in Germany.
1924	Leitz launched the first 35mm camera, the Leica, delayed because of World War I. It became very popular with photojournalists because it was quiet, small, dependable, and had a range of lenses and accessories.
1929	Rolleiflex produced a twin-lens reflex camera in Germany.
1935	In the USA, Mannes and Godowsky invented Kodachrome transparency film, which produced sharp images and rich colour quality. Electronic flash was invented in the USA.
1936	*Life* magazine, significant for its photojournalism, was first published in the USA.
1938	*Picture Post* magazine was introduced in the UK.
1940	Multigrade enlarging paper by Ilford was made available in the UK.
1942	Kodacolour negative film was introduced.
1945	The zone system of exposure estimation was published in the book *Exposure Record* by Ansel Adams.
1947	Polaroid black and white instant process film was invented by Dr Edwin Land, who set up the Polaroid corporation in Boston, Massachusetts. The principles of holography were demonstrated in England by Dennis Gabor.
1955	Kodak introduced Tri-X, a black and white 200 ASA film.
1959	The zoom lens was invented by the Austrian firm of Voigtlander.
1960	The laser was invented in the USA, making holography possible. Polacolor, a self-processing colour film, was introduced by Polaroid, using a 60–second colour film and dye diffusion technique.
1963	Cibachrome, paper and chemicals for printing directly from transparencies, was made available by Ciba-Geigy of Switzerland. One of the most permanent processes, it is marketed by Ilford in the UK.

1966	The International Center of Photography was established in New York.
1969	Photographs were taken on the Moon by US astronauts.
1970	A charge-coupled device was invented at Bell Laboratories in New Jersey, USA, to record very faint images (for example in astronomy). Rencontres Internationales de la Photographie, the annual summer festival of photography with workshops, was founded in Arles, France.
1971	Opening of the Photographers' Gallery, London, and the Photo Archive of the Bibliothéque Nationale, Paris.
1972	The SX70 system, a single-lens reflex camera with instant prints, was produced by Polaroid.
1975	The Center for Creative Photography was established at the University of Arizona.
1980	Ansel Adams sold an original print, *Moonrise: Hernandez*, for $45,000, a record price, in the USA. *Voyager 1* sent photographs of Saturn back to Earth across space.
1983	The National Museum of Photography, Film and Television opened in Bradford, England.
1985	The Minolta Corporation in Japan introduced the Minolta 7000 – the world's first body-integral autofocus single-lens reflex camera.
1988	The electronic camera, which stores pictures on magnetic disc instead of on film, was introduced in Japan.
1990	Kodak introduced PhotoCD which converts 35mm camera pictures (on film) into digital form and stores them on compact disc (CD) for viewing on TV.
1992	Japanese company Canon introduced a camera with autofocus controlled by the user's eye. The camera focuses on whatever the user is looking at. *Girl with a Leica* by Russian photographer Aleksandr Rodchenko sold for £115,500 at Christie's, London – a world-record price for a photograph.

POTTERY AND PORCELAIN

10,000 BC	Earliest known pottery in Japan.
c. 5000	The potter's wheel was developed by the Egyptians.
c. 600–450	Black-and red-figured vases from Greece.
6th C AD	Fine quality stoneware was developed in China, as the forerunner of porcelain.

7th–10th C	Tang porcelain in China.
10th–13th C	Song porcelain in China.
14th–17th C	Ming porcelain in China; Hispano-Moresque ware.
16th C	**Majolica**, an Italian tin-glazed earthenware with painted decoration, often large dishes with figures; **faience** (from Faenza, Italy) glazed earthenware and delftware.
17th C	Chinese porcelain was first exported to the West; it was soon brought in large quantities (for example, the Nanking Cargo) as a ballast in tea clippers; **delftware** tin-glazed earthenware with white with blue decoration was brought to perfection in Delft, the Netherlands. In North America, colonists made bricks and tiles by 1612.
18th C	In 1710 the first European hardpaste porcelain was made in **Dresden**, Germany, by Johann Böttger (1682–1719); the factory later transferred to **Meissen**; from 1769 hardpaste porcelain as well as softpaste was made in **Sèvres**, France, remarkable for its ground colours; c. 1760 cream-coloured earthenware was perfected (superseding delftware) by Josiah **Wedgwood** in England; he also devised stoneware, typically with white decoration in Neo-Classical designs on a blue ground, still among the wares made in Barlaston, Staffordshire; **English softpaste** was made c. 1745–1810, first in Chelsea, later in Bow, Derby, and Worcester; **English hardpaste** was first made in Plymouth 1768–70, and Bristol 1770–81, when the stock was removed to New Hall in Staffordshire; **bone china** c. 1789 was first produced by Josiah Spode, Coalport, near Shrewsbury, and Thomas Minton followed, as did all English tableware of this type from 1815.
19th C	Large-scale production of fine wares, in Britain notably Royal Worcester from 1862, and Royal (Crown) Derby from 1876. In the USA, potteries established in New Jersey, Pennsylvania, Ohio, New England, and the South made earthenware and stoneware utility items and earthenware, stoneware, and bone china for tableware and fine ornaments.
20th C	There has been a revival in the craft of the individual potter, for example, Bernard Leach, Lucie Rie, and Maria Martinez. California potteries entered the world market.

SCULPTURE, WESTERN

c. 25,000 BC	Small clay models and carvings such as The Venus of Willendorf, probably a magic fertility symbol, made by paleolithic man.
4500–400	Western Asian civilisations, including those based at Ur, Nineveh and Persepolis, developed majestic carvings and reliefs.
2700–2300	Figurines produced by the Cycladic culture.
c. 2530	The Sphinx, one of the world's largest sculptures, built in the Egyptian Old Kingdom.
2000–1450	The Minoan civilization, based at Knossos in Crete, produced the 'bull's head' sacrificial vessel.
From 2000	Oceanic culture carved the giant Easter Island statues.
1500–1200	Mycenaean civilization expressed itself in violent images and work in gold.
1379–1361	Heads of Nefertiti and Akhenaten carved in the Egyptian New Kingdom.
From 500	Central and West African sculpture developed.
c. 500	Ancient Greek statues attained a naturalistic style, while Etruscans adapted the Greek style freely yet more crudely.
500 BC–AD 800	Traditional Celtic curvilinear plants, animals and abstract designs flowered again with early British and Irish Christianity.
460–450 BC	Myron's The Discus Thrower, a Greek bronze now surviving only in the form of a Roman marble copy, achieved a striking naturalism and sense of movement.
c. 490–417	The sculptor Phidias supervised the reliefs for the Parthenon in Athens.
c. 400	The Olmecs in Central America created colossal stone heads and fine sculptures in jade, bronze and clay.
350–330	Praxiteles executed the famous Aphrodite of Knidos, the first Greek life-size free-standing female nude.
323–31	The Hellenistic period achieved more complex forms with the Venus de Milo, the Winged Victory of Samothrace, Dying Gaul and Laocoon.
75	Portrait busts (a new form), monuments and sarcophagi celebrated the achievements of great Romans.
AD 106–113	Trajan's Column was the most complex example of Roman monumental art.

330–1453	Byzantine Christianity, established in the eastern Roman Empire, Russia and Greece, specifically excluded religious sculpture.
From 580	Japanese Buddhist and later portrait sculpture flourished.
780–1050	The Carolingian and Ottonian period revived Roman aims.
800–1275	The Romanesque style, epitomized in the work of Gislebertus at Autun, united Celtic and Roman forms in early stone churches.
c. 1154	Chartres Cathedral marked the triumph of the spiritualized Gothic style, incorporating new serenity in the portrayal of figures.
1258–1314	Pulpits carved by the Pisano brothers developed a more classical form of Gothic church sculpture.
1380–1406	Claus Sluter achieved a new psychological realism in work on Philip the Bold's tomb.
1404–1452	Ghiberti sculpted the panels for the four great bronze doors for the Baptistery in Florence. Having begun the first pair in the graceful International Gothic style, his second pair, The Gates of Paradise, represent a masterpiece of the Early Renaissance.
1430–32	Donatello, a pupil of Ghiberti, developed a new vital realism in scupture. His David became the first free-standing life-size bronze since antiquity.
1502–4	Michelangelo's Pietà, completed during the Italian High Renaissance, revealed the artist's grandeur of vision, portraying a Christian subject with all the magnificence of rediscovered classical form.
1540–1600	Cellini achieved fame as a goldsmith and sculptor in the Mannerist style.
1587–95	Giambologna's Rape of the Sabine was a high point of Mannerist movement and the first statue requiring to be seen from all angles.
1615–1680	Bernini produced light and fluid forms that seemed to defy the weight of the marble in the High Baroque style.
1787–1793	Canova's Cupid and Psyche expressed the neo-classical ideal of the late 18th century.
1875–1898	In works such as The Kiss, Balzac, and The Thinker, Rodin's romanticism dissolved the classical tradition of sculpture.
1880	Degas's only displayed piece, The Little 14-year-old Dancer, was acclaimed as the first modern sculpture.
1906–10	Brancusi evolved a simplified, abstract vocabulary for modern sculpture.

1900–1931	Matisse's sculptures revealed formal simplifications that parallel his paintings.
1913	Boccioni developed Futurist sculpture, which aimed to express movement and the space around objects.
1913–1940	Jacob Epstein's achievement in sculpture embraced vorticism, expressionist portraits and religious monuments.
1912–1966	Marcel Duchamp revolutionized traditional notions of art and artist by incorporating ready-made and found objects.
1916–24	Dadaists such as Schwitters and Arp included found objects, collage and unorthodox materials for their anarchistic work.
1909–1973	Picasso's career as a sculptor paralleled and complemented that of his painting throughout his many styles.
c. 1920	Rodchenko, El Lissitisky, Tatlin, Gabo and Pevsner developed a contructivist art to express revolutionary ideals.
1924–1986	Henry Moore explored the human form, in varying degrees of abstraction, often in monumental pieces.
From 1924	Arp, Ernst and Miro developed sculpture as a surrealist medium.
From 1928	Wire and mobile sculptures created by Calder. (Kinetic sculpture subsequently developed from the mid-50s by Tinguely and Takis).
1931–75	Barbara Hepworth developed Brancusi's process of simplification into the realms of pure form.
1933–65	In the USA, David Smith pursued metal sculpture in the wake of Picasso's experiments, an approach further developed by Caro since the 60s.
1935–66	Giacometti's slender, rough figures expressed the alienation of modern mid-century man.
From 1960s	An explosion of new approaches to art, employing a wide variety of new materials or no materials at all, and undermining the traditional notion of sculpture itself: Pop, Minimal, Happenings, Environmental, Performance, Body, Land, Earth and Conceptual Art.

THEATRE

| c. 3200 BC | Beginnings of Egyptian religious drama, essentially ritualistic. |
| c. 600 | Choral performances (dithyrambs) in honour of Dionysus formed the beginnings of Greek tragedy, according to Aristotle. |

500–300	Great age of Greek drama which included tragedy, comedy, and satyr plays (grotesque farce).
468	Sophocles' first victory at the Athens festival. His use of a third actor altered the course of the tragic form.
458	Aeschylus' *Oresteia* first performed.
c. 425–388	Comedies of Aristophanes including *The Birds* 414, *Lysistrata* 411, and *The Frogs* 405. In tragedy the importance of the chorus diminished under Euripides, author of *The Bacchae* c. 405.
c. 320	Menander's 'New Comedy' of social manners developed.
c. 240 BC –AD 100	Emergence of Roman drama, adapted from Greek originals. Plautus, Terence, and Seneca were the main dramatists.
c. 400	Kālidāsa's *Sakuntalā* marked the height of Sanskrit drama in India.
c. 1250–1500	European mystery (or miracle) plays flourished, first in the churches, later in marketplaces, and were performed in England by town guilds.
c. 1375	Nō (or Noh) drama developed in Japan.
c. 1495	*Everyman*, the best known of all the morality plays, was first performed.
1525–1750	Italian commedia dell'arte troupes performed popular, improvized comedies; they were to have a large influence on Molière and on English harlequinade and pantomime.
c. 1540	Nicholas Udall wrote *Ralph Roister Doister*, the first English comedy.
c. 1576	The first English playhouse, The Theatre, was built by James Burbage in London.
c. 1587	Christopher Marlowe's play *Tamburlaine the Great* marked the beginning of the great age of Elizabethan and Jacobean drama in England.
c. 1588	Thomas Kyd's play *The Spanish Tragedy* was the first of the 'revenge' tragedies.
c. 1590–1612	Shakespeare's greatest plays, including *Hamlet* and *King Lear*, were written.
1604	Inigo Jones designed *The Masque of Blackness* for James I, written by Ben Jonson.
c. 1614	Lope de Vega's *Fuenteovejuna* marked the Spanish renaissance in drama. Other writers include Calderón de la Barca.
1636	Pierre Corneille's *Le Cid* established classical tragedy in France.
1642	An act of Parliament closed all English theatres.
1660	With the restoration of Charles II to the English throne, dramatic performances recommenced. The first professional

actress appeared as Desdemona in Shakespeare's *Othello*.

1664	Molière's *Tartuffe* was banned for five years by religious factions.
1667	Jean Racine's first success, *Andromaque*, was staged.
1680	The Comédie Française was formed by Louis XIV.
1700	William Congreve, the greatest exponent of Restoration comedy, wrote *The Way of the World*.
1716	The first known American theatre was built in Williamsburg, Virginia.
1728	John Gay's *The Beggar's Opera* was first performed.
1737	The Stage Licensing Act in England required all plays to be approved by the Lord Chamberlain before performance.
1747	The actor David Garrick became manager of the Drury Lane Theatre, London.
1773	In England, Oliver Goldsmith's *She Stoops to Conquer* and Richard Sheridan's *The Rivals* 1775 established the 'comedy of manners'. Goethe's *Götz von Berlichingen* was the first *Sturm und Drang* play (literally, storm and stress).
1781	Friedrich Schiller's *Die Räuber/The Robbers*.
1784	Beaumarchais' *Le Mariage de Figaro/The Marriage of Figaro* (written 1778) was first performed.
1830	Victor Hugo's *Hernani* caused riots in Paris. His work marked the beginning of a new Romantic drama, changing the course of French theatre.
1878	Henry Irving became actor-manager of the Lyceum with Ellen Terry as leading lady.
1879	Henrik Ibsen's *A Doll's House* was written, an early example of realism in European theatre.
1888	August Strindberg wrote *Miss Julie*.
1893	George Bernard Shaw wrote *Mrs Warren's Profession* (banned until 1902 because it deals with prostitution). Shaw's works brought the new realistic drama to Britain and introduced social and political issues as subjects for the theatre.
1895	Oscar Wilde's comedy *The Importance of Being Earnest* was written.
1896	The first performance of Anton Chekhov's *The Seagull* failed. Alfred Jarry's *Ubu Roi*, a forerunner of Surrealism, produced in Paris.
1904	Chekhov's *The Cherry Orchard* was written. The Academy of Dramatic Art (Royal Academy of Dramatic Art 1920) was founded in London to train young actors. The Abbey Theatre, Dublin, opened by W B Yeats and Lady Gregory, marked the

	beginning of an Irish dramatic revival.
1919	The Theater Guild was founded in the USA to perform less commercial new plays.
1920	*Beyond the Horizon*, Eugene O'Neill's first play, marked the beginning of serious theatre in the USA.
1921	Luigi Pirandello's *Six Characters in Search of an Author* introduced themes of the individual and exploration of reality and appearance.
1927	*Show Boat*, composed by Jerome Kern with libretto by Oscar Hammerstein II, laid the foundations of the US musical.
1928	Bertolt Brecht's *Die Dreigroschenoper/The Threepenny Opera* with score by Kurt Weill; other political satires by Karel Čapek and Elmer Rice. In the USA musical comedies by Cole Porter, Irving Berlin, and George Gershwin, were popular.
1930s	US social-protest plays of Clifford Odets, Lillian Hellman, Thornton Wilder, and William Saroyan.
1935	T S Eliot's *Murder in the Cathedral* was written.
1935–39	WPA Federal Theater Project in the USA.
1938	Publication of Antonin Artaud's *Theatre and Its Double*.
1943	The first of the Rodgers and Hammerstein musicals, *Oklahoma!*, opened.
1944	Jean-Paul Sartre's *Huis Clos/In Camera*; Jean Anouilh's *Antigone*.
post-1945	Resurgence of German-language theatre, including Wolfgang Borchert, Max Frisch, Friedrich Dürrenmatt, and Peter Weiss.
1947	Tennessee Williams' *A Streetcar Named Desire* was written. First Edinburgh Festival, Scotland, with fringe theatre events.
1949	Bertolt Brecht and Helene Weigel founded the Berliner Ensemble in East Germany.
1953	Arthur Miller's *The Crucible* opened in the USA; *En attendant Godot/Waiting for Godot* by Samuel Beckett exemplified the Theatre of the Absurd.
1956	The English Stage Company was formed at the Royal Court Theatre to provide a platform for new dramatists. John Osborne's *Look Back in Anger* was included in its first season.
1957	Leonard Bernstein's *West Side Story* opened in New York.
1960	Harold Pinter's *The Caretaker* was produced in London.
1960s	Off-off-Broadway theatre, a more daring and experimental type of drama, began to develop in New York. Fringe theatre developed in Britain.
1961	The Royal Shakespeare Company was formed in the UK under the directorship of Peter Hall.
1963–64	The UK National Theatre Company was formed at the Old Vic

under the directorship of Laurence Olivier.

1964   Théâtre du Soleil, directed by Ariane Mnouchkine, founded in Paris.

1967   Athol Fugard founded the Serpent Players as an integrated company in Port Elizabeth, South Africa; success in the USA of *Hair*, the first of the 'rock' musicals; Tom Stoppard's *Rosencrantz and Guildenstern are Dead* was produced in London.

1968   Abolition of pre-censorship theatre in the UK.

1970   Peter Brook founded his international company, the International Centre for Theatre Research, in Paris; first festival of Chicano theatre in the USA.

1970s   Women's theatre movement developed in the USA and Europe.

1972   Sam Shepherd's *The Tooth of Crime* performed in London.

1974   Athol Fugard's *Statements After an Arrest under the Immorality Act* performed in London.

1975   *A Chorus Line*, to become the longest-running musical, opened in New York; Tadeusz Kantor's *Dead Class* produced in Poland.

1980   Howard Brenton's *The Romans in Britain* led in the UK to a private prosecution of the director for obscenity; David Edgar's *The Life and Times of Nicholas Nickleby* performed in London.

1985   Peter Brook's first production of *The Mahabharata* produced at the Avignon Festival.

1987   The Japanese Ninagawa Company performed Shakespeare's *Macbeth* in London.

1989   Discovery of the remains of the 16th-century Rose and Globe theatres, London.

1990   The Royal Shakespeare Company suspended its work at the Barbican Centre, London, for six months, pleading lack of funds.

1992   Ariane Mnouchkine's production of *Les Atrides* performed in Paris and the UK; Robert Wilson's production of *Alice* performed in Germany.

TABLES

AUSTRALIAN PRIME MINISTERS FROM 1901

term	name	party
1901–03	Sir Edmund Barton	Protectionist
1903–04	Alfred Deakin	Protectionist
1904	John Watson	Labor
1904–05	Sir George Reid	Free Trade–Protectionist coalition
1905–08	Alfred Deakin	Protectionist
1908–09	Andrew Fisher	Labor
1909–10	Alfred Deakin	Fusion
1910–13	Andrew Fisher	Labor
1913–14	Sir Joseph Cook	Liberal
1914–15	Andrew Fisher	Labor
1915–23	William Morris Hughes	Labor (National Labor from 1917)
1923–29	James H Scullin	Labor
1932–39	Joseph Aloysius Lyons	United Australia–Country coalition
1939–41	Robert G Menzies	United Australia
1941–41	A W Fadden	Country–United Australia coalition
1941–45	John Curtin	Labor
1945	F M Forde	Labor
1945–49	J B Chifley	Labor
1949–66	Robert G Menzies	Liberal–Country coalition
1966–67	Harold Holt	Liberal–Country coalition
1967–68	John McEwen	Liberal–Country coalition
1968–71	John Grey Gorton	Liberal–Country coalition
1971–72	William McMahon	Liberal–Country coalition
1972–75	Gough Whitlam	Labor
1975–83	Malcolm Fraser	Liberal–National coalition
1983–91	Robert Hawke	Labor
1991–	Paul Keating	Labor

BRITISH PRIME MINISTERS

took office	name	party
1721	Sir Robert Walpole	Whig
1742	Earl of Wilmington	Whig
1743	Henry Pelham	Whig
1754	Duke of Newcastle	Whig
1756	Duke of Devonshire	Whig

1757	Duke of Newcastle	Whig
1762	Earl of Bute	Tory
1763	George Grenville	Whig
1765	Marquess of Rockingham	Whig
1766	Duke of Grafton	Whig
1770	Lord North	Tory
1782	Marquess of Rockingham	Whig
1782	Earl of Shelbourne	Whig
1783	William Pitt	Tory
1783	Duke of Portland	Coalition
1801	Henry Addington	Tory
1804	William Pitt	Tory
1806	Lord Grenville	Whig
1807	Duke of Portland	Tory
1809	Spencer Percival	Tory
1812	Earl of Liverpool	Tory
1827	George Canning	Tory
1827	Viscount Goderich	Tory
1828	Duke of Wellington	Tory
1830	Earl Grey	Whig
1834	Viscount Melbourne	Whig
1834	Sir Robert Peel	Conservative
1835	Viscount Melbourne	Whig
1841	Sir Robert Peel	Conservative
1846	Lord J Russell	Liberal
1852	Earl of Derby	Conservative
1852	Lord Aberdeen	Peelite
1855	Viscount Palmerston	Liberal
1858	Earl of Derby	Conservative
1859	Viscount Palmerston	Liberal
1865	Lord J Russell	Liberal
1866	Earl of Derby	Conservative
1868	Benjamin Disraeli	Conservative
1886	W E Gladstone	Liberal
1874	Benjamin Disraeli	Conservative
1880	W E Gladstone	Liberal
1885	Marquess of Salisbury	Conservative
1886	W E Gladstone	Liberal
1886	Marquess of Salisbury	Conservative
1892	W E Gladstone	Liberal
1894	Earl of Rosebery	Liberal
1895	Marquess of Salisbury	Conservative

1905	Sir H Campbell-Bannerman	Liberal
1908	H H Asquith	Liberal
1915	H H Asquith	Coalition
1916	D Lloyd George	Coalition
1922	A Bonar Law	Conservative
1923	Stanley Baldwin	Conservative
1924	Ramsay MacDonald	Labour
1924	Stanley Baldwin	Conservative
1929	Ramsay MacDonald	Labour
1931	Ramsay MacDonald	National
1935	Stanley Baldwin	National
1937	N Chamberlain	National
1940	Sir Winston Churchill	Coalition
1945	Clement Attlee	Labour
1951	Sir Winston Churchill	Conservative
1955	Sir Anthony Eden	Conservative
1957	Harold Macmillan	Conservative
1963	Sir Alec Douglas-Home	Conservative
1964	Harold Wilson	Labour
1970	Edward Heath	Conservative
1974	Harold Wilson	Labour
1976	James Callaghan	Labour
1979	Margaret Thatcher	Conservative
1990	John Major	Conservative

CANADIAN PRIME MINISTERS FROM 1867

term	name	party
1867–73	John A Macdonald	Conservative
1873–78	Alexander Mackenzie	Liberal
1878–91	John A Macdonald	Conservative
1891–92	John J Abbott	Conservative
1892–94	John S D Thompson	Conservative
1894–96	Mackenzie Bowell	Conservative
1896	Charles Tupper	Conservative
1896–1911	Wilfred Laurier	Liberal
1911–20	Robert L Borden	Conservative
1920–21	Arthur Meighen	Conservative
1921–26	William L M King	Liberal
1926–26	Arthur Meighen	Conservative
1926–30	William L M King	Liberal
1930–35	Richard B Bennett	Conservative

1935–48	William L M King	Liberal
1948–57	Louis S St Laurent	Liberal
1957–63	John G Diefenbaker	Conservative
1963–68	Lester B Pearson	Liberal
1968–79	Pierre E Trudeau	Liberal
1979–80	Joseph Clark	Progressive Conservative
1980–84	Pierre E Trudeau	Liberal
1984	John Turner	Liberal
1984–93	Brian Mulroney	Progressive Conservative
1993	Kim Campbell	Progressive Conservative
1993–	Jean Chretien	Liberal

ENGLISH SOVEREIGNS FROM 900

reign	name	relationship
West Saxon kings		
901–25	Edward the Elder	son of Alfred the Great
925–40	Athelstan	son of Edward I
940–46	Edmund	half-brother of Athelstan
946–55	Edred	brother of Edmund
955–59	Edwy	son of Edmund
959–75	Edgar	brother of Edwy
975–78	Edward the Martyr	son of Edgar
978–1016	Ethelred II	son of Edgar
1016	Edmund Ironside	son of Ethelred
Danish kings		
1016–35	Canute	son of Sweyn I of Denmark, who conquered England in 1013
1035–40	Harold I	son of Canute
1040–42	Hardicanute	son of Canute
West Saxon kings (restored)		
1042–66	Edward the Confessor	son of Ethelred II
1066	Harold II	son of Godwin
Norman kings		
1066–87	William I	illegitimate son of Duke Robert the Devil
1087–1100	William II	son of William I
1100–35	Henry I	son of William I
1135–54	Stephen	grandson of William II

House of Plantagenet

1154–89	Henry II	son of Matilda (daughter of Henry I)
1189–99	Richard I	son of Henry II
1199–1216	John	son of Henry II
1216–72	Henry III	son of John
1272–1307	Edward I	son of Henry III
1307–27	Edward II	son of Edward I
1327–77	Edward III	son of Edward II
1377–99	Richard II	son of the Black Prince

House of Lancaster

1399–1413	Henry IV	son of John of Gaunt
1413–22	Henry V	son of Henry IV
1422–61, 1470–71	Henry VI	son of Henry V

House of York

1461–70, 1471–83	Edward IV	son of Richard, Duke of York
1483	Edward V	son of Edward IV
1483–85	Richard III	brother of Edward IV

House of Tudor

1485–1509	Henry VII	son of Edmund Tudor, Earl of Richmond
1509–47	Henry VIII	son of Henry VII
1547–53	Edward VI	son of Henry VIII
1553–58	Mary I	daughter of Henry VIII
1558–1603	Elizabeth I	daughter of Henry VIII

House of Stuart

1603–25	James I	great-grandson of Margaret (daughter of Henry VIII)
1625–49	Charles I	son of James I
1649–60	the Commonwealth	

House of Stuart (restored)

1660–85	Charles II	son of Charles I
1685–88	James II	son of Charles I
1689–1702	William III and Mary	son of Mary (daughter of Charles I); daughter of James II
1702–14	Anne	daughter of James II

House of Hanover

1714–27	George I	son of Sophia (grand-daughter of James I)
1727–60	George II	son of George I

1760–1820	George III	son of Frederick (son of George II)
1820–30	George IV (regent 1811–20)	son of George III
1830–37	William IV	son of George III
1837–1901	Victoria	daughter of Edward (son of George III)

House of Saxe-Coburg

| 1901–10 | Edward VII | son of Victoria |

House of Windsor

1910–36	George V	son of Edward VII
1936	Edward VIII	son of George V
1936–52	George VI	son of George V
1952–	Elizabeth II	daughter of George VI

FRENCH RULERS FROM 751

date of accession	name	title of ruler
751	Pepin III/Childerich III	*kings*
752	Pepin III	
768	Charlemagne/Carloman	
814	Louis I	
840	Lothair I	
843	Charles II (the Bald)	
877	Louis II	
879	Louis III	
882	Charles III (the Fat)	
888	Odo	
893	Charles III (the Simple)	
922	Robert I	
923	Rudolf	
936	Louis IV	
954	Lothair II	
986	Louis V	
987	Hugues Capet	
996	Robert II	
1031	Henri I	
1060	Philippe I	
1108	Louis VI	
1137	Louis VII	
1180	Philippe II	
1223	Louis VIII	

1226	Louis IX	
1270	Philippe III	
1285	Philippe IV	
1314	Louis X	
1316	Jean I	
1328	Philippe V	
1322	Charles IV	
1328	Philippe VI	
1350	Jean II	
1356	Charles V	
1380	Charles VI	
1422	Charles VII	
1461	Louis XI	
1483	Charles VIII	
1498	Louis XII	
1515	François I	
1547	Henri II	
1559	François II	
1560	Charles IX	
1574	Henri III	
1574	Henri IV	
1610	Louis XIII	
1643	Louis XIV	
1715	Louis XV	
1774	Louis XVI	
1792	National Convention	
1795	Directory (five members)	
1799	Napoléon Bonaparte	*first consul*
1804	Napoléon I	*emperor*
1814	Louis XVIII	*king*
1815	Napoléon II	*emperor*
1815	Louis XVIII	*kings*
1824	Charles X	
1830	Louis XIX	
1830	Henri V	
1830	Louis-Philippe	
1848	Philippe Buchez	*heads of state*
1848	Louis Cavaignac	
1848	Louis Napoléon Bonaparte	*president*
1852	Napoléon III	*emperor*
1871	Adolphe Thiers	*presidents*
1873	Patrice MacMahon	

1879	Jules Grevy
1887	François Sadui-Carnot
1894	Jean Casimir-Périer
1895	François Faure
1899	Emile Loubet
1913	Armand Fallières
1913	Raymond Poincaré
1920	Paul Deschanel
1920	Alexandre Millerand
1924	Gaston Doumergue
1931	Paul Doumer
1932	Albert Le Brun
1940	Philippe Pétain (vichy government)
1944	provisional government
1947	Vincent Auriol
1954	René Coty
1959	Charles de Gaulle
1969	Alain Poher
1969	Georges Pompidou
1974	Alain Poher
1974	Valéry Giscard d'Estaing
1981	François Mitterrand

IRISH PRIME MINISTERS

term	name
1931–48	Éamon de Valéra
1948–51	John Costello
1951–54	Éamon de Valéra
1954–57	John Costello
1957–59	Éamon de Valéra
1959–66	Seán F Lemass
1966–73	John M Lynch
1973–77	Liam Cosgrave
1977–79	John M Lynch
1979–81	Charles J Haughey
1981–82	Garrett Fitzgerald
1982	Charles J Haughey
1982–87	Garret Fitzgerald
1987–92	Charles J Haughey
1992–	Albert Reynolds

RUSSIAN RULERS 1547–1917

reign	name
	House of Rurik
1547–84	Ivan 'the Terrible'
1584–98	Theodore I
1598	Irina
	House of Godunov
1598–1605	Boris Godunov
1605	Theodore II
	usurpers
1605–06	Dimitri III
1606–10	Basil IV
1610–13	**interregnum**
	House of Romanov
1613–45	Michael Romanov
1645–76	Alexis
1676–82	Theodore III
1682–96	Peter I 'Peter the Great' and Ivan V (brothers)
1689–1721	Peter I, as tsar
1721–25	Peter I, as emperor
1725–27	Catherine I
1727–30	Peter II
1730–40	Anna Ivanovna
1740–41	Ivan VI
1741–62	Elizabeth
1762	Peter III
1762–96	Catherine II 'Catherine the Great'
1796–1801	Paul I
1801–25	Alexander I
1825–55	Nicholas I
1855–81	Alexander II
1881–94	Alexander III
1894–1917	Nicholas II

SCOTTISH KINGS AND QUEENS 1005–1603

(From the unification of Scotland to the union of the crowns of
Scotland and England)

reign	name	reign	name
Celtic monarchs		**English domination**	
1005	Malcolm II	1292–96	John Baliol
1034	Duncan I	1296–1306	annexed to England
1040	Macbeth	**House of Bruce**	
1057	Malcolm III Canmore	1306	Robert I the Bruce
1093	Donald III Donalbane	1329	David II
1094	Duncan II		
1094	Donald III (restored)	**House of Stuart**	
1097	Edgar	1371	Robert II
1107	Alexander I	1390	Robert III
1124	David I	1406	James I
1153	Malcolm IV	1437	James II
1165	William the Lion	1460	James III
1214	Alexander II	1488	James IV
1249	Alexander III	1513	James V
1286–90	Margaret of Norway	1542	Mary
		1567	James VI
		1603	union of crowns

US PRESIDENTS

year	name and serial no.	party
1789	1. George Washington	Federalist
1792	re-elected	
1796	2. John Adams	Federalist
1800	3. Thomas Jefferson	*D.R.
1804	re-elected	
1808	4. James Madison	*D.R.
1812	re-elected	
1816	5. James Monroe	*D.R.
1820	re-elected	
1824	6. John Quincy Adams	*D.R.
1828	7. Andrew Jackson	Democrat
1832	re-elected	
1836	8. Martin Van Buren	Democrat

1840	9. William Henry Harrison	Whig
1841	10. John Tyler[1]	Whig
1844	11. James K Polk	Democrat
1848	12. Zachary Taylor	Whig
1850	13. Millard Fillmore[2]	Whig
1852	14. Franklin Pierce	Democrat
1856	15. James Buchanan	Democrat
1860	16. Abraham Lincoln	Republican
1864	re-elected	
1865	17. Andrew Johnson[3]	Democrat
1868	18. Ulysses S Grant	Republican
1872	re-elected	
1876	19. Rutherford B Hayes	Republican
1880	20. James A Garfield	Republican
1881	21. Chester A Arthur[4]	Republican
1884	22. Grover Cleveland	Democrat
1888	23. Benjamin Harrison	Republican
1892	24. Grover Cleveland	Democrat
1896	25. William McKinley	Republican
1900	re-elected	
1901	26. Theodore Roosevelt[5]	Republican
1904	re-elected	
1908	27. William H Taft	Republican
1912	28. Woodrow Wilson	Democrat
1916	re-elected	
1920	29. Warren G Harding	Republican
1923	30. Calvin Coolidge[6]	Republican
1924	re-elected	
1928	31. Herbert Hoover	Republican
1932	32. Franklin D Roosevelt	Democrat
1936	re-elected	
1940	re-elected	
1944	re-elected	
1945	33. Harry S Truman[7]	Democrat
1948	re-elected	
1952	34. Dwight D Eisenhower	Republican
1956	re-elected	
1960	35. John F Kennedy	Democrat
1963	36. Lyndon B Johnson[8]	Democrat
1964	re-elected	
1968	37. Richard M Nixon	Republican

1972	re-elected	
1974	38. Gerald R Ford[9]	Republican
1976	39. Jimmy Carter	Democrat
1980	40. Ronald Reagan	Republican
1984	re-elected	
1988	41. George Bush	Republican
1993	42. Bill Clinton	Democrat

*D.R. Democrat-Republican
**D.L. R. Democrat– Liberal Republican
[1] became president on death of Harrison
[2] became president on death of Taylor
[3] became president on assassination of Lincoln
[4] became president on assassination of Garfield
[5] became president on assassination of McKinley
[6] became president on death of Harding
[7] became president on death of F D Roosevelt
[8] became president on assassination of Kennedy
[9] became president on resignation of Nixon

History and politics

ASSASSINATIONS

date	victim	details of assassination
681 BC	Sennacherib of Assyria	murdered by his two sons
514	Hipparchus, tyrant of Athens	killed by Harmodius and Aristogeiton, two Athenians
336	Philip II of Macedon	killed by Pausanias, a Spartan regent and general
44	Julius Caesar, Roman dictator	stabbed by Brutus, Cassius, and others in Senate
AD 41	Caligula, Roman emperor	murdered by Cassius Chaerea, an officer of his guard
96	Domitian, Roman dictator	stabbed in his bedroom by Stephanus, a freed slave
1170	Thomas à Becket	killed by four knights (Fitzorse, Tracy, Morville, and Brito) in Canterbury Cathedral, England
1437	James I of Scotland	murdered in court residence, a Dominican monastery, by assassins led by Sir Robert Graham
1488	James III of Scotland	murdered following defeat of royal army at Sauchieburn by an unknown person
1567	Lord Darnley, husband of Mary, Queen of Scots	blown up near Edinburgh while suffering from smallpox; suspected assassin: the Earl of Bothwell
1584	William the Silent, Prince of Orange	shot at Delft by Balthasar Gérard
1589	Henry III of France	stabbed by Jacques Clément, a fanatical Dominican
1610	Henry IV of France	murdered by Ravaillac, a Catholic fanatic
1628	Duke of Buckingham	stabbed at Portsmouth, England en route for La Rochelle, by John Felton, a discontented subaltern
1634	Prince Wallenstein, German general	killed in private train by Devereux

1793	Jean Paul Marat, French revolutionary	stabbed in bath by Charlotte Corday
1801	Paul I of Russia	strangled by army officers who had conspired to force his abdication
1812	Spencer Perceval, British prime minister	shot while entering lobby of the House of Commons by John Bellingham, a bankrupt Liverpool broker
1865	Abraham Lincoln, US president	shot by actor J Wilkes Booth in theatre
1881	James A Garfield, US president	shot at station by Charles Guiteau, a disappointed office-seeker
1881	Alexander II of Russia	died from injuries after bomb was thrown near his palace by Nihilists
1882	Lord Frederick Cavendish, chief secretary for Ireland	murdered by 'Irish Invincibles' in Phoenix Park, Dublin
1894	Marie François Carnot, French president	murdered by Italian anarchist in Lyon
1897	Antonio Cánovas del Castillo, Spanish premier	shot by Italian anarchist Angiolillo at the bath of Santa Agueda, Vitoria
1900	Umberto I of Italy	murdered by anarchist G Bresci in Monza
1901	William McKinley, US president	shot by anarchist Leon Czolgosz in Buffalo, New York
1903	Alexander Obrenovich King of Serbia, and his wife Draga	murdered by military conspirators
1913	George I of Greece	murdered by a Greek, Schinas, in Salonika
1914	Archduke Francis Ferdinand	shot in car by Gavrilo Princip in Sarajevo (sparked World War I); an alleged Serbian plot
1914	Jean Jaurès, French socialist	shot by nationalist in café
1916	Rasputin, Russian monk	shot and dumped in river Neva by a group of nobles led by Prince Feliks Yusupov
1922	Michael Collins, Irish Sinn Fein leader	killed in an ambush between Bandon and Macroom in Irish Republic

1934	Dr Engelbert Dollfuss, Austrian chancellor	shot by Nazis in the Chancellery
1934	Alexander I of Yugoslavia	murdered; Italian fascists or Croatian separatists suspected
1935	Huey Long, corrupt American politician	murdered by Dr Carl Austin Weiss
1940	Leon Trotsky, exiled Russian communist leader	killed with an ice axe in Mexico by Ramon de Rio
1942	Reinhard Heydrich, second in command of the Nazi secret police	murdered by Czech resistance fighters
1948	Mohandas Gandhi, Indian nationalist leader	shot by a Hindu fanatic, Nathuran Godse
1948	Count Folke Bernadotte, Swedish diplomat	murdered by Jewish extremists in ambush in Jerusalem
1951	Abdullah I of Jordan	murdered by member of Jehad faction
1951	Liaquat Ali Khan, prime minister of Pakistan	murdered in Rawalpindi by fanatics advocating war with India
1958	Faisal II of Iraq	murdered with his entire household during a military coup
1959	Solomon Bandaranaike, Ceylonese premier	murdered by Buddhist monk Talduwe Somarama
1959	Rafael Trujillo Molina, Dominican Republic dictator	machine-gunned in car by assassins including General J T Díaz
1963	John F Kennedy, US president	shot in car by rifle fire in Dallas, Texas; alleged assassin, Lee Oswald, himself shot two days later while under heavy police escort
1963	Malcolm X (Little), US leading representative of the Black Muslims	shot at political rally
1966	Hendrik Verwoerd, South African premier	stabbed by parliamentary messenger (later ruled mentally disordered)
1968	Rev Martin Luther King, US Black civil rights leader	shot on hotel balcony by James Earl Ray in Memphis, Tennessee
1968	Robert F Kennedy, US senator	shot by Arab immigrant Sirhan Sirhan in the Hotel Ambassador, Los Angeles

1975	King Faisal of Saudi Arabia	murdered by his nephew
1976	Christopher Ewart Biggs British ambassador to Republic of Ireland	car blown up by IRA landmine
1978	Aldo Moro, president of Italy's Christian Democrats and five times prime minister	kidnapped by Red Brigade guerrillas and later found dead
1979	Airey Neave, British Conservative MP and Northern Ireland spokesperson	killed by IRA bomb while driving out of House of Commons car park
1979	Lord Mountbatten, uncle of Duke of Edinburgh	killed by IRA bomb in sailing boat off coast of Ireland
1979	Park Chung Hee, president of South Korea	shot in restaurant by chief of Korean Central Intelligence Agency
1980	John Lennon, singer and songwriter	shot outside his apartment block in New York
1981	Anwar al-Sadat, president of Egypt	shot by rebel soldiers while reviewing military parade
1984	Indira Gandhi, Indian prime minister	murdered by members of her Sikh bodyguard
1986	Olof Palme, Swedish prime minister	shot in Stockholm as he walked home with his wife
1988	General Zia ul-Haq military leader of Pakistan	killed in air crash owing to sabotage
1991	Rajiv Gandhi, former Indian prime minister	shot during an election campaign
1992	Muhammad Boudiaf president of Algeria's ruling High State Council	murdered during a speech

BRITISH COMMONWEALTH

country	capital	date joined	area in sq km	constitutional status
in Africa				
Botswana	Gaborone	1966	582,000	sovereign republic
British Indian Ocean Terr.	Victoria	1965	60	British dependent territory
Gambia	Banjul	1965	10,700	sovereign republic

Ghana	Accra	1957	238,300	sovereign republic
Kenya	Nairobi	1963	582,600	sovereign republic
Lesotho	Maseru	1966	30,400	sovereign constitutional monarchy
Malawi	Zomba	1964	118,000	sovereign republic
Mauritius	Port Louis	1968	2,000	sovereign republic
Namibia	Windhoek	1990	824,000	sovereign republic
Nigeria	Lagos	1960	924,000	sovereign republic
St Helena	Jamestown	1931	100	British dependent territory
Seychelles	Victoria	1976	450	sovereign republic
Sierra Leone	Freetown	1961	73,000	sovereign republic
Swaziland	Mbabane	1968	17,400	sovereign republic
Tanzania	Dodoma	1961	945,000	sovereign republic
Uganda	Kampala	1962	236,900	sovereign republic
Zambia	Lusaka	1964	752,600	sovereign republic
Zimbabwe	Harare	1980	390,300	sovereign republic

in the Americas

Anguilla	The Valley	1931	155	British dependent territory
Antigua and Barbuda	St John's	1981	400	sovereign constitutional monarchy*
Bahamas	Nassau	1973	13,900	sovereign constitutional monarchy*
Barbados	Bridgetown	1966	400	sovereign constitutional monarchy*
Belize	Belmopan	1982	23,000	sovereign constitutional monarchy*
Bermuda	Hamilton	1931	54	British dependent territory
British Virgin Islands	Road Town	1931	153	British dependent territory
Canada	Ottawa	1931	9,958,400	sovereign constitutional monarchy*
Cayman Islands	George-town	1931	300	British dependent territory
Dominica	Roseau	1978	700	sovereign republic
Falkland Islands	Port Stanley	1931	12,100	British dependent territory
Grenada	St George's	1974	300	sovereign constitutional monarchy*

Guyana	George-town	1966	215,000	sovereign republic
Jamaica	Kingston	1962	11,400	sovereign constitutional monarchy*
Montserrat	Plymouth	1931	100	British dependent territory
St Christo -pher Nevis	Basseterre	1983	300	sovereign constitutional monarchy*
St Lucia	Castries	1979	600	sovereign constitutional monarchy*
St Vincent & the Grenadines	Kingstown	1979	400	sovereign constitutional monarchy*
Trinidad & Tobago	Port of Spain	1962	5,100	sovereign republic
Turks and Caicos Islands	Grand Turk	1931	400	British dependent territory

in the Antarctic

Australian Antarctic Territory	uninhabited	1936	5,403,000	Australian external territory
British Antarctic Territory	uninhabited	1931	390,000	British dependent territory
Falkland Islands Dependencies	uninhabited	1931	1,600	British dependent territories
Ross Dependency	uninhabited	1931	453,000	New Zealand associated territory

in Asia

Bangladesh	Dhaka	1972	144,000	sovereign republic
Brunei	Bandar Seri Begawan	1984	5,800	sovereign monarchy
Hong Kong	Victoria	1931	1,100	British crown colony
India	Delhi	1947	3,166,800	sovereign republic
Malaysia	Kuala Lumpur	1957	329,800	sovereign constitutional monarchy
Maldives	Malé	1982	300	sovereign republic
Pakistan	Islamabad	1947†	803,900	sovereign republic
Singapore	Singapore	1965	600	sovereign republic
Sri Lanka	Colombo	1948	66,000	sovereign republic

in Australasia and the Pacific

Australia	Canberra	1931	7,682,300	sovereign constitutional monarchy*
Cook Islands	Avarua	1931	300	New Zealand associated territory
Norfolk Island	Kingston	1931	34	Australian external territory
Kiribati	Tawawa	1979	700	sovereign republic
Nauru	Yaren	1968	21	sovereign republic
New Zealand	Wellington	1931	268,000	sovereign constitutional monarchy*
Niue	Alofi	1931	300	New Zealand associated territory
Papua New Guinea	Port Moresby	1975	462,800	sovereign constitutional monarchy*
Pitcairn Islands	Adamstown	1931	5	British dependent territory
Solomon Islands	Honiara	1978	27,600	sovereign constitutional monarchy*
Tokelau	Nukunonu	1931	10	New Zealand associated territory
Tonga	Nuku'alofa	1970	700	sovereign monarchy
Tuvalu	Funafuti	1978	24	sovereign constitutional monarchy*
Vanuatu	Villa	1980	15,000	sovereign republic
Western Samoa	Apia	1970	2,800	sovereign republic

in Europe

Channel Islands		1931	200	UK crown dependencies
Guernsey	St Peter Port			
Jersey	St Helier			
Cyprus	Nicosia	1961	9,000	sovereign republic
Gibraltar	Gibraltar	1931	6	British dependent territory
Malta	Valletta	1964	300	sovereign republic
Isle of Man	Douglas	1931	600	UK crown dependency
United Kingdom:	London	1931	244,100	sovereign constitutional monarchy*
England	London			
Northern Ireland	Belfast			

Scotland	Edinburgh	
Wales	Cardiff	
total		33,089,900

*Queen Elizabeth II constitutional monarch and head of state
† left 1972 and rejoined 1989

COLONIES AND INDEPENDENCE

current name	colonial names and history	colonized	independent
Belgium			
Zaïre	Belgian Congo	1885	1960
France			
Cambodia	Kampuchea 1970–89	1863	1953
Laos	French Indochina (protectorate)	1893	1954
Vietnam	Tonkin, Annam, Conchin-China to 1954	1858	1954
	North and South Vietnam 1954–76		
Burkina Faso	Upper Volta to 1984	1896	1960
Central African Republic	Ubangi-Shari	19th C	1960
Chad	French Equatorial Africa	19th C	1960
Côte d'Ivoire	Ivory Coast to 1986	1883	1960
Madagascar		1896	1960
Mali	French Sudan	19th C	1960
Niger		1912	1960
Algeria	colonized in 19th century – incorporated into France 1881	c. 1840	1962
The Netherlands			
Indonesia	Netherlands Indies	17th C	1949
Suriname	British colony 1650–67	1667	1975
Portugal			
Brazil		1532	1822
Uruguay	province of Brazil	1533	1828
Mozambique		1505	1975
Angola		1491	1975
Spain			
Paraguay	viceroyalty of Buenos Aires	1537	1811

Argentina	viceroyalty of Buenos Aires	16th C	1816
Chile		1541	1818
Costa Rica		1563	1821
Mexico	viceroyalty of New Spain	16th C	1821
Peru		1541	1824
Bolivia		16th C	1825
Ecuador	Greater Colombia 1822–30	16th C	1830
Venezuela	captaincy-general of Caracas to 1822 Greater Colombia 1822–30	16th C	1830
Honduras	federation of Central America 1821–38	1523	1838
El Salvador	federation of Central America 1821–39	16th C	1839
Guatemala	federation of Central America 1821–39	16th C	1839
Dominican Republic	Hispaniola to 1821, ruled by Haiti to 1844	16th C	1844
Cuba		1512	1898
Colombia	viceroyalty of New Granada to 1819, Greater Colombia to 1830	16th C	1903
Panama	part of Colombia to 1903	16th C	1903
Philippines	Spain 1565–1898, US 1898–1946	1565	1946

United Kingdom

India	British E India Co. 18th C–1858	18th C	1947
Pakistan	British E India Co. 18th C–1858	18th C	1947
Sri Lanka	Portuguese, Dutch 1602–1796; Ceylon 1802–1972	16th C 1802	1948
Ghana	Gold Coast	1618	1957
Nigeria		1861	1960
Cyprus	Turkish to 1878, then British rule	1878	1960
Sierra Leone	British protectorate	1788	1961
Tanzania	German E Africa to 1921; British mandate from League of Nations/UN as Tanganyika	19th C	1961

Jamaica	Spanish to 1655	17th C	1962
Trinidad & Tobago	Spanish 1532–1797; British 1797–1962	1532	1962
Uganda	British protectorate	1894	1962
Kenya	British colony from 1920	1895	1963
Malaysia	British interests from 1786; Federation of Malaya 1957–63	1874	1963
Malawi	British protectorate of Nyasaland 1907–53; Federation of Rhodesia & Nyasaland 1953–64	1891	1964
Malta	French 1798–1814	1798	1964
Zambia	N Rhodesia – British protectorate; Federation of Rhodesia & Nyasaland 1953–64	1924	1964
The Gambia		1888	1965
Singapore	Federation of Malaya 1963–65	1858	1965
Guyana	Dutch to 1796; British Guiana 1796–1966	1620	1966
Botswana	Bechuanaland – British protectorate	1885	1966
Lesotho	Basutoland	1868	1966
Mauritius		1814	1968
Bangladesh	British E India Co. 18th C–1858; British India 1858–1947; E Pakistan 1947–71	18th C	1971
Zimbabwe	S Rhodesia from 1923; UDI under Ian Smith 1965– 79	1895	1980

EUROPEAN COMMUNITY MEMBERS

country	date	country	date	country	date
Belgium	1958	France	1958	Germany	1958
Italy	1958	Luxembourg	1958	Netherlands	1958
Denmark	1973	Rep. of Ireland	1973	United Kingdom	1973
Greece	1981	Portugal	1986	Spain	1986

MAJOR BATTLES

battle	date	victorious forces	defeated
Marathon	490 BC	10,000 Athenians and allies	50,000 Persians
Tours	732	The Franks under Charles Martel	Muslim invaders of Europe
Hastings	1066	8,000 Normans under Duke William	8,000 English under Harold II
Agincourt	1415	10,000 English under Henry V	40,000 French
Lepanto	1571	208 galleys under Don John of Austria	230 Turkish galleys under Ali Pasha
Armada	1588	197 English ships	130 Spanish ships
Plassey	1757	3,000 Anglo-Indians under Robert Clive	60,000 Bengali Indians under the Nawab of Bengal
Saratoga	1777	16,000 American colonists under General Gates	3,500 British under General Burgoyne
Yorktown	1781	American colonists under George Washington	8,000 British under Charles Cornwallis
Trafalgar	1805	27 British ships under Horatio Nelson	33 French and Spanish ships under Villeneuve
Austerlitz	1805	65,000 French under Napoleon I	83,000 Austrians and Russians under their emperors
Waterloo	1815	67,000 British, Dutch and Belgians under Wellington	74,000 French under Napoleon I
Gettysburg	1863	Union forces under George Meade	Confederate forces under Robert E Lee
Marne	1914	French and British armies	German invaders of France
Verdun	1916	French forces	German forces in France
Passchendaele	1917	British forces	German forces in France
Britain	1940	British Royal Air Force	German air force
Midway	1942	US ships under Raymond Spruance	Japanese ships under Isoruku Yamamoto
El Alamein	1942	British Eighth Army under General Montgomery	German Afrika Korps under General Rommel
Stalingrad	1942–43	Red Army under Marshal Zhukov	German Sixth Army under General Paulus
Normandy	1944	Allied sea-borne forces	German forces in France

UNITED NATIONS MEMBERS

country	year of admission	UN budget (%)	country	year of admission	UN budget (%)
Afghanistan	1946	0.01	Cyprus	1960	0.02
Albania	1955	0.01	Czech Republic	1993	***
Algeria	1962	0.16	Denmark †	1945	0.65
Angola	1976	0.01	Djibouti	1977	0.01
Antigua & Barbuda	1981	0.01	Dominica	1978	0.01
Argentina †	1945	0.57	Dominican		
Armenia	1992	0.13	Republic †	1945	0.02
Australia †	1945	1.51	Ecuador †	1945	0.03
Austria	1955	0.75	Egypt †	1945	0.07
Azerbaijan	1992	0.22	El Salvador †	1945	0.01
Bahamas	1973	0.02	Eritrea	1993	0.07
Bahrain	1971	0.03	Equatorial		
Bangladesh	1974	0.01	Guinea	1968	0.01
Barbados	1966	0.01	Estonia	1991	***
Belarus †	1945	0.31	Ethiopia †	1945	0.01
Belgium †	1945	1.06	Fiji	1970	0.01
Belize	1981	0.01	Finland	1955	0.57
Benin	1960	0.01	France †	1945	6.00
Bhutan	1971	0.01	Gabon	1960	0.02
Bolivia †	1945	0.01	Gambia	1965	0.01
Bosnia-Herzegovina	1992	0.04	Georgia	1992	0.21
Botswana	1966	0.01	Germany**	1973/1990	8.93
Brazil †	1945	1.59	Ghana	1957	0.01
Brunei	1984	0.03	Greece †	1945	0.35
Bulgaria	1955	0.13	Grenada	1974	0.01
Burkina Faso	1960	0.01	Guatemala †	1945	0.02
Burundi	1962	0.01	Guinea	1958	0.01
Cambodia	1955	0.01	Guinea-Bissau	1974	0.01
Cameroon	1960	0.01	Guyana	1966	0.01
Canada †	1945	3.11	Haiti †	1945	0.01
Cape Verde	1975	0.01	Honduras †	1945	0.01
Central African			Hungary	1955	0.18
Republic	1960	0.01	Iceland	1946	0.03
Chad	1960	0.01	India †	1945	0.36
Chile †	1945	0.08	Indonesia	1950	0.16
China †	1945	0.77	Iran †	1945	0.77
Colombia †	1945	0.13	Iraq †	1945	0.13
Comoros	1975	0.01	Ireland	1955	0.18
Congo	1960	0.01	Israel	1949	0.23
Costa Rica †	1945	0.01	Italy	1955	4.29
Croatia	1992	0.13	Ivory Coast	1960	0.02
Cuba †	1945	0.09	Jamaica	1962	0.01

country	year of admission	UN budget (%)	country	year of admission	UN budget (%)
Japan	1956	12.45	Panama †	1945	0.02
Jordan	1955	0.01	Papua New Guinea	1975	0.01
Kazakhstan	1992	0.35	Paraguay †	1945	0.02
Kenya	1963	0.01	Peru †	1945	0.06
Kuwait	1963	0.25	Philippines †	1945	0.07
Kyrgyzstan	1992	0.06	Poland †	1945	0.47
Laos	1955	0.01	Portugal	1955	0.20
Latvia	1991	0.13	Qatar	1971	0.05
Lebanon †	1945	0.01	Romania	1955	0.17
Lesotho	1966	0.01	Russian Federation*	1945	6.71
Liberia †	1945	0.01	Rwanda	1962	0.01
Libya	1955	0.24	St Christopher–Nevis	1983	0.01
Liechtenstein	1990	0.01	St Lucia	1979	0.01
Lithuania	1991	0.15	St Vincent &		
Luxembourg †	1945	0.06	Grenadines	1980	0.01
Macedonia	1993	***	Samoa	1976	0.01
Madagascar	1960	0.01	San Marino	1992	0.01
Malawi	1964	0.01	São Tomé Príncipe	1975	0.01
Malaysia	1957	0.12	Saudi Arabia †	1945	0.96
Maldives	1965	0.01	Senegal	1960	0.01
Mali	1960	0.01	Seychelles	1976	0.01
Malta	1964	0.01	Sierra Leone	1961	0.01
Marshall Islands	1991	0.01	Singapore	1965	0.12
Mauritania	1961	0.01	Slovak Republic	1993	***
Mauritius	1968	0.01	Slovenia	1992	0.04
Mexico †	1945	0.88	Solomon Isles	1978	0.01
Micronesia	1991	0.01	Somalia	1960	0.01
Moldova	1992	0.15	South Africa †	1945	0.41
Mongolia	1961	0.01	South Korea	1991	0.69
Monaco	1993	***	Spain	1955	1.98
Morocco	1956	0.03	Sri Lanka	1955	0.01
Mozambique	1975	0.01	Sudan	1956	0.01
Myanmar (Burma)	1948	0.01	Surinam	1975	0.01
Namibia	1990	0.01	Swaziland	1968	0.01
Nepal	1955	0.01	Sweden	1946	1.11
Netherlands †	1945	1.50	Syria †	1945	0.04
New Zealand †	1945	0.24	Tajikistan	1992	0.05
Nicaragua †	1945	0.01	Tanzania	1961	0.01
Niger	1960	0.01	Thailand	1946	0.11
Nigeria	1960	0.20	Togo	1960	0.01
North Korea	1991	0.05	Trinidad & Tobago	1962	0.05
Norway †	1945	0.55	Tunisia	1956	0.03
Oman	1971	0.03	Turkey †	1945	0.27
Pakistan	1947	0.06	Turkmenistan	1992	0.06

country	year of admission	UN budget (%)	country	year of admission	UN budget (%)
Uganda	1962	0.01	Vanuatu	1981	0.01
Ukraine †	1945	1.87	Venezuela †	1945	0.49
United Arab Emirates	1971	0.21	Vietnam	1977	0.01
United Kingdom †	1945	5.02	Yemen**	1947	0.01
United States of America †	1945	25.00	Yugoslavia †****	1945	0.16
			Zaire	1960	0.01
Uruguay †	1945	0.04	Zambia	1964	0.01
Uzbekistan	1992	0.26	Zimbabwe	1980	0.01

† founder members

*Became a separate member upon the demise of the USSR which was a founder member 1945

**represented by two countries until unification 1990

***contributions to be determined

****membership suspended 1992

The sovereign countries that are not UN members are Andorra, Kiribati, Monaco, Nauru, Switzerland, Taiwan, Tonga, Tuvalu, and Vatican City.

Science and Nature

EARTHQUAKES

date	place	magnitude (Richter scale)	number of deaths
1906	San Francisco, USA	8.3	450
1908	Messina, Italy	7.5	83,000
1915	Avezzano, Italy	7.5	29,980
1920	Gansu, China	8.6	100,000
1923	Tokyo, Japan	8.3	99,330
1927	Nan-Shan, China	8.3	200,000
1932	Gansu, China	7.6	70,000
1935	Quetta, India	7.5	30,000
1939	Erzincan, Turkey	7.9	30,000
1939	Chillán, Chile	8.3	28,000
1948	USSR	7.3	110,000
1970	N Peru	7.7	66,794
1976	Tangshan, China	8.2	242,000
1978	NE Iran	7.7	25,000
1980	El Asnam, Algeria	7.3	20,000
1985	Mexico	8.1	25,000
1988	Armenia, USSR	6.9	25,000
1989	San Francisco, USA	7.1	300
1990	NW Iran	7.7	50,000

GEOLOGICAL TIME CHART

era	period	epoch	millions of years ago	life forms
Cenozoic	Quaternary	Holocene	0.01	
		Pleistocene	1.64	humans appeared
		Pliocene	5.2	
	Tertiary	Miocene	23.5	
		Oligocene	35.5	
		Eocene	56.5	
		Palaeocene	65	mammals flourished
Mesozoic	Cretaceous		146	heyday of dinosaurs
	Jurassic		208	first birds
	Triassic		245	first mammals and dinosaurs
Palaeozoic	Permian		290	reptiles expanded
	Carboniferous		363	first reptiles
	Devonian		409	first amphibians
	Silurian		439	first land plants
	Ordovician		510	first fish
	Cambrian		570	first fossils
Precambrian	Proterozoic		3,500	earliest living things
	Archaean		4,600	

HURRICANES: TEN WORST OF THE 20TH CENTURY

date	location	deaths
1900 Aug–Sept	Galveston, Texas	6,000
1926 20 Oct	Cuba	600
1928 6–20 Sept	Southern Florida	1,836
1930 3 Sept	Dominican Republic	2,000
1938 21 Sept	Long Island, New York,New England	600
1942 15–16 Oct	Bengal, India	40,000
1963 4–8 Oct	(Flora) Caribbean	6,000
1974 19–20 Sept	(Fifi) Honduras	2,000
1979 30 Aug–7 Sept	(David) Caribbean, E USA	1,100
1989 16–22 Sept	(Hugo) Caribbean, SE USA	504

ICE AGES

name	date (years ago)
Pleistocene	1.64 million–10,000
Permo-Carboniferous	330–250 million
Ordovician	440–430 million
Verangian	615–570 million
Sturtian	820–770 million
Gnejso	940–880 million
Huronian	2,700–1,800 million

NOBEL PRIZE: RECENT WINNERS

Peace

1982	Alva Myrdal (*Sweden*) and Alfonso Garcia Robles (*Mexico*)
1983	Lech Walesa (*Poland*)
1984	Bishop Desmond Tutu (*South Africa*)
1985	International Physicians for the Prevention of Nuclear War
1986	Elie Wiesel (*USA*)
1987	President Oscar Arias Sanchez (*Costa Rica*)
1988	The United Nations peacekeeping forces
1989	The Dalai Lama (*Tibet*)
1990	President Mikhail Gorbachev (*USSR*)
1991	Aung San Suu Kyi (*Myanmar*)
1992	Rigoberta Menche (*Guatemala*)
1993	Nelson Mandela and Frederik Willem de Klerk (*South Africa*)

Economics

1982	George J Stigler (*USA*)
1983	Gérard Debreu (*USA*)
1984	Richard Stone (*UK*)
1985	Franco Modigliani (*USA*)
1986	James Buchanan (*USA*)
1987	Robert Solow (*USA*)
1988	Maurice Allais (*France*)
1989	Trygve Haavelmo (*Norway*)
1990	Harry M Markowitz (*USA*), Merton H Miller (*USA*), and William F Sharpe (*USA*)
1991	Ronald H Coase (*USA*)
1992	Gary S Becker (*USA*)
1993	Robert Fogel and Douglass North (*USA*)

SCIENCE AND NATURE

Chemistry

1982	Aaron Klug (*UK*)
1983	Henry Taube (*USA*)
1984	Bruce Merrifield (*USA*)
1985	Herbert A Hauptman (*USA*) and Jerome Karle (*USA*)
1986	Dudley Herschbach (*USA*), Yuan Lee (*USA*), and John Polanyi (*Canada*)
1987	Donald Cram (*USA*), Jean-Marie Lehn (*France*), and Charles Pedersen (*USA*)
1988	Johann Deisenhofer (*West Germany*), Robert Huber (*West Germany*), and Hartmut Michel (*West Germany*)
1989	Sydney Altman (*USA*) and Thomas Cech (*USA*)
1990	Elias James Corey (*USA*)
1991	Richard R Ernst (*Switzerland*)
1992	Rudolph A Marcus (*USA*)
1993	Kary Mullis (*USA*) and Michael Smith (*Canada*)

Physics

1982	Kenneth G Wilson (*USA*)
1983	Subrahmanyan Chandrasekhar (*USA*) and William A Fowler (*USA*)
1984	Carlo Rubbia (*Italy*) and Simon van der Meer (*Netherlands*)
1985	Klaus von Klitzing (*West Germany*)
1986	Ernst Ruska (*West Germany*), Gerd Binnig (*West Germany*), and Heinrich Rohrer (*Switzerland*)
1987	Georg Bednorz (*West Germany*) and Alex Müller (*Switzerland*)
1988	Leon Lederman, Melvin Schwartz, and Jack Steinberger (*USA*)
1989	Norman Ramsey (*USA*), Hans Dehmeit (*USA*), and Wolfgang Paul (*West Germany*)
1990	Richard E Taylor (*Canada*), Jerome I Friedman (*USA*), and Henry W Kendall (*USA*)
1991	Pierre-Gilles de Gennes (*France*)
1992	Georges Charpak (*France*)
1993	Joseph Taylor (*USA*) and Russell Hulse (*USA*)

Physiology or Medicine

1982	Sune Bergström (*Sweden*), Bengt Samuelson (*Sweden*), and John Vane (*UK*)
1983	Barbara McClintock (USA)
1984	Niels Jerne (*Denmark*), Georges Köhler (*West Germany*), and César Milstein (*UK*)
1985	Michael Brown (*USA*) and Joseph L Goldstein (*USA*)
1986	Stanley Cohen (*USA*) and Rita Levi-Montalcini (*Italy*)

1987	Susumu Tonegawa (*Japan*)
1988	James Black (*UK*), Gertrude Elion (*USA*), and George Hitchings (*USA*)
1989	Michael Bishop (*USA*) and Harold Varmus (*USA*)
1990	Joseph Murray (*USA*) and Donnall Thomas (*USA*)
1991	Erwin Neher (*Germany*) and Bert Sakmann (*Germany*)
1992	Edmond Fisher (*USA*) and Edwin Krebs (*USA*)
1993	Phillip Sharp (*USA*) and Richard Roberts (*UK*)

See also Literary Prizes on p. 295

WORLD POPULATION

Date	Estimated population	Date	Estimated population
2000 BC	100,000,000	1800	900,000,000
1000 BC	120,000,000	1850	1,260,000,000
AD 1	180,000,000	1900	1,620,000,000
1000	275,000,000	1950	2,500,000,000
1250	375,000,000	1960	3,050,000,000
1500	420,000,000	1970	3,700,000,000
1650	500,000,000	1980	4,450,000,000
1700	615,000,000	1990	5,245,000,000
1750	750,000,000	2000	6,100,000,000

Art and Religion

ACADEMY AWARD: RECENT WINNERS

1982 Best Picture: *Gandhi*; Best Director: Richard Attenborough *Gandhi*; Best Actor: Ben Kingsley *Gandhi*; Best Actress: Meryl Streep *Sophie's Choice*

1983 Best Picture: *Terms of Endearment*; Best Director: James L Brooks *Terms of Endearment*; Best Actor: Robert Duvall *Tender Mercies*; Best Actress: Shirley Maclaine *Terms of Endearment*

1984 Best Picture: *Amadeus*; Best Director: Milos Forman *Amadeus*; Best Actor: F Murray Abraham *Amadeus*; Best Actress: Sally Field *Places in the Heart*

1985 Best Picture: *Out of Africa*; Best Director: Sydney Pollack *Out of Africa*; Best Actor: William Hurt *Kiss of the Spider Woman*; Best Actress: Geraldine Page *The Trip to Bountiful*

1986 Best Picture: *Platoon*; Best Director: Oliver Stone *Platoon*; Best Actor: Paul Newman *The Color of Money*; Best Actress: Marlee Matlin *Children of a Lesser God*

1987 Best Picture: *The Last Emperor*; Best Director: Bernardo Bertolucci *The Last Emperor*; Best Actor: Michael Douglas *Wall Street*; Best Actress: Cher *Moonstruck*

1988 Best Picture: *Rain Man*; Best Director: Barry Levington *Rain Man*; Best Actor: Dustin Hoffman *Rain Man*; Best Actress: Jodie Foster *The Accused*

1989 Best Picture: *Driving Miss Daisy*; Best Director: Oliver Stone *Born on the Fourth of July*; Best Actor: Daniel Day-Lewis *My Left Foot*; Best Actress: Jessica Tandy *Driving Miss Daisy*

1990 Best Picture: *Dances With Wolves*; Best Director: Kevin Costner *Dances With Wolves*; Best Actor: Jeremy Irons *Reversal of Fortune*; Best Actress: Kathy Bates *Misery*

1991 Best Picture: *The Silence of the Lambs*; Best Director: Jonathan Demme *The Silence of the Lambs*; Best Actor: Anthony Hopkins *The Silence of the Lambs*; Best Actress: Jodie Foster *The Silence of the Lambs*

1992 Best Picture: *Unforgiven*; Best Director: Clint Eastwood *Unforgiven*; Best Actor: Al Pacino *Scent of a Woman* ; Best Actress: Emma Thompson *Howard's End*

1993 Best Picture: *Schindler's List*; Best Director: Steven Spielberg *Schindler's List*; Best Actor: Tom Hanks *Philadelphia*; Best Actress: Holly Hunter *The Piano*

CANNES FILM FESTIVAL: BEST FILM

1985	*When Father Was Away on Business* (Yugoslavia)
1986	*The Mission* (UK)
1987	*Under the Sun of Satan* (France)
1988	*Pelle the Conqueror* (Denmark)
1989	*Sex, Lies and Videotape* (USA)
1990	*Wild at Heart* (USA)
1991	*Barton Fink* (USA)
1992	*The Best Intentions* (Sweden)
1993	*The Piano* (USA) / *Farewell, My Concubine* (China)
1994	*Pulp Fiction* (USA)

LITERARY PRIZES: RECENT WINNERS

Booker Prize for Fiction

1982	Thomas Keneally *Schindler's Ark*
1983	J M Coetzee *The Life and Times of Michael K*
1984	Anita Brookner *Hotel du Lac*
1985	Keri Hulme *The Bone People*
1986	Kingsley Amis *The Old Devils*
1987	Penelope Lively *Moon Tiger*
1988	Peter Carey *Oscar and Lucinda*
1989	Kazuo Ishiguro *The Remains of the Day*
1990	A S Byatt *Possession*
1991	Ben Okri *The Famished Road*
1992	Barry Unsworth *Sacred Hunger*; Michael Ondaatje *The English Patient* (joint winners)
1993	Roddy Doyle *Paddy Clarke Ha Ha Ha*

Nobel Prize for Literature

1982	Gabriel García Marquez *(Colombia)*
1983	William Golding *(UK)*
1984	Jaroslav Seifert *(Czechoslovakia)*
1985	Claude Simon *(France)*
1986	Wole Soyinka *(Nigeria)*
1987	Joseph Brodsky *(USSR/USA)*
1988	Naguib Mahfouz *(Egypt)*
1989	Camilo José Cela *(Spain)*
1990	Octavio Paz *(Mexico)*
1991	Nadine Gordimer *(South Africa)*

1992 Derek Walcott *(St Lucia)*
1993 Toni Morrison *(USA)*

Pulitzer Prize for Fiction

1982 John Updike *Rabbit is Rich*
1983 Alice Walker *The Color Purple*
1984 William Kennedy *Ironweed*
1985 Alison Lurie *Foreign Affairs*
1986 Larry McMurtry *Lonesome Dove*
1987 Peter Taylor *A Summons to Memphis*
1988 Toni Morrison *Beloved*
1989 Anne Tyler *Breathing Lessons*
1990 Oscar Hijuelos *The Mambo Kings Play Songs of Love*
1991 John Updike *Rabbit at Rest*
1992 Jane Smiley *A Thousand Acres*
1993 Robert Olen Butler *A Good Scent from a Strange Mountain*

Whitbread Literary Award for fiction (British)

1982 John Wain *Young Shoulders*
1983 William Trevor *Fools of Fortune*
1984 Christopher Hope *Kruger's Alp*
1985 Peter Ackroyd *Hawksmoor*
1986 Kazuo Ishiguro *An Artist of the Floating World*
1987 Ian McEwan *The Child in Time*
1988 Salman Rushdie *The Satanic Verses*
1989 Lindsay Clarke *The Chymical Wedding*
1990 Nicholas Mosley *Hopeful Monsters*
1991 Jane Gardam *The Queen of the Tambourine*
1992 Alasdair Gray *Poor Things*
1993 Joan Brady *Theory of War*

PHILOSOPHERS AND POLITICAL THINKERS

name	dates	nationality	representative work
Confucius	551–479 BC	Chinese	*The Analects*
Heraclitus	c. 544–483 BC	Greek	*On Nature*
Parmenides	c. 510–c. 450 BC	Greek	fragments
Socrates	469–399 BC	Greek	—
Plato	428–347 BC	Greek	*Republic; Phaedo*
Aristotle	384–322 BC	Greek	*Nichomachaen Ethics; Metaphysics*

Epicurus	341–270 BC	Greek	fragments
Lucretius	c. 99–55 BC	Roman	*On the Nature of Things*
Plotinus	AD 205–270	Greek	*Enneads*
Augustine	354–430	N African	*Confessions; City of God*
Aquinas	c. 1225–1274	Italian	*Summa Theologica*
Duns Scotus	c. 1266-1308	Scottish	*Opus Oxoniense*
William of Occam	c. 1285–1349	English	*Commentary of the Sentences*
Nicholas of Cusa	1401–1464	German	*De Docta Ignorantia*
Machiavelli	1469–1527	Italian	*Il principe; Discorsi*
Giordano Bruno	1548–1600	Italian	*De la Causa, Principio e Uno*
Bacon	1561–1626	English	*Novum Organum; The Advancement of Learning*
Hobbes	1588–1679	English	*Leviathan*
Descartes	1596-1650	French	*Discourse on Method; Meditations on the First Philosophy*
Pascal	1623–1662	French	*Pensées*
Spinoza	1632–1677	Dutch	*Ethics*
Locke	1632–1704	English	*Essay Concerning Human Understanding*
Leibniz	1646-1716	German	*The Monadology*
Vico	1668–1744	Italian	*The New Science*
Berkeley	1685–1753	Irish	*A Treatise Concerning the Principles of Human Knowledge*
Hume	1711–1776	Scottish	*A Treatise of Human Nature*
Rousseau	1712–1778	French	*The Social Contract*
Diderot	1713–1784	French	*D'Alembert's Dream*
Kant	1724–1804	German	*The Critique of Pure Reason*
Burke	1729–1797	Irish	*Thoughts on the Present Discontents*
Paine	1737–1809	English	*The Rights of Man*
Bentham	1748–1832	English	*Fragments on Government*
Fichte	1762–1814	German	*The Science of Knowledge*
Hegel	1770–1831	German	*The Phenomenology of Spirit*

Fourier	1772–1837	French	Le nouveau Monde industriel
Schelling	1775–1854	German	System of Transcendental Idealism
Schopenhauer	1788–1860	German	The World as Will and Idea
Comte	1798–1857	French	Cours de philosophie positive
Mill	1806-1873	English	Utilitarianism
Proudhon	1809–1865	French	Qu'est-ce que la propriété?
Kierkegaard	1813–1855	Danish	Concept of Dread
Marx	1818–1883	German	Economic and Philosophical Manuscripts
Engels	1820–1895	German	The Communist Manifesto (with K Marx)
Dilthey	1833–1911	German	The Rise of Hermeneutics
Pierce	1839–1914	US	How to Make our Ideas Clear
Nietzsche	1844–1900	German	Thus Spake Zarathustra
Bergson	1859–1941	French	Creative Evolution
Husserl	1859–1938	German	Logical Investigations
Russell	1872–1970	English	Principia Mathematica
Lukács	1885–1971	Hungarian	History and Class Consciousness
Wittgenstein	1889–1951	Austrian	Tractatus Logico-Philosophicus; Philosophical Investigations
Heidegger	1889–1976	German	Being and Time
Gramsci	1891–1937	Italian	Quaderni di Carcere
Gadamer	1900–	German	Truth and Method
Sartre	1905–1980	French	Being and Nothingness
Merleau Ponty	1908–1961	French	The Phenomenology of Perception
Quine	1908–	US	Word and Object
Foucault	1926–1984	French	The Order of Things

POETS LAUREATE

1668	John Dryden (1631–1700)
1689	Thomas Shadwell (1642?–1692)
1692	Nahum Tate (1652–1715)
1715	Nicholas Rowe (1674–1718)
1718	Laurence Eusden (1688–1730)
1730	Colley Cibber (1671–1757)
1757	William Whitehead (1715–1785)
1785	Thomas Warton (1728–1790)
1790	Henry James Pye (1745–1813)
1813	Robert Southey (1774–1843)
1843	William Wordsworth (1770–1850)
1850	Alfred, Lord Tennyson (1809–1892)
1896	Alfred Austin (1835–1913)
1913	Robert Bridges (1844–1930)
1930	John Masefield (1878–1967)
1968	Cecil Day Lewis (1904–1972)
1972	Sir John Betjeman (1906–1984)
1984	Ted Hughes (1930–)

SHAKESPEARE'S PLAYS

title	performed/written (approximate)
early plays	
Henry VI Part I	1589–92
Henry VI Part II	1589–92
Henry VI Part III	1589–92
The Comedy of Errors	1592–93
The Taming of the Shrew	1593–94
Titus Andronicus	1593–94
The Two Gentlemen of Verona	1594–95
Love's Labours Lost	1594–95
Romeo and Juliet	1594–95
histories	
Richard III	1592–93
Richard II	1595–97
King John	1596–97
Henry IV Part I	1597–98
Henry IV Part II	1597–98
Henry V	1599

Roman plays

Julius Caesar	1599–1600
Antony and Cleopatra	1607–08
Coriolanus	1607–08

the 'great' or 'middle' comedies

A Midsummer Night's Dream	1595–96
The Merchant of Venice	1596–97
Much Ado About Nothing	1598–99
As You Like It	1599–1600
The Merry Wives of Windsor	1600–01
Twelfth Night	1601–02

the great tragedies

Hamlet	1601–02
Othello	1604–05
King Lear	1605–06
Macbeth	1605–06
Timon of Athens	1607–08

the 'dark' comedies

Troilus and Cressida	1601–02
All's Well That Ends Well	1602–03
Measure for Measure	1604–05

late plays

Pericles	1608–09
Cymbeline	1609–10
The Winter's Tale	1610–11
The Tempest	1611–12
Henry VIII	1612–13

THE BIBLE

name of book	chapters	date written
The Books of the Old Testament		
The Pentateuch or the Five Books of Moses		
Genesis	50	mid-8th C BC
Exodus	40	950–586 BC
Leviticus	27	mid-7th C BC
Numbers	36	850–650 BC
Deuteronomy	34	mid-7th C BC
Joshua	24	c. 550 BC
Judges	21	c. 550 BC

Ruth	4	end 3rd C BC
1 Samuel	31	c. 900 BC
2 Samuel	24	c. 900 BC
1 Kings	22	550–600 BC
2 Kings	25	550–600 BC
1 Chronicles	29	c. 300 BC
2 Chronicles	36	c. 300 BC
Ezra	10	c. 450 BC
Nehemiah	13	c. 450 BC
Esther	10	c. 200 BC
Job	42	600–400 BC
Psalms	150	6th–2nd C BC
Proverbs	31	350–150 BC
Ecclesiastes	12	c. 200 BC
Song of Solomon	8	3rd C BC
Isaiah	66	end 3rd C BC
Jeremiah	52	604 BC
Lamentations	5	586–536 BC
Ezekiel	48	6th C BC
Daniel	12	c. 166 BC
Hosea	14	c. 732 BC
Joel	3	c. 500 BC
Amos	9	775–750 BC
Obadiah	1	6th–3rd C BC
Jonah	4	600–200 BC
Micah	7	end 3rd C BC
Nahum	3	c. 626 BC
Habakkuk	3	c. 600 BC
Zephaniah	3	3rd C BC
Haggai	2	c. 520 BC
Zechariah	14	c. 520 BC
Malachi	4	c. 430 BC

The Books of the New Testament

The Gospels

Matthew	28	before AD 70
Mark	16	before AD 70
Luke	24	AD 70–80
John	21	AD 90–100
The Acts	28	AD 70–80
Romans	16	AD 120

1 Corinthians	16	AD 57	
2 Corinthians	13	AD 57	
Galatians	6	AD 53	
Ephesians	6	AD 140	
Philippians	4	AD 63	
Colossians	4	AD 140	
1 Thessalonians	5	AD 50–54	
2 Thessalonians	3	AD 50–54	
1 Timothy	6	before AD 64	
2 Timothy	4	before AD 64	
Titus	3	before AD 64	
Philemon	1	AD 60–62	
Hebrews	13	AD 80–90	
James	5	before AD 52	
1 Peter	5	before AD 64	
2 Peter	3	before AD 64	
1 John	5	AD 90–100	
2 John	1	AD 90–100	
3 John	1	AD 90–100	
Jude	1	AD 75–80	
Revelation	22	AD 81–96	

RELIGIOUS FESTIVALS

date	festival	religion	event commemorated
6 Jan	Epiphany	Western Christian	coming of the Magi
6–7 Jan	Christmas	Orthodox Christian	birth of Jesus
18–19 Jan	Epiphany	Orthodox Christian	coming of the Magi
Jan–Feb	New Year	Chinese	Return of Kitchen god to heaven
Feb–March	Shrove Tuesday	Christian	day before Lent
	Ash Wednesday	Christian	first day of Lent
	Purim	Jewish	story of Esther
	Mahashivaratri	Hindu	Siva
March–April	Palm Sunday	Western Christian	Jesus' entry into Jerusalem
	Good Friday	Western Christian	crucifixion of Jesus
	Easter Sunday	Western Christian	resurrection of Jesus
	Passover	Jewish	escape from slavery in Egypt
	Holi	Hindu	Krishna
	Holi Mohalla	Sikh	(coincides with Holi)

	Rama Naumi	Hindu	birth of Rama
	Ching Ming	Chinese	remembrance of the dead
13 April	Baisakhi	Sikh	founding of the Khalsa
April–May	Easter	Orthodox Christian	death and resurrection of Jesus
May–June	Shavuot	Jewish	giving of ten Commandments to Moses
	Pentecost (Whitsun)	Western Christian	Jesus' followers receiving the Holy Spirit
	Wesak	Buddhist	day of the Buddha's birth, enlightenment and death
	Martyrdom of Guru Arjan	Sikh	death of fifth guru of Sikhism
June	Dragon Boat Festival	Chinese	Chinese martyr
	Pentecost	Orthodox Christian	Jesus' followers receiving the Holy Spirit
July	Dhammacakka	Buddhist	preaching of Buddha's first sermon
Aug	Raksha Bandhan	Hindu	family
Aug–Sept	Janmashtami	Hindu	birthday of Krishna
Sept	Moon Festival	Chinese	Chinese hero
Sept–Oct	Rosh Hashana	Jewish	start of Jewish New Year
	Yom Kippur	Jewish	day of atonement
	Succot	Jewish	Israelites' time in the wilderness
Oct	Dusshera	Hindu	goddess Devi
Oct–Nov	Divali	Hindu	goddess Lakshmi
	Divali	Sikh	release of Guru Hargobind from prison
Nov	Guru Nanak's birthday	Sikh	founder of Sikhism
Nov–Dec	Bodhi Day	Buddhist (Mahayana)	Buddha's enlightenment
Dec	Hanukkah	Jewish	recapture of Temple of Jerusalem
	Winter Festival	Chinese	time of feasting

25 Dec	Christmas	Western Christian	birth of Christ
Dec–Jan	Birthday of Guru Gobind Sind	Sikh	last (tenth) human guru of Sikhism
	Martyrdom of Guru Tegh Bahadur	Sikh	ninth guru of Sikhism

Sport

AMERICAN FOOTBALL: RECENT WINNERS

Super Bowl

1984	Los Angeles Raiders	1990	San Francisco 49ers
1985	San Francisco 49ers	1991	New York Giants
1986	Chicago Bears	1992	Washington Redskins
1987	New York Giants	1993	Dallas Cowboys
1988	Washington Redskins	1994	Dallas Cowboys
1989	San Francisco 49ers		

BASEBALL: RECENT WINNERS

World Series

1983	Baltimore Orioles	1989	Oakland Athletics
1984	Detroit Tigers	1990	Cincinnati Reds
1985	Kansas City Royals	1991	Minnesota Twins
1986	New York Mets	1992	Toronto Blue Jays
1987	Minnesota Twins	1993	Toronto Blue Jays
1988	Los Angeles Dodgers		

COMMONWEALTH GAMES: VENUES

1930	Hamilton, Canada	1970	Edinburgh, Scotland
1934	London, England	1974	Christchurch, New Zealand
1938	Sydney, Australia		
1950	Auckland, New Zealand	1978	Edmonton, Canada
1954	Vancouver, Canada	1982	Brisbane, Australia
1958	Cardiff, Wales	1986	Edinburgh, Scotland
1962	Perth, Australia	1990	Auckland, New Zealand
1966	Kingston, Jamaica	1994	Victoria, Canada

CRICKET: RECENT WINNERS

County Championship

1983	Essex
1984	Essex
1985	Middlesex
1986	Essex
1987	Nottinghamshire
1988	Worcestershire
1989	Worcestershire
1990	Middlesex
1991	Essex
1992	Essex
1993	Middlesex

AXA Equity and Law League
(formerly Refuge Assurance League)

1982	Sussex
1983	Yorkshire
1984	Essex
1985	Essex
1986	Hampshire
1987	Worcestershire
1988	Worcestershire
1989	Lancashire
1990	Derbyshire
1991	Nottinghamshire
1992	Middlesex
1993	Glamorgan

Nat West Trophy

1983	Somerset
1984	Middlesex
1985	Essex
1986	Sussex
1987	Nottinghamshire
1988	Middlesex
1989	Warwickshire
1990	Lancashire
1991	Hampshire
1992	Northamptonshire
1993	Warwickshire

Benson and Hedges Cup

1980	Northamptonshire
1983	Middlesex
1984	Lancashire
1985	Leicestershire
1986	Middlesex
1987	Yorkshire
1988	Hampshire
1989	Nottinghamshire
1990	Lancashire
1991	Worcestershire
1992	Hampshire
1993	Derbyshire
1994	Warwickshire

Sheffield Shield

1990–91	Victoria
1991–92	Western Australia

World Cup

1975	West Indies
1979	West Indies
1983	India
1987	Australia
1992	Pakistan

FOOTBALL: RECENT WINNERS

World Cup
1950	Uruguay
1954	West Germany
1958	Brazil
1962	Brazil
1966	England
1970	Brazil
1974	West Germany
1978	Argentina
1982	Italy
1986	Argentina
1990	West Germany
1994	Brazil

European Championship
1960	USSR
1964	Spain
1968	Italy
1972	West Germany
1976	Czechoslovakia
1980	West Germany
1984	France
1988	Holland
1992	Denmark

European Champions Cup
1983	SV Hamburg (West Germany)
1984	Liverpool (England)
1985	Juventus (Italy)
1986	Steaua Bucharest (Romania)
1987	FC Porto (Portugal)
1988	PSV Eindhoven (Holland)
1989	AC Milan (Italy)
1990	AC Milan (Italy)
1991	Red Star Belgrade (Yugoslavia)
1992	Barcelona (Spain)
1993	Marseille (France)
1994	AC Milan (Italy)

European Cup Winners' Cup
1983	Aberdeen (Scotland)
1984	Juventus (Italy)
1985	Everton (England)
1986	Dinamo Kiev (USSR)
1987	Ajax (Holland)
1988	Mechelen (Belgium)
1989	Barcelona (Spain)
1990	Sampdoria (Italy)
1991	Manchester United (England)
1992	Werder Bremen (Germany)
1993	AC Parma (Italy)
1994	Arsenal (England)

UEFA Cup
1983	Anderlecht (Belgium)
1984	Tottenham Hotspur (England)
1985	Real Madrid (Spain)
1986	Real Madrid (Spain)
1987	IFK Gothenburg (Sweden)
1988	Bayer Leverkusen (West Germany)
1989	Napoli (Italy)
1990	Juventus (Italy)
1991	Internazionale Milan (Italy)
1992	Ajax (Holland)
1993	Juventus (Italy)
1994	Internazionale Milan (Italy)

UK championships:

FA Cup
1983	Manchester United
1984	Everton
1985	Manchester United

1986	Liverpool
1987	Coventry City
1988	Wimbledon
1989	Liverpool
1990	Manchester United
1991	Tottenham Hotspur
1992	Liverpool
1993	Arsenal
1994	Manchester United

Football League Cup

1983	Liverpool
1984	Liverpool
1985	Norwich City
1986	Oxford United
1987	Arsenal
1988	Luton Town
1989	Nottingham Forest
1990	Nottingham Forest
1991	Sheffield Wednesday
1992	Manchester United
1993	Arsenal
1994	Aston Villa

Premier League Champions
(formerly Division One Champions)

1981–82	Liverpool
1982–83	Liverpool
1983–84	Liverpool
1984–85	Everton
1985–86	Liverpool
1986–87	Everton
1987–88	Liverpool
1988–89	Arsenal
1989–90	Liverpool
1990–91	Arsenal
1991–92	Leeds United
1992–93	Manchester United
1993–94	Manchester United

Scottish Premier Division Champions

1982–83	Dundee United
1983–84	Aberdeen
1984–85	Aberdeen
1985–86	Celtic
1986–87	Rangers
1987–88	Celtic
1988–89	Rangers
1989–90	Rangers
1990–91	Rangers
1991–92	Rangers
1992–93	Rangers
1993–94	Rangers

Scottish FA Cup

1983	Aberdeen
1984	Aberdeen
1985	Celtic
1986	Aberdeen
1987	St Mirren
1988	Celtic
1989	Celtic
1990	Aberdeen
1991	Motherwell
1992	Rangers
1993	Rangers
1994	Dundee United

GOLF: RECENT WINNERS

British Open

1982	Tom Watson	(*USA*)
1983	Tom Watson	(*USA*)
1984	Severiano Ballesteros	(*Spain*)
1985	Sandy Lyle	(*UK*)
1986	Greg Norman	(*Australia*)
1987	Nick Faldo	(*UK*)
1988	Severiano Ballesteros	(*Spain*)
1989	Mark Calcavecchia	(*USA*)
1990	Nick Faldo	(*UK*)
1991	Ian Baker-Finch	(*Australia*)
1992	Nick Faldo	(*UK*)
1993	Greg Norman	(*Australia*)
1994	Nick Price	(*Zimbabwe*)

US Open

1982	Tom Watson	(*USA*)
1983	Larry Nelson	(*USA*)
1984	Fuzzy Zoeller	(*USA*)
1985	Andy North	(*USA*)
1986	Ray Floyd	(*USA*)
1987	Scott Simpson	(*USA*)
1988	Curtis Strange	(*USA*)
1989	Curtis Strange	(*USA*)
1990	Hale Irwin	(*USA*)
1991	Payne Stewart	(*USA*)
1992	Tom Kite	(*USA*)
1993	Lee Janzen	(*USA*)
1994	Ernie Els	(*S. Africa*)

US Masters

1982	Craig Stadler	(*USA*)
1983	Severiano Ballesteros	(*Spain*)
1984	Ben Crenshaw	(*USA*)
1985	Bernhard Langer	(*West Germany*)
1986	Jack Nicklaus	(*USA*)
1987	Larry Mize	(*USA*)
1988	Sandy Lyle	(*UK*)
1989	Nick Faldo	(*UK*)
1990	Nick Faldo	(*UK*)
1991	Ian Woosnam	(*UK*)
1992	Fred Couples	(*USA*)
1993	Bernard Langer	(*Germany*)
1994	José Maria Olazabal	(*Spain*)

US PGA Championship

1981	Larry Nelson	(*USA*)
1982	Ray Floyd	(*USA*)
1983	Hal Sutton	(*USA*)
1984	Lee Trevino	(*USA*)
1985	Hubert Green	(*USA*)
1986	Bob Tway	(*USA*)
1987	Larry Nelson	(*USA*)
1988	Jeff Sluman	(*USA*)
1989	Payne Stewart	(*USA*)
1990	Wayne Grady	(*Australia*)
1991	John Daly	(*USA*)
1992	Nick Price	(*Zimbabwe*)
1993	Paul Azinger	(*USA*)

OLYMPIC VENUES

summer games/winter games

1896	Athens, Greece
1900	Paris, France
1904	St Louis, USA
1908	London, UK
1912	Stockholm, Sweden
1916	Not held
1920	Antwerp, Belgium
1924	Paris, France/Chamonix, France
1928	Amsterdam, Holland/St Moritz, Switzerland
1932	Los Angeles, USA/Lake Placid, New York, USA
1936	Berlin, Germany/Garmisch-Partenkirchen, Germany
1940	Not held
1944	Not held
1948	London, UK/St Moritz, Switzerland
1952	Helsinki, Finland/Oslo, Norway
1956	Melbourne, Australia*/Cortina d'Ampezzo, Italy
1960	Rome, Italy/Squaw Valley, Colorado, USA
1964	Tokyo, Japan/Innsbruck, Austria
1968	Mexico City, Mexico/Grenoble, France
1972	Munich, West Germany/Sapporo, Japan
1976	Montréal, Canada/Innsbruck, Austria
1980	Moscow, USSR/Lake Placid, New York, USA
1984	Los Angeles, USA/Sarajevo, Yugoslavia
1988	Seoul, South Korea/Calgary, Canada
1992	Barcelona, Spain/Albertville, France
1994	Lillehammer, Norway (winter games)
1996	Atlanta, Georgia, USA (summer games)
1998	Nagano, Japan (winter games)
2000	Sydney, Australia (summer games)

*Because of quarantine restrictions, equestrian events were held in Stockholm, Sweden.

RUGBY LEAGUE: RECENT WINNERS

Challenge Cup
1982	Hull
1983	Featherstone Rovers
1984	Widnes
1985	Wigan
1986	Castleford
1987	Halifax
1988	Wigan
1989	Wigan
1990	Wigan
1991	Wigan
1992	Wigan
1993	Wigan
1994	Wigan

Premiership Trophy
1982	Hull Kingston Rovers
1983	Widnes
1984	Hull Kingston Rovers
1985	St Helens
1986	Warrington
1987	Wigan
1988	Widnes
1989	Widnes
1990	Widnes
1991	Hull
1992	Wigan
1993	St Helens
1994	Wigan

RUGBY UNION: RECENT WINNERS

World Cup
1987	New Zealand
1991	Australia

International championship
1982	Ireland
1983	France and Ireland
1984	Scotland
1985	Ireland
1986	France
1987	France
1988	France and Wales
1989	France
1990	Scotland
1991	England
1992	England
1993	France
1994	Wales

County championship
1982	Lancashire
1983	Gloucestershire
1984	Gloucestershire
1985	Middlesex
1986	Warwickshire
1987	Yorkshire
1988	Lancashire
1989	Durham
1990	Lancashire
1991	Cornwall
1992	Lancashire
1993	Lancashire
1994	Yorkshire

Pilkington Cup
(formerly the **John Player Special Cup**)
1982	Gloucester and Moseley
1983	Bristol
1984	Bath
1985	Bath
1986	Bath
1987	Bath
1988	Harlequins

1989 Bath
1990 Bath
1991 Harlequins
1992 Bath
1993 Leicester
1994 Bath

Scottish Club Championship
1982 Hawick
1983 Gala
1984 Hawick
1985 Hawick
1986 Hawick
1987 Hawick
1988 Kelso
1989 Kelso
1990 Melrose
1991 Boroughmuir
1992 Melrose

1993 Melrose
1994 Melrose

Swalec Welsh Cup
(formerly the **Schweppes Welsh Cup**)
1982 Cardiff
1983 Pontypool
1984 Cardiff
1985 Llanelli
1986 Cardiff
1987 Cardiff
1988 Llanelli
1989 Neath
1990 Neath
1991 Llanelli
1992 Llanelli
1993 Llanelli
1994 Cardiff

TENNIS: RECENT WINNERS

Australian Open
men's singles

1982	Johan Kriek	*(South Africa)*
1983	Mats Wilander	*(Sweden)*
1984	Mats Wilander	*(Sweden)*
1985	Stefan Edberg	*(Sweden)*
1987	Stefan Edberg	*(Sweden)*
1988	Mats Wilander	*(Sweden)*
1989	Ivan Lendl	*(Czechoslovakia)*
1990	Ivan Lendl	*(Czechoslovakia)*
1991	Boris Becker	*(Germany)*
1992	Jim Courier	*(USA)*
1993	Jim Courier	*(USA)*
1994	Pete Sampras	*(USA)*

women's singles

1982	Chris Evert-Lloyd	*(USA)*
1983	Martina Navratilova	*(USA)*
1984	Chris Evert-Lloyd	*(USA)*
1985	Martina Navratilova	*(USA)*

1987	Hana Mandlikova	(*Czechoslovakia*)
1988	Steffi Graf	(*West Germany*)
1989	Steffi Graf	(*West Germany*)
1990	Steffi Graf	(*Germany*)
1991	Monica Seles	(*Yugoslavia*)
1992	Monica Seles	(*Yugoslavia*)
1993	Monica Seles	(*Yugoslavia*)
1994	Steffi Graf	(*Germany*)

(Australian Open not held 1986).

French Open
men's singles

1982	Mats Wilander	(*Sweden*)
1983	Yannick Noah	(*France*)
1984	Ivan Lendl	(*Czechoslovakia*)
1985	Mats Wilander	(*Sweden*)
1986	Ivan Lendl	(*Czechoslovakia*)
1987	Ivan Lendl	(*Czechoslovakia*)
1988	Mats Wilander	(*Sweden*)
1989	Michael Craig	(*USA*)
1990	Andres Gomez	(*Ecuador*)
1991	Jim Courier	(*USA*)
1992	Jim Courier	(*USA*)
1993	Sergi Bruguera	(*Spain*)
1994	Sergi Bruguera	(*Spain*)

women's singles

1982	Martina Navratilova	(*USA*)
1983	Chris Evert-Lloyd	(*USA*)
1984	Martina Navratilova	(*USA*)
1985	Chris Evert-Lloyd	(*USA*)
1986	Chris Evert-Lloyd	(*USA*)
1987	Steffi Graf	(*West Germany*)
1988	Steffi Graf	(*West Germany*)
1989	Arantxa Sanchez Vicario	(*Spain*)
1990	Monica Seles	(*Yugoslavia*)
1991	Monica Seles	(*Yugoslavia*)
1992	Monica Seles	(*Yugoslavia*)
1993	Steffi Graf	(*Germany*)
1994	Arantxa Sanchez Vicario	(*Spain*)

US Open
men's singles

1982	Jimmy Connors	(*USA*)
1983	Jimmy Connors	(*USA*)
1984	John McEnroe	(*USA*)
1985	Ivan Lendl	(*Czechoslovakia*)
1986	Ivan Lendl	(*Czechoslovakia*)
1987	Ivan Lendl	(*Czechoslovakia*)
1988	Mats Wilander	(*Sweden*)
1989	Boris Becker	(*West Germany*)
1990	Pete Sampras	(*USA*)
1991	Stefan Edberg	(*Sweden*)
1992	Stefan Edberg	(*Sweden*)
1993	Pete Sampras	(*USA*)

women's singles

1982	Chris Evert-Lloyd	(*USA*)
1983	Martina Navratilova	(*USA*)
1984	Martina Navratilova	(*USA*)
1985	Hana Mandlikova	(*Czechoslovakia*)
1986	Martina Navratilova	(*USA*)
1987	Martina Navratilova	(*USA*)
1988	Steffi Graf	(*West Germany*)
1989	Steffi Graf	(*West Germany*)
1990	Gabriela Sabatini	(*Argentina*)
1991	Monica Seles	(*Yugoslavia*)
1992	Monica Seles	(*Yugoslavia*)
1993	Steffi Graf	(*Germany*)

Wimbledon
men's singles

1982	Jimmy Connors	(*USA*)
1983	John McEnroe	(*USA*)
1984	John McEnroe	(*USA*)
1985	Boris Becker	(*West Germany*)
1986	Boris Becker	(*West Germany*)
1987	Pat Cash	(*Australia*)
1988	Stefan Edberg	(*Sweden*)
1989	Boris Becker	(*West Germany*)
1990	Stefan Edberg	(*Sweden*)
1991	Michael Stich	(*Germany*)

1992	Andre Agassi	(USA)
1993	Pete Sampras	(USA)
1994	Pete Sampras	(USA)

women's singles

1982	Martina Navratilova	(USA)
1983	Martina Navratilova	(USA)
1984	Martina Navratilova	(USA)
1985	Martina Navratilova	(USA)
1986	Martina Navratilova	(USA)
1987	Martina Navratilova	(USA)
1988	Steffi Graf	(West Germany)
1989	Steffi Graf	(West Germany)
1990	Martina Navratilova	(USA)
1991	Steffi Graf	(Germany)
1992	Steffi Graf	(Germany)
1993	Steffi Graf	(Germany)
1994	Conchita Martinez	(Spain)

COLLINS POCKET REFERENCE